LAST ROUND

'*Life's the best gift nature can bestow;*
the first that we receive,
the last which we forgo.'

DANIEL DEFOE, *The Spanish Descent*

LAST ROUND

The Battle of Majar al-Kabir

Mark Nicol

WEIDENFELD & NICOLSON

'Exemplo Decemus'

Sergeant Simon Hamilton-Jewell

Corporal Russ Aston

Corporal Paul Long

Corporal Simon Miller

Lance Corporal Ben Hyde

Lance Corporal Thomas Keys

First published in Great Britain in 2005
by Weidenfeld & Nicolson

1 3 5 7 9 10 8 6 4 2

A CIP catalogue record for this book
is available from the British Library

ISBN 0 297 84641 8

Printed in Great Britain by
Butler & Tanner Ltd, Frome and London

Weidenfeld & Nicolson

The Orion Publishing Group Ltd
Orion House, 5 Upper Saint Martin's Lane
London, WC2H 9EA

www.orionbooks.co.uk

Contents

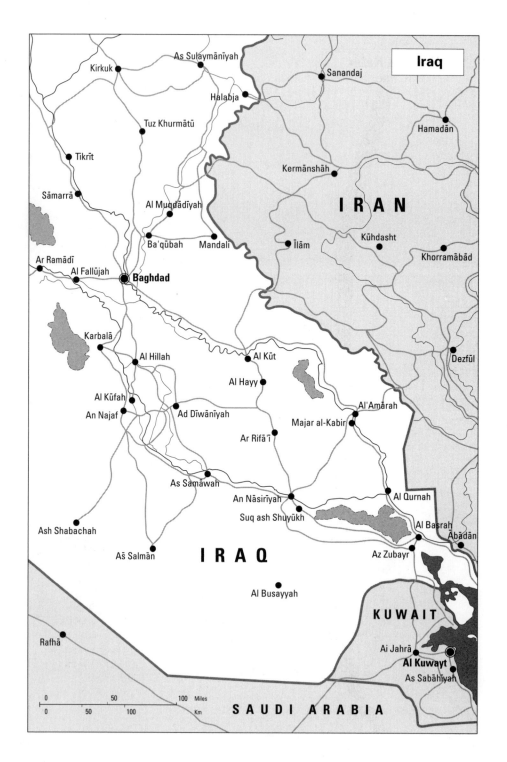

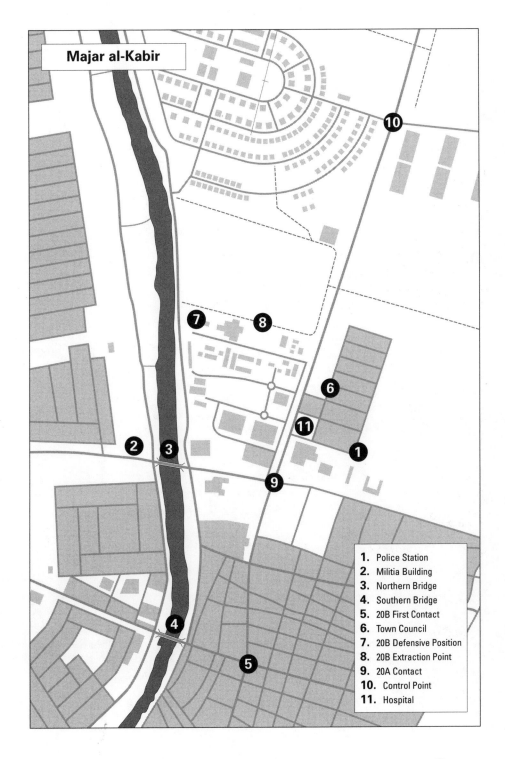

Majar al-Kabir

1. Police Station
2. Militia Building
3. Northern Bridge
4. Southern Bridge
5. 20B First Contact
6. Town Council
7. 20B Defensive Position
8. 20B Extraction Point
9. 20A Contact
10. Control Point
11. Hospital

Acknowledgements

LAST ROUND has not been easy to write or research as there have been differences of opinion over what the legacy of this book might be. As there were no British witnesses to events at the police station, it will never be known precisely what happened there, and to think otherwise would be foolish. So I have been guided by the Special Investigation Branch account of events at that location, which is supported by forensic evidence, scores of interviews and the statement of the interpreter who worked with H-J, Russ, Paul, Si, Ben and Tom.

In the aftermath of such a tragedy it is too easy to cast blame. While *Last Round* contains many constructive criticisms it should be remembered that errors were inevitable with such excruciating demands placed on so many personnel. There are so many to whom I am indebted for assistance. I will begin with the families of the six Royal Military Policemen. The families may have wanted *Last Round* to focus more on their ordeal since June 2003, the secrecy of the Board of Inquiry and the government's failure to make good its promise to bring the killers to justice. I wanted to write the most complete book I could, ensuring the accuracy of the account of the passage of 8 Platoon and 156 Provost Company through the war and the day in Majar al-Kabir, which, inevitably, has left less time to spend on a detailed discussion of other issues.

I would like to thank the families for their generosity in permitting the use of letters from the six, which have proved invaluable sources of information and, I believe, stand as fitting testimony to their humour, humility and bravery. The following deserve special thanks: Adele, Anna, Andy, Glenice and Mike Aston, Teresa, Tony and Eileen Hamilton-Jewell, John Hyde, Reg and Sally Keys, Pat Long and John and Marilyn Miller.

All the members of the 1st Battalion, the Parachute Regiment I spoke to expressed deep sorrow at the deaths of the RMPs. I am in no doubt had they known H-J, Russ, Paul, Si, Ben and Tom were stranded they would have fought and perhaps died trying to save them; that is the mark of them as soldiers and men. They did not abandon the RMPs, as has so often been made out.

As much as I would like to credit publicly all those who shared their recollections, this is impossible. I trust I have made clear how much I value your contributions and hope that on reading *Last Round* you feel I have done justice to you and your comrades. You spent hundreds of hours with me, detailing events and checking my work; thank you again.

On a personal level, I would like to thank my family and friends, the usual suspects: Ian, James, John, the two Jonathans, Michal and Mike.

Andrew Lownie knew this book would work and secured a deal with Ian Drury, my editor at Weidenfeld & Nicolson, who was likewise enthused and supportive. I would also like to mention Lord Westbury and my security team in Maysan province.

Mark Nicol, London, January 2005

Author's Note

BEFORE embarking on the Prologue, readers may benefit from a brief familiarisation with the diagrams, maps and photographs of Majar al-Kabir. There is also a comprehensive Glossary and Notes section at the back of the book.

Prologue

'HAPPY fire' heralded the dawn over the city: and free of Saddam there was much to celebrate for the people of Amarah. Five kilometres away, British soldiers stirred where they slept on the rooftops. Awakened by gunfire, trained ears recognised the AK47's deep, slow rate of fire. Some were scornful, the Arabs wasting ammunition on celebration when they had so little. They always fired on automatic, the British more often on single shot.

Chanted verses of the Koran followed, echoing the recordings sent home by Royal Military Policeman (RMP) Si Miller. Listening to tapes of the call to prayer confirmed to Si's parents what a country their son occupied – separated by language, culture and belief, he and they would never understand its people. His colleague Paul Long, who had taken to wearing aviator sunglasses on patrol, likened singing imams to rap artists, renaming them 'DJ Az and Co', and complained they sang out of tune.

Paul used humour to make Op (Operation) TELIC bearable, as he had written to his brother: 'Bush and Blair tours, never going on holiday with this club again. The brochure said "state of the art war, luxury hotels two to a room". No murder mystery holiday here, Bush did it. War, what war? Have I been to war?'

EARLY sunlight glinted on the Tigris, the river running through the city like a seeping wound. Since 1920, the Amarah plains had been drenched in the blood of Her Majesty's soldiers, thousands of whom died in that year's Shia uprising against British occupation. By mid-morning it would be 'hot enough to cook off the rocks' as RMP Russ Aston had written to his wife. Russ, 30, missed Derbyshire's dark, moist earth, wooded hills and his local pub's 'flat beer and ugly women'.

Pain in Tom Keys' right ankle registered in his brain. Nervously energetic, he loathed injuries and this was a recent sprain. Making a fuss was out of the question, however, as there were scarcely enough RMPs for him to cry off. Only a third of 156 Provost Company's personnel remained, fifty of the original deployment, including Major Bryn Parry-Jones, the 156 Officer Commanding (OC), having returned to Colchester. His departure had particularly rankled – those left behind felt the principles of leadership dictated he should remain. Si, Paul, Russ and Tom were among the unlucky twenty-five staying on until July; their morale had suffered as efforts to train the Iraqi police had produced little by way of results. Tom had described Iraq to his parents as 'this shithole of a country'.

The RMP accommodation area was sandwiched between the 1st Battalion, the Parachute Regiment's A, B and C rifle companies but there was little social interaction beyond the Paras leering at the Red Cap 'chicks'. Male and female RMPs were working too hard to take as much advantage of Camp Abu Naji's recently installed home comforts as some units, notably the Army Air Corps (AAC). When the heat grounded their Lynx helicopters they basked like lizards while the RAF took every opportunity to fly to Kuwait by Chinook, its more powerful engine equal to the temperature. Kuwait, with its children fattened on American brands of fast food, was where RMP Sergeant Simon Hamilton-Jewell should have been this morning, but his rest and recreation break had been cancelled. He would instead lead his six-man section, C Section, as it toured police stations south of the camp.

The perimeter of Abu Naji was marked every 150 metres by sangars – field fortifications built with sandbags and rocks – from where sentries scanned the crusty, brown landscape. Protective trenches and sandbanks had also been dug and a gravel track ran along its 2,600-metre circumference. Every morning the Paras ran around it carrying 40-lb bergens (rucksacks). This was the kind of pursuit on which the ex-1 PARA recruit Tom Keys thrived, when fit. His parents, Reg and Sally, had moved to early retirement in north Wales. They found Bala a rural idyll, set beside the lake of the same name and under the shadow of the Cambrian Mountains. On leave, Tom would run up them, hoping every time to beat his personal best.

Russ visited the Regimental Aid Post (RAP) with a stomach complaint, where he was met by the 'warry-looking' Corporal Lenny Thorne, a former rat catcher and 1 PARA medic. His nose, battered by bare-knuckle fighting, was as flat as his examination table. Lenny also wore a hound-dog expression and a moustache which drooped to a point just below the level of his lips – the 'Fu Manchu' look was a throwback to the 1980s when a bushy 'tache was de rigueur in airborne forces. Though surpassed by Major Bill Hayward's walrus whiskers, Lenny's were a matter of personal pride.

Clouds of steam carried the promise of bacon and eggs as 8 Platoon (8 Pl), 1 PARA queued by the scoff house. After four months of eating the same rations the Toms* waited impatiently. Many carried their own pint-sized mugs inside, where water bottles were piled to the ceiling. They passed along the hotplate, gazing avidly at the bacon but disappointedly at the plastic knives, forks and spoons; using their own battlefield utensils had been banned for hygiene reasons. Men had routinely lost two stone or more over the course of Op TELIC and there was no spare flesh on Danny Connolly or Barry McAdam; their uniforms looked two sizes bigger than when they had arrived in Kuwait. The Ulsterman Jason Davidson was one of the few who appeared to have kept his bulk, while Serge Lynch looked healthier for having spent less time 'in theatre' – he had been too young to deploy in February. Now 18, the 'Baby Para' from London looked forward to home and his parachuting course at RAF Brize Norton – Serge was one of 8 Platoon's two 'penguins' (Paras without

---

* 'Tom' – Para shorthand for soldiers ranked as private. Tom is an abbreviation of Tommy Atkins, the generic sobriquet for the English soldier in use since the eighteenth century.

wings), the other being Ritchie Clement. Animated conversations drowned out the live Sky TV news feed – the failure to find Weapons of Mass Destruction (WMD) dominated; with home beckoning, however, concerns over the Allies' case for war were far from their minds.

8 Platoon consisted of two 'multiples' – call signs Two Zero Alpha and Two Zero Bravo – and breakfasts had to be eaten fast as both were visiting Majar al-Kabir. The task, as outlined to their Officer Commanding (OC), Lieutenant Ross Kennedy, was to show a 'strong presence' in this volatile town where every local had access to weapons and saw it as a right to hold them.

Two days previously, Alpha had been on 'tan ops' (sunbathing) at the police station when a chanting, hissing mob surrounded them. Humanitarian aid shortages and weapons searches of nearby villages had angered the locals – they were protesting to protect their homes and keep their guns. As naked Paras got their kit together the crowd stoned the building, smashed windows and wrecked their vehicles – a Land Rover and a DAF truck. To Ross Kennedy's annoyance his second-in-command (2IC) Mark Weadon fired warning shots above the crowd, in breach of standard operating procedures (SOPs). Having been inside the police station sending a quick reaction force (QRF) request by satellite phone, Ross climbed up to the roof and ordered him to cease fire. The QRF arrived and the crowd was pushed back by the column of Scimitars (armoured vehicles) and WMIKs (heavily armed open-top Land Rovers).

This morning, Bravo would accompany Alpha, a doubling of manpower in response to the increased threat. Bravo had some 'heavy call signs' – hardened soldiers. The presence of Jock Robbo, John 'The Dolmanator' Dolman and 'Big Steve' Oellerman would reassure the Toms. Prior to departure, Ross's duty was to check out and leave a 'trace' of his platoon's intended movements. It was 08.40hrs.

Entering the Ops Room, a hard-shelled building little bigger than a squash court, he hit a wall of sweaty air. The 0300hrs divisional conference call had suggested a still night in southern Iraq, perhaps too still. Between 0630 and 0700hrs two WMIKs had swept through Majar al-Kabir. On their return the crews said it was 'eerily quiet' and that they had received 'death stares' from the locals.

Ross headed for the 'bird table', the 10 feet by 6 feet epicentre of the Ops Room. His battalion's area of operations (AO) was spread across it; as and when required, see-through plastic sheets were draped over it to show man-made features, area boundaries and positions of friendly forces. Next to it was the watch keeper's desk – his job being to log the course of events – and on the other side sat Airborne signallers hunched over radio sets. The duty watch keeper was Eric Sekwalor, a.k.a. 'Bobsleigh Bob', a veteran of the British bobsleigh team.

A, B and C Companies' desks were each equipped with their own VHF nets and satellite phones; the walls were weighed down with charts, maps and schedules. Behind a partition of filing cabinets was the 'Intelligence Cell', led by Captain Stuart Morgan and staffed by lower ranks such as Piers Roberts, a skydiving Canadian with officer ambitions. He had fought alongside Tom Keys on Op BARRAS in Sierra Leone but had seen less of him since Tom, partly at his father's behest, left 1 PARA to become a military policeman. The Int Cell's task was to provide the man in charge of Camp Abu Naji, Lieutenant Colonel Tom Beckett, with knowledge of the enemy threat. Intelligence sources were graded from A to F, and their information snippets from 1 to 6. The reliability of Iraqi-sourced 'humint' had been questioned during Op JASMINE, the local arms amnesty programme. Detailed tip-offs about the whereabouts of weapons caches were received but none would be found when the locations were searched. The intelligence was either inaccurate, or the Iraqis were eavesdropping using British-spec radios sold to them during the Iran–Iraq War.

This morning, as on so many others, Beckett was meeting local officials – the drive to restore law and order, rebuild schools and repair water and electricity supplies being the commanding officer's (CO's) 'main effort' in the post-war period. Accustomed to good living, Beckett looked as much an officer and a gentleman out of uniform as in it and his natural diplomacy impressed the sheikhs. The CO's voice seemed almost too soft for a man of his position and height. That he presented himself as less the conqueror was suited to negotiations with those who commanded tens of thousands of men and were opposed to the British presence. Beckett described the security situation as 'benign but fragile'. In his absence, Major Stuart Tootal led the Battle Group. He shared an office next door to the Ops Room with Captain Richard Todd. 'Toddy' had begun Op TELIC as training officer before attending the Ops Officers' course at Army Staff College.

While Tootal, with his effeminate hairstyle and slight build, broke Para officer conventions, Toddy looked the part. His gregarious behaviour enlivened the dullest of battalion functions and he had a penchant for exotic girlfriends. 'Dushka', the latest, had been renamed after the Russian-made heavy machine gun, as Toddy could not pronounce her Eastern European name. Her party piece was to strip and reassemble the AK47 kept behind the bar at the Officers' Mess. Most of Toddy's girlfriends only saw one function before being demobilised; she was due a Long Service Good Conduct medal. While both men were respected by their officer brethren, many of the battalion's lower ranks dismissed them as 'Ruperts' preoccupied with personal career advancement at others' expense – although they thought this of most officers. Tootal in particular was a target of ridicule for the 'Toms Liberation Front' (TLF) – as the battalion's unofficial union for perpetually disgruntled private soldiers was known.

Ross filled out a flap sheet – a hand-sized piece of white paper onto which he wrote his route and times of departure and return. He also gave the registration numbers of his three vehicles – two Pinzgauers and a DAF truck – and the names of his men, their blood groups and nick numbers/Zap numbers for use in radio communications. Each number comprised the first two letters of a soldier's surname followed by the last four digits of his army serial number. Ross's flap sheet – which gave his estimated time of departure from Abu Naji as 0900hrs – was placed on an A4-sized clipboard and his information transferred onto the current situation, call sign and location status boards. He was all too aware of the signal problems, having struggled to get through to the Ops Room during the riot two days previously. The strength of his satellite phone reception had been reduced by the dry air, lack of moisture in the ground and the power lines hanging outside the police station.

With the Majar al-Kabir area being so flat, there had been no height-gain factor to assist, while the scale of the area restricted HF and VHF signals. Even when in range, there were black spots where communications were impossible. This made the procedure of making 'check calls' to the Ops Room from radio-friendly areas all the more important.

Alpha and Bravo would take Personal Role Radios (PRRs), portable VHF radios and two iridium satellite phones, which looked like mobile phones from the 1980s. If Ross dialled the C Company desk when its satellite phone was in use, he would be put through to a network voicemail – unsatisfactory under fire. The satellite phones were a Battle Group asset, kept in the Ops Room and booked out as and when required by all units: they were, in the words of one senior officer, 'a precious commodity' and it was known to all that they represented the best chance, albeit not guaranteed, of summoning assistance.

The RMP duty Ops Room representative was Warrant Officer Matthew 'Bob' Marley, whom Sergeant Hamilton-Jewell informed of his patrol's proposed journey – as discussed with his OC Lieutenant Richard Phillips the previous evening. The C Section leader wrote that he was due to reach Al Uzayr by 1400hrs and would return to Abu Naji at approximately 1700hrs. He did not say how long he would be spending in Majar al-Kabir or Qalat Salih while en route. On the bird table, a map pin-marked with the letters MP (Military Policeman) was moved to Majar al-Kabir, their first intended stop-off point. Hamilton-Jewell gave C Section's estimated time of departure as 0910hrs. The RMPs and the Paras would be travelling seperately to Majar al-Kabir, unaware of each others' specific tasks.

LOADING his helmet and body armour onto the Pinzgauer, John Dolman felt it getting hotter. He glanced at his digital timepiece, the sort that still worked after being smashed against concrete. With the day's temperature likely to exceed 45°C, the army's dress recommendation 'sleeves up and down as per first and last light' had seldom seemed more academic. Sewn onto his upper right sleeve was a red square, his 1 PARA Drop Zone (DZ) flash. Just as Hell's Angels decorated their helmets with chapter colours and winged skulls, so Dolman, from Ollerton, wore his with pride. Dolman's battalion was his clan and he was an elder. Pitbull-like in stature, he had, in army vernacular, a short 'flash to bang' time: if his security was threatened he shot first. Ammunition took priority in the organisation of his operational waistcoat: magazines were kept in the front-left pouches, which were easiest to reach, while shell dressings and bandages were also handily placed. Magazine charger, weapons cleaning kit, water bottles and his PRR were stored to the rear and side.

Dolman and Robbo were hard men. When the latter broke the world military marathon record, running the 1999 London Marathon in boots and carrying a 40 lb bergen in 4 hours 14 minutes, he barely looked tired. Photographs of him crossing the line with Corporal John West were pinned up at 1 PARA's barracks in Dover so every new Tom knew what 'Daddy' was about. Robbo was, in Para argot, 'Regted up' and regarded as a Regimental Sergeant Major (RSM) in waiting. The Scot, from Dalrymple, Ayrshire, would be IC (In Command) Wagon on the lead Pinzgauer, driven by Billy Brown. Dolman would take charge of the rear Pinzgauer and sit alongside its driver, 'Big Steve' Oellerman.

With circular headlights for eyes and a small, box-shaped grille of a mouth, the wagons looked like toy trucks. Made in Austria by Steyr-Daimler-Puch, a company better known for manufacturing motorbikes, the four-wheel-drive turbos were used across NATO and were popular with the Toms, who raced Pinzgauers across the mudflats, shouting, 'Let's off-road!', aping characters from *The Fast Show*.

Ross jumped into the DAF cabin alongside Tim May. The first leg of the journey was a 2 kilometre drive around Abu Naji's one-way system with the four-tonner's engine spitting out grains of sand. C Company used four DAFs – renamed 'Deliverers of Airborne Forces' – all of which had suffered mechanical problems. For reasons unknown, spraying antiperspirant into the truck's external air intake often helped to start it, with Lynx proving most effective. The multiple's second-in-command, Mark Weadon, sat in the cargo hold. His Personal Role Radio (PRR) head strap pushed up a fringe of dark-brown hair.

Low enemy threat status and lazy administration combined to grant them more leg room. The 1st Battalion, the King's Own Scottish Borderers

(1KOSB) was in the process of replacing 1 PARA, and the Paras had to sacrifice ammunition for the Jocks. This exchange and the belief that British forces would not be attacked had reduced the Paras to 100 rounds each for their A2s (personal rifles) and 200 rounds for 'the gun', as the general purpose machine gun (GPMG) was known – one sixth of that issued for Op TELIC's 'war-fighting' phase.

Because of its awkwardness and weight, junior Toms Serge Lynch and Mark Lewis had been 'dicked' to carry the light support weapon (LSW). They hated the 'Crow's Cannon' as the LSW had been renamed. A more 'ally' weapon was Mick Haines' Minimi (light machine gun). Three types of grenade, Red Phosphorous, Signal Smoke and High Explosive, had also been withdrawn from 8 Platoon as they were on peace-support operations. They had not carried bayonets since Barry McAdam had his stolen by children in Amarah.

The convoy turned right past the Lynx pad, passed through the camp gate and drove alongside the Chinook Helicopter Landing Site (HLS). The HLS was outside Abu Naji because the transport helicopters created small-scale sandstorms on take-off and landing. As Alpha and Bravo gazed from their vehicles, they noticed that the once vast, muddy pools formed by spring floods had dried into a plaster-of-Paris-like mould. The three vehicles rolled beneath a stone archway, a landmark representing the boundary between the worlds: British and Iraqi, safe and unsafe. This was the junction with Route 6, the main Basra to Baghdad highway.

Since February, 8 Platoon had driven thousands of kilometres across marshland, desert and track. They would take home so many memories: the worst being corpses strewn by the roadside and the wreckage of burnt-out tanks. There had been lighter moments: playing football, the 'Dushka Challenge' and when platoons of elfish boys greeted their arrival in villages, staring in wonder at the white tribe. The children were too young to have been imbued with political and religious dogma. 8 Platoon knew better than to ask about their mothers and sisters – that female RMPs had been punched, stoned and spat at told them it was better not to enquire.

The 'craic' was 'same old, same old': one less morning before coming home. Overall, however, the war had bored the Paras. They had trained

25

hard for it, been impressed by the size of the initial ammunition supply – not that there was much more should it run out – but were then denied any significant enemy contacts. Hence, with just a week to go, Op TELIC had been unofficially renamed 'Exercise TELIC'.

Aware of the rocket-propelled grenade (RPG) threat and roadside bombs, the drivers varied the distances between their vehicles and occasionally swerved from side to side. Beneath a layer of sandy brown smog the ground was as flat as the sea. Chimneys shaped like old naval cannons fired clouds of thick grey smoke. Tiny female figures in black *burkha*s scurried about as men sat in the tea tents; such were the working practices of the brick foundries. For Iraqi men, treating their females as cattle bred for labour seemed one of their primary pleasures.

Around 20 minutes later, the Paras' destination appeared through the heat haze. Lieutenant Kennedy was unaware that he would shortly be joined in the town by Sergeant Hamilton-Jewell's RMP section, his men carrying just fifty rounds. Major Parry-Jones had backed the ammunition de-scaling, against his men's wishes, as according to him 'everything looked rosy'.

Majar al-Kabir was less than half the size of a British town with the same population, 60,000, approximately 4 kilometres in length between its northern and southern perimeters and 3 kilometres from east to west. The poor shared mud huts, the middle classes cube-shaped homes painted white and with flat, concrete roofs – ideal firing positions against Coalition aircraft. Every man, woman and child was hardened by resistance to Saddam and believed themself to be entirely self-sufficient; a view compounded by winning their own freedom – the last of the Ba'athists had fled long before the British arrived.

Attacking the police station on 22 June, the Iraqis had expressed their unwillingness to embrace a new occupancy or the guns amnesty. Perhaps 8 Platoon would be given a few rusted, unusable rifles, but any new weapons would remain hidden. They had not fired at Alpha that day, limiting their protest to intense stone throwing and vandalism. It was a warning – return and the locals would take resistance to the next level.

The sloping warehouse roofs knelt to meet the horizon and the sugar factory shimmered in sunlight. To 8 Platoon's right was a reservoir, and as their vehicles drew alongside the gentlest of waves broke the dark blue surface. Here the roads were partially hidden beneath a layer of yellow sand. Each day the traffic brushed the grains one way before the summer breeze blew them back. Tyre tracks were etched into the earth as if scribbled by a child's crayon. They criss-crossed and turned, scarring the crust but leading nowhere. There were signs of recent affluence: satellite dishes and imported cars, while locals dressed smartly in slip-on leather shoes, belted casual slacks and imitation designer shirts.

The more impoverished wore *shalwar kameez* (the familiar baggy trousers and long loose shirts) and flip-flops. Traditional black and white head cloths were folded on top of their heads and secured with black rope. These were Joseph's people. Joseph, 8 Platoon's interpreter, lived with his family in a northern suburb, and the convoy stopped at a round-about to collect him. Joseph was aged around 50 but looked older, and his skin was lighter than most Iraqis'. At two dollars a day Joseph was good value and could have earned far greater sums working for US civilian contractors nearer Baghdad. It would not be safe for him to return home after today.

On Route 6 Iraqi drivers switched carriageways according to mood and though a modicum of self-discipline was exercised in the towns, concrete blocks had been placed between lanes. Municipal buildings came into view, set back from the main road. 8 Platoon knew the biggest to be the council offices and the white building on the crossroads to be a hospital.

'Right at the next,' Ross reminded Tim; he usually turned left to park up outside the police station.

A man of few, gruff words, Tim nodded and the DAF headed towards the town's northern bridge over the River Majar. This major tributary of the Tigris flowed north to south, or right to left as he approached. On reaching the militia headquarters (also known as the FAWJ from the Arabic for the militia: Fawj ad-Dwaara), Alpha debussed. They were to patrol with the militia, a trigger-happy outfit who enjoyed the power trip of patrolling with the British – but as collaborators they were also risking their lives. 8 Platoon considered them a liability. It was 0930hrs.

EACH scene along the RMPs' route was interchangeable with the last: scrubland, salt deposits and frenzied dogs on both sides of Route 6. It was as if the Red Caps were actors in an early Hollywood Western, driving in front of the same backdrop rotated before the camera. The sun exposed the landscape's dry ugliness making it hard to envisage the lives of its people before Saddam's ecocide.

Amid 6,000 square miles of marshlands, the locals had caught fish with spears and nets, farmed water buffalo and slept in huts made of bulrushes. Amarah, a major port on the Tigris, was then the northern tip of the marshland triangle, with Nasiriyah, on the Euphrates, and Basra being the triangle's other two points. The rivers met at Al Qurnah to form the Shatt al-Arab waterway. Saddam had destroyed a way of life unchanged since biblical times, draining 90 per cent of the marshes, sending 10,000 of its inhabitants to prison camps and making many more refugees as punishment for their support of Iran. The Marsh Arabs' champion in the UK, Baroness Nicholson of Winterbourne, had predicted: 'Soon there will be no waters of Babylon beside which to sit down and weep – only cracked, barren earth, not suitable for agriculture.' Only refugees' testimonies remained: 'The birds died, the animals died, the people died, the world died. There is no water, there is no life, we are naked in our misery.'

Maysan province was 'inhabited by Arabs noted for their predatory habits, they are brigands', according to the historian Ibn Batuta, and was populated by a mosaic of feuding clans and titled families, while the British explorer Wilfred Thesiger, who lived with the Marsh Arabs for seven years, wrote: 'You can usually get on terms with people by helping them kill something.'

BRAVO remained at the FAWJ building, while Alpha's foot patrol began.

'Move out, staggered file.'

'Stay tight, yeah? And watch your arcs.'

Ross walked back towards the bridge. Danny Connolly, who carried his OC's iridium phone in a daysack, stayed close – because of the phone's low battery life it was only switched on when Ross wanted to make a call. To get a signal he would have to stand still, outside.

Ross's Toms walked within 5 metres of each other, constantly turning back to see the militia, unsure where they would be or who they were about to threaten.

'Watch for those carrying stones.'

'Roger that; we had enough of that on Sunday [22 June at the police station].'

Having crossed the northern bridge – marked out as Yellow 2 on British maps – the patrol approached the crossroads.

'Right turn here.'

'Head south down the main street.'

WHEN Simon Hamilton-Jewell's section arrived at the police station, at around 0940hrs, his interpreter was waiting and his bicycle was parked against a wall. All was quiet.

IT was just after 1000hrs when a 4x4 vehicle drove towards Ross, kicking up dust as it braked. Talal Abid Ahmed Zubaida appeared: 'You can't go into the town.'

Ross frowned. 'Sorry?'

'It's not safe. Bad men.' The militia leader poked his bald head out of the car and gestured. 'You will be shot at.'

'I see.'

'Not good.'

Ross's men had been shot at on a weekly, if not daily basis. The subaltern's orders from Major Chris Kemp were to 'show a presence'. Major Kemp and Zubaida had negotiated an agreement yesterday over weapons searches and access to the town; their interpretations of what this deal meant in practice were different.

Zubaida was insistent: 'If you go then you cannot take my men with you. The town is too dangerous.'

A compromise was required.

'What if we remount our vehicles and your militia follow us in theirs?'

Zubaida paused. 'Err...It is the route as well. That is a problem.'

'OK.'

Ross squinted as he checked the whereabouts of his men. 'Back here, get back here.' He gestured with his hand and the Toms retreated. A new route would have to be devised.

'Go this way,' the militia leader pointed.

Via PRR, Ross briefed Robbo: 'We're returning to your location. It'll have to be a vehicle patrol. We need to keep him onside, over.'

'Roger that. We're already mounted.'

'There's a route change as well.'

'Oh?'

'Don't cross that bridge. Head south down this bank and cross over the southern bridge [Yellow 3]. I'll stay here; the militia will accompany you.'

Bravo left militia headquarters and the air was heavy with sewage as Billy Brown drove down the western riverbank. The Pinzgauers crossed the town's southern bridge and entered the souk – a labyrinth of bazaars, stalls and booths. As they did so, barefooted children played in the dirt and angry eyes bored into their backs.

'OK, not a drama, guys,' an NCO reassured.

'Yup.'

'Just keep an eyes on…We're not bothered.'

Iraqis crowded around – either the sight of British vehicles was the day's highlight or they had hostile intentions.

'Watch your arcs. Shout if you see anyone armed.'

'Everyone switch on,' Robbo echoed.

'It's got the look of Mogadishu,' said one Tom – he had not been to Somalia but he had seen *Black Hawk Down*.

'At least at night time you can't see how shit it is.'

Narrow streets filled with youths who pushed against Billy and Steve's wagons.

'Don't like the look of this.'

8 Platoon had inherited responsibility for Majar al-Kabir from a platoon from 3 PARA when the other battalion returned to the UK – and at this moment it seemed remarkable that they had chatted freely to locals and regarded the town as easy to patrol.

Billy Brown cursed the 'crusties' beneath his breath as speakers perched on the mosque minarets crackled into life.

'They are coming to search for weapons, to tear our houses apart. We mustn't let them. Arm yourselves, they want to fight us. *La, la Amerika.* [No, no America'] *La, la Amerika.'*

The crowd chanted louder, *'La, la Amerika!! La, la Amerika!!'*

Bravo took a deep breath. 'Fucking hell, they're on top of us here.'

'This is well cheeky – another glorious day in the regiment, eh?'

Iraqis pointed at them with grubby hands. Joseph's kindly face contorted as his fellow Iraqis hissed through their beards. 'Stay calm,' he urged, as much to himself. *This is crazy,* he thought.

Robbo sensed he was losing control – the mob was on top. There were 200 of them and their intentions were definitely hostile; this seemed more of an ambush than a protest. Today, the soldiers thought the Iraqis looked and smelt as if it had been weeks since their last wash. Some appeared to have more gaps in their mouths than teeth; their dental hygiene was worse even than Freddy Ellis's, an 8 Platoon Tom with teeth described as 'a fighting patrol, well spaced out'.

'This isn't good,' said one. 'I don't like this one fucking bit,' said another, ducking to avoid a rock.

ROSS'S pulse quickened; he had lost radio communications with Robbo and was faced with an angry crowd outside militia headquarters. Mark Weadon ordered the Toms into firing positions around the DAF as youths showered them with rocks.

Fear was a bully who tapped on every soldier's shoulder. By 1020hrs the locals were gradually closing in around Alpha and Bravo. They had anticipated a hot reception, hence both multiples had deployed, but not one as fractious as this. The mob wanted to make Majar al-Kabir a no-go zone for British forces.

Meanwhile, the RMP had been at the police station for around half an hour. H-J, Russ and Ben were inside the building, Paul, Si and Tom had stayed with the Land Rovers.

Six months earlier...

ONE Deployment

THE party on Saturday, 11 January 2003 was a small family affair at the Marquis of Granby in Esher, Surrey. Teresa was to receive her presents on 14 January, her birthday proper, but the best arrived today: her son Simon. Her elder son Tony and his wife Eileen were as happy to see him as she was. Simon knew his mother's eightieth birthday lunch would be the last time he saw her before the war began, a conflict he supported and she opposed. In spite of Saddam Hussein, what had the Iraqis done to us? That was Teresa's logic. What evidence was there of an immediate threat to Britain? As Chief Weapons Inspector Dr Hans Blix had told the United Nations: 'We now have been there for some two months and have been covering the country in ever-wider sweeps, and we haven't found any smoking guns.'

Across the country the feeling was spreading that war was getting closer. The previous day, Britain's largest maritime deployment for twenty years had sailed from Portsmouth while 1,000 soldiers from 16 Air Assault Brigade (16 Air Asslt Bde) were relieved from Op FRESCO – where they had been providing emergency cover for striking firemen. Soldiers, lower-paid than the men taking industrial action, would be heading to the Gulf.

Teresa beamed as she held Simon's hand. Aged 41, he was one of the RMP's most experienced soldiers, having spent nine years in the Territorial Army (TA) and fifteen as a regular, serving on operations in Northern Ireland and the former Yugoslavia. His friends called him 'H-J' or 'Hammy'. To Teresa he was simply her loving, loyal son. Simon wore a black RMP Close Protection Team shirt, a souvenir of his service in Sarajevo. Armed with a Sig Sauer P228 pistol and an automatic assault rifle, he had protected the deputy commander of SFOR (Stabilisation Force) operations, Lieutenant General John Kiszely MC; before that he had stood bodyguard to the British ambassador to Sudan. Simon had served in 21 (TA) SAS and been attached to 1 PARA before transferring to the RMP. In 1997 he overcame Crohn's disease, a severe inflammation of the small intestine, and a bout of pneumonia so severe he was read the last rites.

From his mother Simon had inherited a strong sense of justice and determination. Born in the South Yorkshire mining village of Maltby in 1923, Teresa Scholey was one of Percy and Martha Scholey's brood of nine, and the family could trace local roots back to the sixteenth century. While her siblings were at school, Teresa fed and mucked out the pigs, ducks and chickens on the family's smallholding. She attended church every Sunday and life was to deal her faith many tests. Teresa's sister Emma died as a baby; her favourite brother George from pulmonary pneumonia, aged 27; and when her mother lost her sight Teresa became her carer until her death in 1945. Aged 25, she left home for London, disapproving of her father's liaison with a much younger woman. Teresa married, but things went badly. Somehow the family managed after the disappearance of Simon's father and he attended Hinchley Wood Secondary School.

It was a feature of Simon's character that he enjoyed helping the less fortunate, which led him to become a Duke of Edinburgh's Award Scheme instructor. He also liked a joke. In the Brecon Beacons, he convinced a gullible fellow team leader that the quickest way to gut a fish was to 'blow up its arse'.

At the pub in Esher, the family settled down to eat. Teresa, who retained a broad Yorkshire accent, chose a roast, Eileen the vegetarian dish and the brothers opted for sausages and mash. Then Eileen remembered: 'Tony, we haven't got a camera with us. I really wanted some pictures.' Tony admitted he had forgotten. 'Go and buy one of those instant ones,' Eileen told him. 'We've got to have some pictures of Simon before he goes away.'

Tony Fisher, fourteen years older than Simon and born to Teresa during an earlier relationship, was a half-brother and yet more than a brother, having helped raise Simon. Their most treasured moments were spent in Tony's rally car, with Simon as co-driver. Tony, a warm-hearted man whose Fire Brigade career had been curtailed by a back injury, shared his mother's pride in Simon's achievements. He would let his lunch go cold, knowing what it meant to his mother to record the day. The meal compensated for Simon missing Tony and Eileen's wedding whilst serving in Bosnia. Since becoming Tony's fourth wife Eileen had gradually grown closer to Simon as he gained confidence that she would last longer than his brother's previous partners.

'I'll take you up in a helicopter when I get back, Eileen. Would you like that?' Simon leaned back in his chair.

'That would be wonderful,' Eileen replied. Then he teased her about making a parachute jump. When Eileen asked Simon how he felt about going to Iraq, he replied, 'It's my job, Eileen. It's what I do.'

'Aren't you scared?'

'No, I'm just looking forward to getting out there and getting down to work. I've had to buy my own desert boots, but I'm not the only one. Apart from that everything's fine. We've got an important job to do there.'

Tony returned and everyone smiled for the camera. After Irish coffee the party moved to Teresa's flat in Thames Ditton. Simon kissed his mother goodbye and promised he would write. She hugged him and wished him luck. Eileen and Tony drove Simon to his flat, where the brothers shook hands and Simon and Eileen kissed goodbye. Then he turned away, waving as he disappeared through his front door.

H-J was twice the age of many of the RMPs based with him, one being Si Miller, a gregarious 21-year-old from Washington, Tyne and Wear. Already promoted to corporal and engaged to one of 156 Provost Company's most attractive women, Si was admired and envied in equal measure. He and Emma Morris planned to marry in Barbados in July.

Unlike H-J, Si was from a stable family and his father John, who had served in the Royal Army Ordnance Corps (RAOC), had passed on a sense of duty and achievement. Aged 12, Si won a black belt in karate and later joined Sunderland AFC's School of Excellence. Trials at Cambridge United followed, with his father driving him there and back, before he joined the RMP, to be followed by his elder brother. Si enjoyed tours to Kenya and general police duties alike – such was life as a Red Cap, dodging baboons and giraffes in his Land Rover one week and arresting drunken soldiers in Colchester the next.

Corporal Russ Aston was one of 156 Provo's more complex, intelligent characters. Since marching around his mother's lounge as a 3-year-old to recordings of the Grenadier Guards' band, Russ had wanted to be a soldier. His mother Glenice had attempted to dissuade him, but he was adamant. Aged 18 he attended his local recruiting office and applied to join one regiment: the Grenadier Guards. Russ would be promoted to lance sergeant and spend two and a half years in Northern Ireland before joining the RMP. Russ enjoyed being one of his unit's physical training instructors (PTIs) and in 2002 put his fitness to good use, running 50 kilometres to raise money for a youth football team – he had also passed P Company – a series of physical tests beyond the capabilities of most RMPs. A little vain, he packed his weights for use in the Gulf.

Russ was shrewd, selling his mother a Citroën AX hatchback for considerably more than he paid for it, then redeeming himself with a gentle smile and a fulsome apology. His mother always forgave him and this was one of many nice little earners for 'Aston's Autos', as his back-pocket deals were known. Glenice had doted upon her three children and Russ was protective of her and his younger sister Adele, interrogating her potential suitors with, 'Do you like yer beer? 'Ave yer got a bitta money?' Russ's partner Anna, attractive and with a forceful personality, thought the RMP families in Colchester were marginalised in this Para-dominated garrison. After she moved from the married quarters back to Derbyshire, Russ talked of life outside the army.

Russ Aston's distinctive white PTI vest was coveted by Lance Corporal Thomas Keys. Having passed out from the Army Foundation

College he had alarmed his parents by announcing his intention to join the Parachute Regiment – that he weighed a mere 10 stone and looked 14 years old was of no consequence to him.

'Why don't you wait until you've filled out, son? Until you've put on a stone and got stronger?' his father Reg pleaded. Even failing his first attempt at P Company did not blow Tom off course. Having dropped off the 10 mile battle march Tom told him: 'Don't worry, Dad, take a chill pill. I'll get through next time, I know I will.' He retook P Company three weeks later and spoke to his father the night before 'milling'. Combatants in the one-minute test faced each other in a ring and wore gloves, but there the similarities with boxing ended. In milling, defensive actions lost marks and the more aggressive fighter, rather than the more skilled, was determined the victor. Reg feared for his son's safety: 'Remember your kung fu skills, Tom.'

'No, Dad, it's not like that, you just have to go for it.'

'Oh, I see...'

'Don't worry, Dad. I'll be fine, you'll see.'

Tom was paired with a similarly sized cadet, whom he dispatched within seconds and continued thumping to win the bout. Tom also passed every other test: the 10 mile battle march which he completed before the 1 hour 50 minute cut-off point; the aerial assault course, the 2.9 kilometre steeplechase, the 3.1 kilometre log race, during which he helped carry a 55 kg log, the 2 mile speed march, numerous endurance marches and, finally, the 7 kilometre stretcher race.

It was a proud day in November 1999 when Private Thomas Keys of 650 Athens Platoon toasted Her Majesty the Queen with a tot of port, received his maroon beret and heard the words of Field Marshal, the Viscount Montgomery of Alamein:

What manner of men are these who wear the maroon beret? They are firstly, all volunteers and are then toughened by hard physical training. As a result they have that infectious optimism and that offensive eagerness that comes from physical well being. They have jumped from the air and by doing so have conquered fear.

Their duty lies in the van of battle; they are proud of their honour and have never failed in any task. They have the highest standards in all things whether it be skills in battle or smartness in the execution of our peacetime duties. They have shown themselves to be as tenacious and determined in defence as they are courageous in attack. They are in fact, men apart. Every man an Emperor.

Of all the factors which make for success in battle the spirit of the warrior is the most decisive. That spirit can be found in full measure in the men who wear the maroon beret.

Less than a year later Tom was standing inside a Chinook as it hovered over the West African jungle. With 600 rounds draped around his shoulders and cradling a GPMG, Tom was on Op BARRAS – the joint A Company (1 PARA) and D Squadron (22 SAS) mission to rescue the Royal Irish Rangers. A big, grisly NCO, face blackened and eyes burning, bellowed at him: 'You ready to go, Keys?'

'Yeah!' Tom screamed back.

'You get those fucking rounds down! You hear?'

The West Side Boys, for all their voodoo and hallucinogenic drugs to raise their pain thresholds, were less formidable than the NCO.

'Go!'

Once on the ground he had looked up to see smoke wafting above the jungle canopy, and heard the almighty crack of the helicopter cannons. The hostages were freed and Op BARRAS was successful. Afterwards an SAS soldier told Tom, 'The next time we have a party we'll invite you lot again.'

As they watched the TV news Reg told his wife: 'He won't even be there, Sal, they'll have sent seasoned Paras. Our Tom's just a boy.'

On his return from Sierra Leone, the reluctant hero posed for his local newspaper in the family's back garden. He was a veteran of combat but seldom needed to shave. Reg begged him to consider joining a 'safer' regiment and Tom, whose next tour of duty was Northern Ireland, said he would think about it.

General Sir Mike Jackson, Colonel Commandant of the Parachute Regiment, said, 'I must emphasise that the action in Sierra Leone has been widely admired. It is also worth noting that of the twelve casualties six were officers or NCOs (including the company commander) and eight soldiers had been out of training for only two weeks.' It had always been this way – there had never been a cosseted introduction into airborne forces and officers were expected to lead from the front.

IT was to the disappointment of many in 1 PARA that by late 2002 the battalion was led by a former cavalryman, his ethos and culture being anathema to his men. Lieutenant Colonel T. A. Beckett had transferred from the Queen's Royal Hussars (QRH) – the senior light cavalry regiment with 300 years' service to the Crown and a policy of recruiting officers almost exclusively from prominent public schools. This then was a sea change for Beckett when he was appointed second-in-command 2 PARA, his job before transferring battalions. By Royal assent the QRH were allowed to sit for the national anthem and from 1745 were absolved from drinking a loyal toast: the King decreed that their loyalty was beyond question. Beckett was politically astute, softly spoken and suave, three attributes lost on his men – with the exception of Captain Al Truett (OC 1 PARA Mortars), nicknamed 'the poshest man in NATO', and the Air Adjutant, Captain Joe Sinclair, an Old Etonian. Beckett's appointment was indicative of an army policy that encouraged officers of differing types to broaden their horizons. It was, however, a risky career move; for while it would look good on Beckett's CV, the position CO 1 PARA entailed dealing with disciplinary problems and operational tours where much could and often did go wrong. Beckett would either 'fly or die'.

His second-in-command, Major Tootal, was a 'Surrey Highlander' – an officer from an originally Scottish infantry regiment which now attracted as many English as Scottish officers. Stuart Tootal was a mere 5 feet 7 inches tall but had a natural air of authority and apparent ease in command. With Beckett loftily detached, it appeared Tootal ran 1 PARA.

In his pre-Christmas address of 2002, Beckett had urged his men to pray for their battalion's inclusion on the Op TELIC ORBAT (Order of Battle): an appropriate suggestion for a CO whose leadership style was considered pastoral. Prayers were answered and 1 PARA returned to Dover a week early to deploy with 3 PARA and the Royal Irish Regiment (1 RI). Op TELIC would be 2nd Lieutenant Ross Kennedy's first tour. One of only a few teetotallers in the Parachute Regiment, his refusal to participate in alcohol-driven initiations to the Officers' Mess had saved him embarrassment. Sometimes his officer brethren went too far, dousing one unconscious subaltern in Sambucca then setting fire to him – having collapsed in the bar he was considered fair game. Ross was popular with his Toms; at 23 years old he was young enough to relate to them and they knew him as 'Ross the Boss' or 'Mr Kennedy'.

They headed to Northumberland to carry out manoeuvres knee-deep in snow – not ideal Gulf War training – while at Connaught Barracks their vehicles were sprayed in desert colours and red squares stuck on the windscreens – the DZ flash denoting a 1 PARA vehicle. That little of their equipment was used or worn exactly as its manufacturers intended was indicative of the Paras seeking to preserve their distinctive culture. The Toms maintained their own argot and this formed part of being 'ally' or 'warry'. A Tom who dismissed such rituals was guilty of 'being hattish'. Netting was added to the Airborne helmet and secured by tyre inner tubes around the rim. The Toms also personalised chest webbing, belt kit and combat vests. While belt kit was the most comfortable on patrol, it was impractical getting in and out of vehicles. Chest webbing, though easier in transit, had a far smaller storage capacity. The compromise option was a combat vest – as favoured by Robbo and Dolman – which allowed soldiers to manoeuvre storage pouches around their upper bodies.

The party heading for RAF Brize Norton – 1 PARA's departure airfield – included 'Gus the Gorilla' and the 'Phantom Chicken of Stevenage', alias two B Company corporals who brought animal fancy dress outfits on every tour. On arrival in Kuwait the emphasis on operational security became apparent when a major from 16 Air Assault Brigade HQ was sent home after being spotted using a mobile telephone; all personnel had been ordered to hand in mobiles before leaving the UK.

RAF Odiham, Hampshire, also moved to a war footing as 7, 18 and 27 Squadrons completed pre-deployment preparations. Among the Chinook pilots was Wing Commander Guy van den Berg, known to many army officers as a former lecturer at the Royal Military Academy, Sandhurst. He was also a veteran of Sierra Leone and Afghanistan.

By 10 February, war looked even more inevitable as Russia, Germany and France issued a joint declaration at the United Nations in favour of further weapons inspections, an option neither Washington nor London was going to accept:

> Russia, Germany and France, acting in close cooperation with one another, reaffirm that the disarming of Iraq in accordance with the relevant UN Security Council resolutions adopted since Resolution 687 constitutes the common objective of the international community and that this process must be brought to a conclusion as quickly as possible.
>
> Resolution 1441, which was unanimously adopted by the Security Council, provides a framework, the options of which have not yet been fully exhausted. The inspections carried out by UNMOVIC and the IAEA have already produced results. Russia, Germany and France advocate a continuation of the inspections as well as a substantial increase of their human and technical capabilities.
>
> There is still an alternative to war. The use of force can only be a last resort. Russia, Germany and France are determined to give every possible chance to the option of disarming Iraq peacefully. Russia, Germany and France note that the position they take is congruent with that of a large number of other countries, particularly among those on the Security Council.

AS the curtain fell on diplomacy, H-J (Sergeant Simon Hamilton-Jewell) was in Farnborough with his girlfriend Katie and her one-year-old son.

H-J made a natural step-parent, providing the love and attention his own father had denied him. Ollie would miss trips to the park with H-J to feed the ducks. H-J and Katie tried to keep the mood light, with the soldier joking that should the worst happen in Iraq he would ensure she received one of his feet to put on the mantelpiece. The 'family' shared a full English breakfast and kissed each other goodbye in Sainsbury's car park.

Russ Aston was about to leave Derbyshire when his father Mike hugged him and held him by the shoulders. It was a crisp, early spring morning. 'For God's sake be careful, Russ.'

'*You're* worried? How do you think I feel?'

'Just keep your head down, son,' Mike said, tearfully.

On 14 February, H-J and his colleagues flew to Kuwait, and Katie opened his card to her. As usual, he had used a calligraphy pen: 'I will really miss you, I will be thinking of you and I love you.'

Tom Keys had listened to his father's suggestion and moved to the RMP, reasoning that having used his brawn he now wanted to use his brain. Tom sat next to his new girlfriend, Lance Corporal Joanne Richardson, on the Tristar flight, and Lance Corporal Emma Morris sat with her fiancé Corporal Si Miller – 156 Provo was something of a love-in.

Si had spent his last afternoon bowling with his parents in Colchester. When John and Marilyn cried he consoled them: 'Don't worry, I'll be fine.'

TWO On the shell *

Camp Eagle, Kuwait, late February 2003

THE RMPs did their best to settle into the desert environment. With so many sharing cramped living quarters, disagreements were inevitable. Tempers frayed as H-J liked to spread out his kit – he laughed off accusations of being a 'dirty bastard' and a 'grot', replying: 'Yeah, but I'm a real soldier.' Major Parry-Jones, 156 Provost Company's Officer Commanding (OC), had included females in his party. The wisdom of this was to be severely tested as Arab men refused to be told what to do by women.

The deployment list read 'LCpl' after 'LCpl' as upon completion of training all RMPs started as lance corporals. Immediate promotion from private supposedly made it easier for junior military police officers to make arrests but did nothing for their popularity outside their number; infantry soldiers often waited many years for their first stripe. Faster routes to NCO level attracted soldiers to the corps from outside while Ben Hyde was one of many to have joined after first seeking to become a civilian police officer.

On his arrival in Kuwait, Tom Keys wrote to his parents:

---

* Carrying the 'shell', a heavy dummy round, was a punishment for misdemeanours such as being late for parade or 'being drunk the morning after'.

Ma and Pa,

Well we arrived, and it's supposed to be winter and the weather is 25–30 degrees during the day and drops to about 5 degrees at night. So expect to see me with a tan like an Arab when I return home. Just imagine what the summer will be like.

The conditions are pretty poor. We have the whole Company about 70 people in one tent, have to take a leak in a hole in the ground and shit in a portaloo and use solar showers, which I will get about once a week. We get fresh food twice a day and one American ration pack – loads of Americans here with humvees, the lot! If I start to get low on stuff like toiletries I will let you know as its OK to send parcels. So send me a small surprise on my B-Day but no alcohol as it is illegal. Then again I'm sure I could hide a miniature Jack Daniels in the bottom of my sleeping bag! And nothing that will melt and it must be small.

We are working very hard with a lot of long nights getting ready. Let me know in the next letter if my car payments, insurance, tax, refunds, visa card and anything else that I should have all sorted out. I think my visa bill was all paid anyway.

It would be good if you could send me the sports pages out of The News of the World so I can keep in touch with all the sports news and results. It doesn't look like I will get the chance to use a phone at all so its letters all the way. As for how long I am going to be out here I have no idea. There are rumours of 3 months varying to 8 so I won't give you a date until I get something more concrete.

The weather is getting hotter during the day and colder at night. Had a few sandstorms and the odd shower; not getting much chance for sunbathing. Let me know how Rich [Tom's brother] is getting on. If you can get hold of a head torch with a red filter it would come in very handy over here, a travel pillow that you can inflate, the one that goes around your neck would be nice to have. Tanning oil is in the bathroom, if you could get hold of all that stuff it would be very much appreciated, and there would be a meal in the Vic on the house. See you when I see you!!

Love Tom xxx

LANCE Corporal Ben Hyde had been a sporty youth, competing for North Yorkshire in cross-country and long jump before joining the Royal Marines. He left after sixteen weeks' training when his girlfriend gave him an ultimatum: her or military life. He chose her and headed back north but they soon split up. Ben realised he had let down himself and his family: his grandfather was a World War Two veteran, fighting in Alamein and Sicily and landing on Gold Beach on D-Day, while his father John had always regretted not joining the forces himself. Ben applied for the civilian police but his local constabulary considered him too young. The 23-year-old from Northallerton had joined the RMP as a stop-gap but came to enjoy Red Cap life. His friends, chief among them Russ and Tom, favoured his company as he, in their words, 'liked a bit of nonsense'. In Kuwait Ben found himself working as platoon commander James Hibbert's driver and radio operator. He referred to him, informally at least, as 'Mr H'.

Having joined the regular army in 1999, Op TELIC was 24-year-old Corporal Paul Long's first operational deployment. Born in Portsmouth, Paul had lived in various towns, including Aldershot and South Shields. He was married to Gemma and they had a baby boy, Benjamin. Paul opposed the war but kept his views private. Lack of sleep in Kuwait came as a shock, as he told his mother on 23 February: 'I have only been here eight days; seems like a couple of months. Sorry it's a short letter but I have only had six hours sleep since Friday 07.00hrs…Anyway, Mum, I love you and missing everyone so much. Hope it is not too long till I come home.'

Tom Keys sought to reassure his father: 'Don't worry too much, the Yanks go in first, then the Brits of which we are the last ones to go. We might not even cross the border.'

His former 1 PARA colleagues wanted to get 'danger close' to the enemy and the sooner the better. Si Miller wrote home:

Hey dudes, how's it going? We're both good but getting sand in places I never thought possible. The weather is about 28 degrees, not bad for winter. Sandstorms are a pain in the rectum. We're living in Camp Eagle – joint British and American forces (US Marines 'Hoo-Ha') in the middle of the Kuwait desert. The camp is a big old boy with very limited facilities. We've been washing in big bowls of cold water, nice!!! We've been doing plenty of training and acclimatising and filling sand bags.

Thank you for the lovely letter and goodies. Keep them coming; they are morale boosters. I'll have to get some photos of Emma in her desert uniform. Let me know how 'The Spud' is getting on, oh and by the way I got to start wearing my second stripe on the day we left (loads of money). We're getting to see quite a lot of each other which is really nice but that will change before much longer. Emma is sitting here with me now. She sends all her love and a big thanks for the goodies. Oh and by the way the address is BFPO 660 not 663 but not to worry, it still got here.

We'll write again soon, loads of love,

Cpl Si Miller and LCpl Emma Morris

As a show of élan was required to impress the war planners, 1 PARA carried out a parachute jump in NBC (nuclear, biological and chemical) suits, using US Hercules planes to demonstrate they were not tied to the RAF. It was devilishly hot on board, the men close to fainting. As this was his eighth jump, there was a special moment for one 'penguin' on the Drop Zone, Private John Bayliss. With this jump he qualified for his Para wings, which were presented by Major Andy Harrison. Tom remembered Harrison, the officer having been captured in Sierra Leone before making his own escape, while Tom's OC in Sierra Leone was Major Matt Lowe, aka 'Major Low Morale', who was wounded by a stray British mortar round. Recovered and promoted, Lowe led the brigade's recce party to Kuwait and was the CO-in-waiting of 3 PARA. Lowe and Harrison, the latter now OC A Company, had received OBEs after Op BARRAS. *Typical gung-ho Paras*, thought many RMP of 1 PARA's drop – the same response met 3 PARA's 10 mile battle march, after which around thirty soldiers collapsed with heat exhaustion.

One unit had to direct traffic and enforce speed limits and this was the RMP. During the war-fighting phase the corps' tasks would include regulating the flow of personnel and logistics, route reconnaissance, traffic posts and controlling prisoners of war and refugees. Their time of greatest opportunity would fall in post-war Iraq.

156 Provost Company was a distant relative in the Airborne family, by marriage rather than birth, and relations between the corps and 1 PARA were tense. In the 1980s the Paras used to overturn RMP Land Rovers in Aldershot. A more recent thorn was an incident in Kosovo in July 1999 when members of 1 PARA shot and killed locals belonging to the Kosovo Liberation Army (KLA). The British commander in country, General Jackson, described it as a 'regrettable incident', claiming his men 'felt they had no other choice but to open fire in self defence'. The RMP's Special Investigation Branch (SIB) tentatively reached a darker conclusion, suggesting grounds for a murder investigation. To Red Caps, the Army Board's subsequent dismissal of their findings was a whitewash, proof that the Ministry of Defence would always cover up controversial misdemeanours. The legacy was deep mistrust.

At least two of the Paras involved in the shooting were still serving in 1 PARA, and their tasks during and after the war-fighting phase would include responsibility for the Red Caps' security. Disharmony would compromise operational effectiveness.

THERE were 32,000 UK personnel and 6,500 vehicles in theatre. Given the challenge of moving a large percentage of them across the border, a 24 hour desert driving and navigation exercise was carried out. Dubbed 'the drive from hell', it highlighted flaws in British vehicles, particularly the DAF trucks. By day they were steaming hot tin cans, by night they were freezing. The exercise took place during the worst sandstorms reported for thirty years: drivers became lost, trucks broke down or got stuck in the sand dunes, gravel plains and salt marshes. The drivers learnt that soft sand was only passable during hours of darkness, when surface moisture was present, and that rocky areas caused tyre damage. Temperatures dictated vehicle maintenance: tyres inflated to the correct pressure for night driving burst during the day and petrol tanks filled at night overflowed. It was impossible to keep sand out of the engines. Cooling systems had to be serviced, radiators cleared, fan belts adjusted, oil changed and coolant levels constantly topped up – there were many hours when Tim May cursed being 8 Platoon's sole holder of a Heavy Goods Vehicle licence.

Sand also caused rifle stoppages and scratched weapon sights. To prevent this, A2 rifles were wrapped in bin liners and clingfilm stuck over the sights. Every spare moment was used to clean weapons. When Jock Robbo was seen zig-zagging across the desert during a 'Nav-Ex' he blamed his new Global Positioning System (GPS). He was ribbed for this moment of navigational embarrassment but got off lightly compared to Eldon Raymond, a Tom who spent half an hour searching for his daysack only to find it on his back.

On 24 February the United States, United Kingdom and Spain introduced a new UN resolution:

> Noting that Iraq has submitted a declaration pursuant to its resolution 1441 containing false statements and omissions and has failed to comply with and cooperate fully in the implementation of that resolution.
>
> Mindful of its primary responsibility under the charter of the United Nations for the maintenance of international peace and security.
>
> Recognising the threat of Iraq's non-compliance with council resolutions and proliferations of weapons of mass destruction and long-range missiles poses to international peace and security.
>
> Determined to secure full compliance with its decisions and to restore international peace and security in the area, decides that Iraq has failed to take the final opportunity afforded to it in resolution 1441.

As the Prime Minister told the House of Commons:

> We will not put it to a vote immediately. Instead we will delay it to

give Saddam one further, final chance to disarm voluntarily. The UN Inspectors are continuing their work. They have a further report to make in March. But this time Saddam must understand. Now is the time for him to decide. Passive rather than active cooperation will not do. Cooperation on process not substance will not do. Refusal to declare properly and fully what has happened to the unaccounted for WMD will not do. Resolution 1441 called for full, unconditional and immediate compliance. Not 10 per cent, not 20 per cent, not even 50 per cent, but 100 per cent compliance. Anything less will not do. That is all we ask; that what we said in Resolution 1441 we mean; and that what it demands, Saddam does.

Is it not reasonable that Saddam provides evidence of destruction of the biological and chemical agents and weapons the UN proved he had in 1999? So far he has provided none. Is it not reasonable that he provides evidence that he has destroyed 8,500 litres of anthrax that he admitted possessing, and the 2,000 kilos of biological growth material, enough to produce over 26,000 litres of anthrax? Is it not reasonable that Saddam accounts for up to 360 tonnes of bulk chemical warfare agent, including one and a half tonnes of VX nerve agents, 3,000 tonnes of precursor chemicals and over 30,000 special munitions?

To those who say we are rushing to war, I say this. We are now 12 years after Saddam was first told by the UN to disarm; nearly six months after President Bush made his speech to the UN accepting the UN route to disarmament; nearly 4 months on from Resolution 1441 and even now today we are offering Saddam the prospect of voluntary disarmament through the UN.

I detest his regime. But even now he can save it by complying with the UN's demand. Even now we are prepared to go the extra step to achieve disarmament peacefully.

I do not want war. I do not believe anyone in this House wants war. But disarmament peacefully can only happen with Saddam's active cooperation.

THE invasion, or at least the pre-war air raids, had already begun. Operation DENY FLIGHT knocked out key enemy military installations in southern and central Iraq. Officially, United States Central Command (CENTCOM) declared the missions had been carried out in response to violations of the UN-stipulated Southern No Fly Zone. The result was that by 17 March, the final deadline for Iraq to comply on disarmament, most of its mobile surface-to-air missiles systems would be knocked out.

To Russ, war seemed a foregone conclusion, but with the temperature rising daily there was only so long he and his colleagues could sit in the desert before their health and battle readiness suffered.

> Dear Anna,
>
> I hope you and Paygan are well. The sand and dust is worse than I thought, it gets everywhere. All we are doing at the moment is training ready for war. We are unfortunately going to be here for a long time, possibly 7–9 months. But things are always changing so we will have to see. Our main job is to follow the Americans into Iraq. So we will have a lot of traumatic sights and jobs to do. So you'll have to bear with me when I'm home. Anyway, that is all I've been told so far. I hope all your family are well. Say hello to your Dad and Tosh etc.
>
> Well, we have only been rationed two bottles of water a day. Fuck knows why. Something to do with a shortage! Give our daughter a big cuddle and a kiss from her daddy and tell her I love her. I love you dearly sweetheart, I know I don't always show it but I do. So remember that. I've had a lot on my plate lately, but it will calm down on my return. The letters I write to you can take up to nine days to get to you so be patient sweety. This is due to the logistics of the Army. Anyway I have decided to buy a nice new motorbike so this will be a present to myself for my birthday and anniversary. It's a bit of shit but I'm here for both. I'll make it up to you at a later date. Give those furry critters a cuddle for me too. How are the wooflets doing – all well and blind? Well babes, there

really isn't anything else I can tell you about the war but keep watching the news and you might catch a glimpse of me. Hopefully when we are fully established here we will be able to get 20 minutes of phone calls a week, so I will hopefully be able to speak to you soon, don't know when, likely by the end of the month, so don't wait in. I will always get back to you.

When I get back we will have a little holiday somewhere, I don't know where yet (as long as there's not much sand). Can you send me some batteries (AAA) the same as the ones in the video remote please, and some chocolate and other goodies. All we eat is rations. I'm getting thin already, I've only been here a week. Also some multi-vitamins please. Put something in that you think I might like. Thanks. I miss you both very much indeed and love you both dearly. Everybody here is going down with illnesses, I'm alright though, which is the main thing. I love you very much and miss you more. Give Paygan a kiss and a cuddle from her Daddy and tell her I love her very much. See you soon.

All my love and cuddles,

Russ xxxx

1 PARA Quartermaster (QM) Major Pete 'Swiss Toni' Lodge was concerned about ammunition. The Toms had been ripping through 'training ammo' on the assumption that a re-supply would be forthcoming. Training ammo was now all that 1 PARA would receive – range practice was scaled down. There were also insufficient ceramic plates for personal body armour – Paras were issued with one plate each, rather than two, which they strapped across their chests. Lack of rounds and ceramic plates were but two of a number of glitches in the supply chain suffered by British units. By way of compensation, more kit was 'borrowed' from US forces.

By order, there was to be no 'chuntering' when the media corps arrived. If questioned, Toms were to say: 'Morale is high. I'm ready to do what I've been trained for.'

Had 7 Armoured Brigade arrived sooner, the war may already have been underway, yet General Jackson earned a rebuke from Downing Street for suggesting what he and the world knew: Gulf War II remained a matter of when, not if: 'If it's today, it's good to go.' The Prime Minister's spokesman offered 'clarification': 'As I am sure he [General Jackson] acknowledges, the decision whether troops are ready is one thing. The decision as to their use is another.'

On 10 March President Jacques Chirac said France would vote no to the United Kingdom's new resolution, 'whatever the circumstances, because we do not think war is necessary to achieve the goal we've established', adding that waging war without UN backing set a 'dangerous' precedent. Igor Ivanov, Russia's Foreign Minister, agreed: 'Russia believes that no further resolutions of the UN Security Council are necessary. Therefore Russia openly declares that if the draft resolution that currently has been introduced for consideration and which contains demands in the form of an ultimatum that cannot be met, is nonetheless put to a vote then Russia will vote against.'

TONY Blair joined US President George W. Bush and Spanish President José Maria Aznar in the Azores on 16 March for a tri-state council of war. Bush emphasised the invasion's humanitarian dimension:

> Action to remove the threat from Iraq would also allow the Iraqi people to build a better future for their society. And Iraq's liberation would be the beginning, not the end of our commitment to its people. We will supply humanitarian relief, bring economic sanctions to a swift close and work for the long-term recovery of Iraq's economy.
>
> We'll make sure that Iraq's natural resources are used for the benefit of their owners, the Iraqi people. Iraq has the potential to be a great nation. Iraq's people are skilled and educated. We'll push as quickly as possible for an Iraqi interim authority to draw upon the talents of Iraq's people to rebuild their nation. We're committed to the goal of a unified Iraq, with democratic institutions of which members of all ethnic and religious groups are treated with dignity and respect.

Crucial days lie ahead for the world. I want to thank the leaders here today and many others for stepping forward and taking leadership and showing their resolve in the cause of peace and the cause of security.

President Aznar:

I would like to remind you that we all said before we came here that we were not coming to the Azores to make a declaration of war; that we were coming after having made every possible effort. After having made this effort, continuing to make this effort, to working to achieve the greatest possible agreement and for international law to be respected and for UN resolutions to be respected.

We are well aware of the international world public opinion, of its concern. And we are also very well aware of our responsibilities and obligations. If Saddam Hussein wants to disarm and avoid the serious consequences that he has been warned about by the United Nations, he can do so. Nothing in our document, nor in our statement, can prevent him from doing so if he wants to. So his is the sole responsibility.

The Prime Minister:

Even some days ago we were prepared to set out clear tests that allowed us to conclude whether he was cooperating fully or not, with a clear ultimatum to him if he refused to do so. And the reason we approached it in that way is that that is what we agreed in Resolution 1441.

This was his final opportunity; he had to disarm unconditionally. Serious consequences would follow if he failed to do so.

And this is really the impasse that we have, because some say there should be no ultimatum, no authorisation for force in any new UN resolution; instead more discussion in the event of non-compliance. But the truth is that without a credible ultimatum authorising force in the event of non-compliance, then more discussion is just more delay, with Saddam remaining armed with weapons of mass destruction and continuing a brutal murderous regime in Iraq.

And this game that he is playing is, frankly, a game that he has played over the last 12 years. Disarmament never happens. But instead the international community is drawn into some perpetual negotiation, gestures designed to divide the international community, but never real and concrete cooperation leading to disarmament.

THE next day, 17 March, Sir Jeremy Greenstock, the British Ambassador to the UN, confirmed the diplomatic process was at an end – the co-sponsors of the crucial second resolution had withdrawn. UN Secretary General Kofi Annan ordered weapons inspectors to leave Iraq; President Bush gave Saddam Hussein 48 hours to leave the country and Robin Cook MP, Leader of the House of Commons, resigned. By consensus, Cook gave one of the most moving speeches heard in the chamber for many years:

> I applaud the heroic efforts that the Prime Minister has made in trying to secure a second resolution. I do not think that anybody could have done better than the Foreign Secretary in working to get support for a second resolution within the Security Council. But the intensity of those attempts underlines how important it was to succeed. Now that those attempts have failed we cannot pretend that getting a second resolution was of no importance.
>
> The reality is that Britain is being asked to embark on a war without agreement in any of the international bodies of which we are a leading partner – not NATO, not the European Union and, now, not the Security Council. To end up in such diplomatic weakness is a serious reverse.
>
> Only a year ago, we and the United States were part of a coalition against terrorism that was wider and more diverse than I would ever have imagined possible. History will be astonished at the diplomatic miscalculations that led so quickly to the disintegration of that powerful coalition.

The US can afford to go it alone, but Britain is not a superpower. Our interests are best protected not by unilateral action but by multilateral agreement and a world order governed by rules. Yet tonight the international partnerships most important to us are weakened: the European Union is divided; the Security Council is in stalemate. Those are heavy casualties of a war in which a shot has yet to be fired.

Only a couple of weeks ago, Hans Blix told the Security Council that the key remaining disarmament tasks could be completed within months. I have heard it said that Iraq has had not months but 12 years in which to complete disarmament and that our patience is exhausted. Yet it is more than 30 years since Resolution 242 called on Israel to withdraw from the occupied territories. We do not express the same impatience with the persistent refusal of Israel to comply.

From the start of the present crisis, I have insisted, as Leader of the House, on the right of this place to vote on whether Britain should go to war. It has been a favourite theme of commentators that this House no longer occupies a central role in British politics. Nothing could better demonstrate that they are wrong than for this House to stop the commitment of troops in a war that has neither international agreement nor domestic support. I intend to join those tomorrow night who will vote against military action now. It is for that reason and for that reason alone and with a heavy heart that I resign from the Government.

ON the same day, H-J wrote from Kuwait:

Hello Mum,

I hope all is well. Everything is OK here but we will probably be here for quite a long time. I can't phone at the moment, because there are no phones, that's why I thought I'd write. If you have any problems, call Mike and Maria. I think you have their numbers but just in case...I hope you can read my writing because I'm doing it by torchlight in a sandstorm. Anyway, I'll write again when it is easier to do so and I'll make it a bit longer.

Things are busy here, as we are waiting to breach the Iraqi border and have been doing lots of training and preparation. I don't think we will be here more than a few months, so I should be home before the summer.

Because we will be invading soon mail will be stopped for a while, so if you don't hear from me for a while you know why. There is not much to tell really, every day is much the same as the last, we just want to get on with the job. Not too long now, but most of the Iraqi troops have deserted already, so there won't be much fighting, just picking up prisoners of war. It's St Patrick's Day today, but no Guinness for us. I'm looking forward to a pint and some decent food. I've lost quite a lot of weight out here!!! At least when I come home this time I'll be back for a while, so I can enjoy some normality for a while. Say hello to Tony and Eileen, no doubt I'll see them when I come back, but for now, I'll sign off. So take care and I'll write when I can.

Love
Simon

THERE was now no telling what fate held for 8 Platoon or 156 Provost Company. G-Day minus 1 – the day before the start of ground operations – was Lieutenant Colonel Beckett's last chance to brief his Battle Group. The media were present, but only on condition that he would not be quoted:

Gentlemen, even though I am confident that you will, I want you to remember to look after each other, as you always do. This is not the first time for us, but this operation does have the potential to be one of the riskiest we've undertaken, even though our role remains unclear. Do not get disheartened; even if our part turns out to be small, it will be as part of an important overall plan.

We are starting a new chapter in the regiment's history; as each day passes we are writing new pages in this history. I have every confidence in your ability. There is no doubt you will uphold the traditions of the regiment. Hopefully at the end of this, whenever it might be, we will all be able to stand here and I will be able to address you all in a similar fashion. Best of luck.

Next to speak was the 1 PARA RSM, 'Winker' Watson, the Toms' father figure and disciplinarian-in-chief. He waited until the CO and 'Ruperts' were out of earshot: 'Right…to anyone I have put on the shell or charged in the last year I would like to say sorry! And to reinforce what the CO said, it is time to look after each other, irrespective of rank. If we don't, people will die. There is no more time for fun and games.'

Excerpts from the Prime Minister's final pre-war address to the House of Commons, 18 March 2003

At the outset, I say that it is right that the House debate this issue and pass judgment. That is the democracy that is our right, but that others struggle for in vain. Again, I say that I do not disrespect the views in opposition to mine. This is a tough choice indeed, but it is also a stark one: to stand British troops down now and turn back, or to hold firm to the course that we have set. I believe passionately that we must hold firm to that course. The question most often posed is not 'Why does it matter?' but 'Why does it matter so much?'

The country and the Parliament reflect each other. This is a debate that, as time has gone on, has become less bitter but no less grave. So why does it matter so much? Because the outcome of this issue will now determine more than the fate of the Iraqi regime and more than the future of the Iraqi people who have been brutalised by Saddam for so long, important though those issues are. It will determine the way in which Britain and the world confront the central security threat of the 21st century, the development of the United Nations, the relationship between Europe and the United States, the relations within the European Union and the way in which the United States engages with the rest of the world. So it could hardly be more important. It will determine the pattern of international politics for the next generation.

And what is the claim of Saddam today? Why, exactly the same as before: that he has no weapons of mass destruction. Indeed, we are asked to believe that after seven years of obstruction and non-compliance, finally resulting in the inspectors' leaving in 1998 – seven years in which he hid his programme and built it up, even when the inspectors were there in Iraq – when they had left, he voluntarily decided to do what he had consistently refused to do under coercion.

When the inspectors left in 1998, they left unaccounted for 10,000 litres of anthrax; a far-reaching VX nerve agent programme; up to 6,500 chemical munitions; at least 80 tonnes of mustard gas, and possibly more than 10 times that amount; unquantifiable amounts of sarin, botulinum toxin and a host of other biological poisons; and an entire Scud missile programme.

We are asked now seriously to accept that in the last few years – contrary to all history, contrary to all intelligence – Saddam decided unilaterally to destroy those weapons. I say that such a claim is palpably absurd.

This is the choice before us. If this House now demands that at this moment, faced with this threat from this regime, British troops are pulled back, that we turn away at the point of reckoning – this is what it means – what then? What will Saddam feel? He will feel strengthened beyond measure. What will the other states that tyrannise their people, the terrorists who threaten our existence, take from that? They will take it that the will confronting them is decaying and feeble. Who will celebrate and who will weep if we take our troops back from the Gulf now?

The House wanted this discussion before conflict. That was a legitimate demand. It has it, and these are the choices. In this dilemma, no choice is perfect, no choice is ideal, but on this decision hangs the fate of many things: of whether we summon the strength to recognise the global challenge of the 21st century, and meet it; of the Iraqi people, groaning under years of dictatorship; of our armed forces, brave men and women of whom we can feel proud, and whose morale is high and whose purpose is clear; of the institutions and alliances that will shape our world for years to come. To retreat now, I believe, would put at hazard all that we hold dearest. To turn the United Nations back into a talking shop; to stifle the first steps of progress in the Middle East; to leave the Iraqi people to the mercy of events over which we would have relinquished all power to influence for the better; to tell our allies that at the very moment of action, at the very moment when they need our determination, Britain faltered: I will not be party to such a course.

This is not the time to falter. This is the time not just for this Government – or, indeed, for this Prime Minister – but for this House to give a lead.

THAT evening Tony Blair secured the backing of MPs for British troops to participate in the invasion of Iraq by a majority of 179.

THREE Qalat Sikar

FORT Pegasus, 10 kilometres south of the Iraqi border, held its breath on the last night before war. Electric lights powered by generators illuminated the canvas of the Operations Tent. At close quarters voices could be heard, at a lower pitch than the laughter that by day carried above the makeshift washing lines and volleyball courts drawn in the sand. As Lieutenant Colonel Beckett appeared in the doorway those sitting braced up and those standing stood to attention. The top button of his desert camouflage shirt was undone, but the collar was rigid. A Union Jack was sewn onto his upper left sleeve and immediately beneath was his brigade's new insignia. The badge, which was similar to the US Airborne's Screaming Eagle, had replaced the Pegasus motif and been christened the 'Screaming Budgie' by his men. Slung from Beckett's 58 pattern webbing belt and encased in an olive-green belt holster was a pistol. He nodded to those closest to him and sat down.

Major Kemp was among those already present. His Parachute Regiment service dated back to the late 1980s and included a claim to fame neither recalled with fondness nor known to all. As a 2 PARA subaltern, Kemp had led a four-man team on *Combat*, an ITV reality show which pitched infantry units against each other in military exercises. Kemp's battalion and the Scots Guards had won through to the final, presented by Emlyn Hughes and Anneka Rice. Had Kemp's quartet lost to 'hats', they would have been blackballed. They won, assisted by the Scots' navigational error which caused them to set off for phase one, a cross-country drive, in the wrong direction. The Regular Army sighed; they would have cheered a Guards victory over the Paras who, unfairly, poured scorn on them all. Kemp had risen through the junior officer ranks and been awarded the Queen's Commendation for Valuable Service (QCVS) in the 2003 New Year's Honours. He was now awaiting promotion to lieutenant colonel.

1 PARA had been tasked to carry out an aerial assault on the Qalat Sikar airfield close to the Tigris and Euphrates rivers. The mission was to be spearheaded by Kemp's company and heavy casualties were a distinct possibility. C Company would infiltrate in two waves of Chinook helicopters and hold their positions under enemy bombardment until A and B Companies arrived.

Tootal stood, greeted the men and moved through the 'actions on' in the event of an immediate Iraqi air strike. He then asked someone from 23 Engineer Regiment to start with 'ground', a description of the airfield 310 kilometres north of their current location and 150 kilometres south of Baghdad, including the routes and transport links to and from the target and all relevant geographical details. Intelligence Officer Captain Morgan followed with 'Situation: Enemy Forces': two Iraqi divisions, the 10 Armoured and 24 Mechanised, plus elements of the Republican Guard were in the area. However, it was hoped that desertions and heavy aerial bombardment would reduce their fighting capacity by 50 per cent. Captain Morgan concluded with enemy defences, strengths, morale, intentions, likely ambush positions, Iraqi installations, camps and reinforcements.

As those before him leaned forwards in anticipation of another whispered delivery, Beckett produced his aide-memoire notebook, his thoughts on the 'concept of operations' neatly written out:

> As you are all aware we have been tasked to carry on an ABTF
> [Airborne Task Force] mission to attack and to hold the Qalat Sikar
> airfield. There are two objectives: to seize the airfield and to secure the
> eastern flank for the United States Marine Corps [USMC]. In order to

carry out the operation the Battle Group will be separated into four groups. An advance party of Pathfinders [the brigade's elite reconnaissance force, similar to the SAS] and 23 Engineer Regiment Recce Troop will survey the HLS [Helicopter Landing Site] for enemy.

The first wave of the assault will be carried out by C Company. A Company will then arrive with MSGs [Manoeuvre Support Groups]. All being well C Company will then move into screening positions and B Company will infil by road. The USMC will then take over the airfield from us.

The briefing then became more specific and 'what ifs' followed – including who would be in command throughout each phase. Kemp would assume authority from the recce party before handing over to Beckett, who would arrive with A Company. In the event of Beckett's death, command would pass from the CO's Tactical Headquarters to 'Alt HQ': Major Tootal. After procedures for casualty evacuation, reinforcements, situation friendly forces, civilian population, dress, customs and attachments were all covered, the Orders Group closed.

Exactly one hour had passed. The last order was to synchronise watches, in keeping with tradition, to the artillery officer's timepiece.

TWENTY-FOUR hours later, on the night of 19 March, an assassination attempt on Saddam Hussein and his sons failed. A CIA source had reported that they would be staying at the Doha Farm complex near Baghdad University. A pair of 2,000 lb satellite-guided 'Bunker Buster' bombs struck Saddam's bunker, but the President escaped.

In a live broadcast at 10.15 p.m. Eastern Standard Time President Bush proclaimed, 'My fellow citizens, at this hour, American and Coalition forces are in the early stages of military operations to disarm Iraq, to free its people and to defend the world from grave danger.' His audience neither heard nor saw the President's off-camera gesture as he pumped his fist and shouted, 'I feel good!' It was, however, reported by the US media.

This was the start of Defence Secretary Donald Rumsfeld's game plan – dubbed 'War-lite' – relying on less than half the troops used to liberate Kuwait twelve years earlier. His inspiration cast aside the traditional military doctrine of overwhelming force and was drawn from the business school lecture hall: a minimal outlay of assets to achieve maximum results, precision-guided missiles to disrupt command and limit civilian casualties, and simultaneous air and land strikes before a rapid advance to Baghdad by fewer, better-equipped troops – harder work for those who had been deployed. When Rumsfeld referred to 'better equipped' troops he must have been thinking of his own, rather than British soldiers.

Air strikes on Baghdad followed on 20 March as the Special Boat Service (SBS), 40 and 42 Commando Royal Marines and US Navy Seals moved ashore on Iraq's southern coast. Resistance around Umm Qasr was fierce and the first British casualties came that night when five Royal Marines, two army gunners and a Royal Navy specialist died on a US CH-46 Sea Knight helicopter, which crashed after a mechanical failure.

On Friday 21 March, 1 PARA's A, B and D Companies left Fort Pegasus to drive to Qalat Sikar. As they did so Iraq's capital came under fire from 500 aerial munitions. Two hours later, at around 0130 GMT, 22 March, two Royal Navy Sea King helicopters collided over the northern Arabian Gulf, costing one American and six British lives; again there were no survivors.

The following day C Company, including 2nd Lieutenant Kennedy's 8 Platoon and 1 PARA Battalion Headquarters, were airlifted to within striking distance of the target.

ALTHOUGH the front ceramic plate looked tiny on Russ Aston's 13 stone, six-foot-two-inch frame and would only have protected him from a shot to the heart, the charismatic RMP was thankful for his flak jacket. His sleeves were rolled up to an inch below the lowest of four badges on his right arm: a red square with the black letters MP. Snaking its way down his left arm past his elbow was his Maori tattoo. He and Anna thought it looked fantastic; his mum, Glenice, did not.

In the Land Rover's front passenger seat, identically attired and with his helmet chin strap pulled tight, was Steve Brown, one of Russ's best mates. As they crossed the border into Iraq a disposable camera was produced. Russ took his right hand off the wheel and wrapped it around Steve as the fellow corporal leant in and got them both into the frame: a definite Kodak moment. The RMP's war had begun.

PROGRESS towards Qalat Sikar by Recce Troop (RE) and Pathfinders (PF) was halted by US forces near Nasiriyah – the Americans had lost men in a firefight and the main road was an avenue of armoured personnel carriers (APCs) destroyed by RPGs.

As darkness fell they were authorised to proceed and US helicopter gunships screeched above them as they crossed Nasiriyah's north bridge. Although the British killed their lights and used night vision goggles (NVGs), Iraqis located the convoy and put the lead vehicle under fire, bursting a tyre. The wagon limped on to a US position three kilometres away and sent a sitrep via Tactical Satellite (TACSAT). The convoy drove on 40 kilometres before sighting more enemy. This time they turned off-road to find an observation position. Up to a dozen Iraqi vehicles passed, armed with RPGs and Dushka, Russian-made 12.7 mm heavy machine guns. The British party was surrounded by heavily armed Iraqi Army units – emergency action was required. The suggestion made by a Pathfinder officer to blow up their own vehicles and 'tab' the 40 kilometres across country to their final destination was outvoted in favour of a mounted thrust to break the enemy cordon.

Within minutes the convoy was once again under fire, as four RPGs fizzed over the men's heads and one skidded beneath one of the Land Rovers. A Recce Troop NCO was hit by small arms fire and thrown to the ground. Gazing at his midriff he saw the round had lodged against his pistol. Using the Browning .50 cal to maximum effect the convoy succeeded in breaking through, and in doing so destroyed a number of enemy vehicles. Grenades and further heavy machine gun fire finished off Iraqi resistance and the convoy made it to a US-held area. The Americans were relieved to see them: they had lost sixteen soldiers that night; Recce Troop and Pathfinders, none.

Yet, as Tom told his parents, neither heroism nor professionalism could prevent the stream of inadvertent British deaths: 'More people have been killed by accidents than through enemy fire.' On 23 March, two RAF officers were killed when their Tornado was hit by a US Patriot missile as it flew south into Kuwait, returning from an operational mission. On the same day, two members of 33 Engineer Regiment were reported missing in southern Iraq. With British servicemen dying, the Prime Minister's interview with the British Forces Broadcasting Service (BFBS) was aired. Asked about the accidental fatalities, he responded: 'These things are never easy; there will be some tough times ahead. But it is going to plan, despite the tragedies that have occurred and once again we have to thank and take pride in the professionalism, skill and courage of our Armed Forces.'

Russ had mentioned a lack of water in his latest letter to Anna, and the media was also reporting kit shortages. But Blair was unrepentant:

> It is a huge logistical exercise to move tens of thousands of people out into the sand and at the beginning of it you are bound to get problems. But, in fact, the British Army is not one of the finest simply, it is one of the best equipped in the world and we have regular exercises like the Saif Sareea Exercise in Oman [the dry run for Britain's participation in Gulf War II in all but name] in which British troops are constantly training and in a state of readiness, so I think these problems are bound to occur, they do with the Americans too. But we get them sorted out and one of the extraordinary things about the British Armed Forces is just their ability to go into any situation and make the best of it.

On 24 March such kit shortages would have fatal consequences when Sergeant Steven Roberts of 2nd Royal Tank Regiment was killed by friendly fire during a riot in Al Zubayr. Roberts had sacrificed his body armour to give to 'frontline' soldiers whom senior commanders deemed more at risk. Lance Corporal Barry Stephen of the 1st Battalion, the Black Watch, also died.

The length of time the troops were going to spend in Iraq was also a

concern. BFBS asked Blair: 'How full a role would you like to see British troops having once the fighting is over? And are your Defence Secretary and Service Chiefs telling you they have enough personnel to replace the troops that have been fighting to do the peacekeeping?'
He answered:

> This is obviously something we have to discuss with our allies and with other people who may come in and assist in that process and we have got to watch. We have got a certain limit to the capability that British troops can take on. We do a fantastic job in terms of peacekeeping. I would say British troops are probably as admired, if not the most admired, as any in the world. So, you know, we have got that facility; we do it extremely well, but we have got to be careful that we don't overstretch ourselves.
>
> We want to try and bring them [the fighting troops] home as safe and secure as possible. The most important thing we can do for those of our Armed Forces who have gone and put their lives on the line and in some cases lost their lives for their country and for the wider world, is to make sure that they are brought home as soon as possible. I am well aware of our obligations to them and also to their families.

On 25 March, as British and US forces took control of Umm Qasr, two Queen's Royal Lancers were killed when their Challenger 2 tank took incoming fire from another British tank. A third crew member suffered severe burns.

On 26 March, 8 Platoon heard the Qalat Sikar raid was off. By the afternoon the raid was back on and 2nd Lieutenant Kennedy's men were warned to move forward by air from 0600hrs on 27 March. During that night's sandstorm there were two accommodation options, a 'shell scrape' (self-dug trench), or to lie beneath a poncho slung from the side of a vehicle.

The first wave of Chinooks was expected at first light and, sick from sleep deprivation, Alpha and Bravo organised themselves into 'chalks' (numbered queues). Visibility was less than 200 yards. They waited, sitting on their bergens and tugging at every strap until drawn tight and knotted so not an inch could catch on any protruding metal. This kind of discipline was second nature, an early lesson on every parachute jump course and one drummed in until the 'Crows' retained the knowledge.

They peered into the murky distance: no helicopters, just a file of 4-tonne trucks, their outline a blur. At 1500hrs Qalat Sikar was called off again; operational priorities had apparently changed. C Company was instead tasked to guard a gas/oil separation plant (GOSP), which would involve sitting around in the desert doing very little, receiving no training and living in holes in the mud – a huge disappointment after such a dramatic mission had loomed. As they were idle, it was all the more galling to watch the convoys of US vehicles heading to Baghdad.

Meanwhile, in Maysan province the Iraqi Army planned its retreat, unable to defend its positions in Amarah or prevent the uprising in Majar al-Kabir.

On 28 March, 16 Air Assault Brigade suffered its first fatality. 'Dear Anna and Paygan,' wrote Russ Aston, 'The Americans have just blown up one of our tanks with an A-10 Tankbuster. We have just heard about it so I suppose there's more dead there. They always fucking do it don't they. So it's all a bit shit really.'

The attack happened on a road known to British forces as Route Spear, next to the Shatt al-Arab waterway. Eighteen-year-old Trooper Chris Finney of D Squadron, Household Cavalry Regiment, had been driving north when an explosion rocked his armoured vehicle. He assumed he had been hit by an Iraqi RPG; in fact he had been engaged by US aircraft with 30 mm cannon shells. Fire broke out and Finney turned to see his gunner, Al Tudball, wounded. In shock, Finney reversed his Scimitar into the one behind. He climbed out and found cover – but seeing his gunner stuck in the turret he returned to pull him clear. Finney radioed for help and carried Tudball towards dead ground.

The crew of a Spartan threw red smoke to warn the Americans, but to no avail, the attack continued. Matty Hull was trapped in another Scimitar and despite the efforts of Finney and others he died in his vehicle. Iraqi tanks then arrived and Lance Corporal Mick Flynn and Corporal

Dave Telling drew the enemy fire for half an hour while the wounded and deceased were evacuated. Thanks to good fortune and remarkable bravery only one life had been lost. Finney was awarded the George Cross and Flynn the Conspicuous Gallantry Cross.

SICKNESS, substantial weight loss and a recent engagement with Iraqi forces were testing Russ's spirits. As he confided in a phone call to his mother: 'It's just killing for killing's sake out here, mum, and it's the children I worry about. When I get back to the UK I just don't know how I am going to cope with what I've seen.'

'You had to do what you did, Russ, you would have been killed otherwise,' Glenice told him. Russ claimed in a letter to Anna: 'I've shot 4–5 Iraqis* and one of them was quite young, about 15–16 years old. So I felt bad at the time but I'm OK now…' The Iraqis' attitude to death also shocked him:

> There are lots of wild dogs around the location we are at, at the moment. One of them was eating a dead soldier so I buried the soldier properly so he could rest. It is a horrible place here. Nine out of ten times you don't know who the enemy is. They all dress in civilian clothes so you need to be careful.

Russ's experiences were leading him to consider a different life:

> I am thinking of joining the prison service. If you have time you could try to get me some info on it, wages, etc. I have had enough of the Army; I know I have said it before, but I have now.
>
> I don't know how long it is going to last for, we will have a nice holiday when I come home, just me, you and pyklet [Russ's pet name for his daughter] – nowhere with desert please. How are all the family? (yours that is) I hope they are all fine and well.'

He looked to his wife and daughter as a source of strength:

> I will keep my head down because I have you and Paygan to get back to. I can't wait to be back with you both again. I love you

* This claim is disputed.

totally and miss you and Paygan; I cannot begin to describe how much. Anyway, sweetheart, try not to worry about me. 'Ruskins' are superhuman after all. I will get back to you both. Keep smiling and be happy. Kisses and cuddles to you both. All my love,

Russ xxx

FOR Tom Keys the enemy existed on operational maps, in sitreps, and on media broadcasts; everywhere but in the flesh. He wrote home to his parents: 'We are right at the dud end of the action, so try not to worry too much. But it looks like the Yanks are getting it tough. I am really bored so a new book to read would be good for something to do on my rest periods.' Tom wanted to feel he was making a difference: 'All we are doing over here is vehicle check points [VCPs] on civilians and controlling the military traffic around the various areas that have been set up. All in all it's a dull job.'

Tom knew his unit had not deployed to engage the enemy but Op TELIC was failing to provide the mental stimulation he had cited for joining the RMP. He wrote again, a few days later: 'We are still manning TCPs [Traffic Control Points] surrounded by other British units, so I am as safe as I possibly could be at the moment. All we do is direct and monitor military traffic, check routes are serviceable and search any civvy vehicles that come through our location.'

Tom was so far removed from danger that he could afford to bemoan taking precautions: 'No chance to bask in the sun. Have to wear helmet and body armour everywhere.'

ON 30 March, Marine Chris Maddison of 539 Assault Squadron was killed when his landing craft was hit by a Milan fired by 42 Commando, Royal Marines. His vessel was mistaken for an Iraqi tug boat after 42 Commando had been told no other friendly call signs were working in their area of operations. Four other marines were injured – all victims of the 'fog of war'; coordination ceased, communication systems broke down and casualties were self-inflicted. Despite clear evidence pointing to 'blue on blue', the Special Investigation Branch of the RMP said an

RPG had struck Maddison's vessel. It would be many months before its findings were reversed.

The following day, Lance Corporal Shaun Brierley of 212 Signal Squadron was killed in a road traffic accident and Staff Sergeant Chris Muir of the Royal Logistics Corps died conducting explosive ordnance disposal. 16 Air Assault Brigade suffered its second fatality on 1 April when Lance Corporal Karl Shearer was killed when his vehicle over-turned. The crash severely wounded Lieutenant Alexander Tweedie, who died after being airlifted to the UK.

1 PARA had regrouped at Logistical Supply Area 'Rhyl', where the Toms continued chuntering about the lack of 'ally' tasks. Predictably they blamed Beckett – even suggesting this failure was somehow linked to him being a former cavalryman, which was misjudged. Beckett had always been the outsider, his Toms wishing he led in the warrior-esque fashion of his predecessors, whose gruff informality played better with them than Beckett's quiet affability. As he had little influence either with Major General Robin Brims, leading Britain's land invasion force, or Lieutenant General John Reith at Permanent Joint Headquarters (PJHQ), and none with CENTCOM, Beckett was beyond guilt.

His men were the British Army's 'swanks', eager – too eager, many said – to close with the enemy, and when such opportunities were denied they reacted badly. The Paras' detractors, the RMP chief among them, claimed competition between Toms to be 'blooded' made them blasé about the consequences of their actions and a liability to units serving alongside them. They were, more impartially, as one RAF officer put it, 'a sharp tool to be used with care'.

Ahead of 1 PARA now was an array of peace-support tasks, which was not what any infantry battalion, Para or otherwise, had travelled thousands of miles for. The RMPs were about to come into their own.

AS Corporal John West, Jock Robbo's marathon running buddy, led his section around Drilling Station 7 he spotted a lone Iraqi riding a motor-cycle and looking for British troops. Aware the Arab might possess useful intelligence and not wanting to give away his own position, West ordered his men not to fire and they took cover in a ditch. Just metres before the enemy drew level West leapt up and launched himself. A right hook knocked his enemy flying. West stood over him as he came round, 'introduced himself' and his questions were answered. The retelling of this episode lifted the spirits, as did Major Hayward's impression of the Iraqi youth, who, complaining about the shortage of humanitarian aid, had asked forlornly: 'Where is the helping?' This became a 1 PARA catchphrase, admittedly funnier when Hayward repeated it in his best Iraqi accent.

Beckett's men were yet to experience much of it, but interviewed by Abu Dhabi TV, the Prime Minister was questioned on the early signs of civilian resistance, something neither the British nor Americans had 'war-gamed' for:

INTERVIEWER If this resistance carries on and proves that the capture of Iraq is not only to fight Saddam Hussein but to also fight an unconvinced population for a long time, which kind of option would you accept to take in order to end the conflict?

BLAIR I don't believe that is what is happening. What you have got is the security apparatus around Saddam. Now there are tens of thousands of those but they are not the Iraqi population. In the south where the British troops are now patrolling some of these towns, even without their helmets but in ordinary berets and talking to the local people, the moment the local people know that Saddam has gone they are coming out and they are talking about their experiences. And it is important to realise this – the repression of those people and the terror that they had in relation to his regime.

Once that goes then I think you will find that the local people, the ordinary Iraqi people, are out there talking about their experiences. And it is true they don't then want the British or American troops to stay there a moment longer than we need to. We don't want to stay there a moment longer than we need to. As soon as we can get to an interim authority, run by Iraqis, we will do so [leave].

And on the biological and chemical weapons issue Blair continued:

> I have no doubt that we will [find Saddam's WMD]. We have got
> absolutely no doubt that these weapons exist. But there has been a
> campaign of concealment by Saddam ever since he knew that UN
> inspectors were coming back into the country and I have got
> absolutely no doubt that those weapons are there.
>
> You can never find these things unless you have the cooperation
> of the regime itself and once we have the cooperation of the scien-
> tists and the experts I have no doubt that we will find them.

TOM wrote again on 3 April, the day US forces reached Baghdad: 'I have
really brown arms and face but the rest of me is still white, have to even
it out on a sun bed or on holiday because I look stupid at the moment.'
And the next day:

> I saw an advertisement in the back of the Mirror for shorts,
> swimwear you can get a tan through. If you could order a pair of
> black or blue shorts – any colour, just not pink or purple! I should be
> able to get an all-over tan for when I come home. It was only a small
> ad so you will have to look carefully, size 30–32 waist, best go for 32,
> and tins of fruit juice would be good (find advertisement enclosed).

Bored of Traffic Control Points (TCPs), Tom was chuffed to receive an
illicit parcel: 'Thanks a lot. Especially for the "JD". I'll make that last
as long as possible.' His letter on 6 April continued:

> No problems apart from being bored out of my head. I am getting a
> good tan on my top half, but the bottom half is still milk bottle
> white. It looks like I am two different people at the moment, so if
> you can get me a pair of those shorts, any decent pattern or colour
> will do, it would be great. Hope they are not too expensive.
>
> I'll get a few drinks in for all the bits and bobs you have sent
> over. The torch and the travel pillow have been especially useful.
> Another thing that would come in handy is a cheap pair of flip-flops
> to chill out in and some new clean pants. All everyone wants to

know over here is when we are going home, but I still have no date. There are rumours ranging from May to August. So when I can eventually find out I'll let you know soon as!

Stationed far from the enemy, Paul Long's morale was high :

You said you thought you saw me on telly on 20th Mar. If I was riding a motorbike it was me because we crossed the border on about that date, my section + Platoon Commander. I was caught on camera, two of us on motorbikes, side by side, I was the one wearing sunglasses, soaking up the sunny day, cruising into IRAQ, one of us was wearing a green jacket and one wearing a sandy jacket, that was me.

Working with Emma helped Si stay positive:

I'm fine, well, as well as can be expected when you work all day and night in blistering heat with nothing to eat but stinking rat packs, but it ain't so bad. I bet there's a lot of things you would love to know but unfortunately I can't really tell you, I'm afraid your gonna have to wait until I get home.

I can tell you that we are running info posts and traffic posts along the route up north. We haven't gone too far north yet but close enough to see some shit going down. But still I'm further north than you might think. Being in PL HQ [Platoon Headquarters] has its moments but we're attached to A Section which is Emma's, so that's cool because I can look after her. I've just taken on a new job recently, gathering media intelligence and preparing and giving briefings on the Media Int every night to all the hierarchy. It's not a bad little number. I have been receiving all your letters, even though I'm in the middle of nowhere the mail still gets through OK.

I can't wait to get home because living in a place like this under the stress of war 24/7 makes you realise how precious life is and that you've got to make the most of every single second and believe me when I get back I'm gonna.

Emma was having a more difficult time – an Arab had punched her in the face:

> Emma sends her love. She is also fed up of this shit and can't
> wait to get home. Poor girl has only had two letters from her
> family since we've been here so I write her one a day to keep her
> chin up. Well, duty calls, so I'll sign off. I love you guys so much
> and can't wait to see ya's. Hopefully it won't be too long.

On 6 April, C Company, 1 PARA led an advance to contact – albeit a one-way contact – with support from four artillery batteries and a flight of Lynx helicopters from the 3rd Regiment Army Air Corps (3 AAC). After initial high expectations this was another non-event, the enemy retreating before the Paras arrived, leaving behind their mortars and heavy machine guns.

Basra's peaceful liberation and light British casualties – three fatalities – was in no small part due to Major General Brims resisting political pressure to venture sooner into the city he called a 'vipers' nest'. In London, British forces had apparently to be seen to be making faster progress. Brims waited for Saddam's loyalists to flee and they obliged; a bloody street-by-street battle was avoided. 111 Provost Company, RMP took responsibility for resurrecting the defunct Iraqi police in the city and 115 Company had the same task in the surrounding rural area. Initial assessments of the job were bleak. Roads were strewn with the debris of war and law-abiding citizens cowered in their homes as the 'Ali Babas' (thieves) ran amok. The corps had to restore a 9,000-strong police force with insufficient uniforms, equipment and weapons to some kind of operational status. There were also 55 police buildings in need of repair, and 100 police cars and 5,000 missing weapons to find.

In the afterglow of victory, security was reduced, as Tom confirmed: 'I am wearing a beret as the threat in our area is considered low.' Like many fellow Red Caps Tom's next-of-kin letter, written before the war, was returned to him. He burnt it.

On 7 April, 1 PARA moved north to Al Qurnah, the fabled home of the Garden of Eden. Other elements of 16 Air Assault Brigade, with H-J and Si among them, headed further north to Amarah. 'You're probably getting to see more than me on the news,' Si told his parents. 'But we're moving tomorrow, about 200 km. We're going to do some policing in one of the towns as there's a big problem with looters and robberies. The town has a population of about 300,000 so it won't be an easy task by any means.'

He had been thrilled by a recent day's work:

I know I should be careful what I write but I have to tell you I took 3 POWs to the interrogation centre and it weren't just any 3 Arabs. It was the 2IC [second-in-command] of the Ba'ath Party and 2 of his cronies. I had them lying on the floor in the back of a Pinz [Pinzgauer], handcuffed, sandbags on their heads and my shooter pointed straight at their heads, so that was a pretty crazy experience.

Former Ba'ath Party officials, Iraqi Army generals and ex-Special Forces were regarded as Category A prisoners of war and received closer attention. It was a coup for Si to handle their arrest: 'It would be good if you could record the news and stuff so I could see it when I get back. Oh yeah, and I'm going to get interviewed by a reporter soon and my article will be sent home and put in a local paper. I'll let you know more when I do.'

There was less excitement in the next letter sent by H-J:

Hello Mum,

I hope you are well. Everything is OK here even though we have been pretty busy. I hope you are not worrying unnecessarily because of what is in the papers; things really are OK.

Most of the enemy we come across just surrender, so there is very little fighting in our area and when there is, their soldiers are not anywhere near as professional as us.

I don't know if they are showing any maps on the news but we are between Al Basrah and Al Rumaylah, and gradually moving North West...I don't think my brigade will be going to Baghdad.

H-J was not to know that a forty-four-strong 1 PARA team led by Captains Tom McDade and Danny Matthews MC was to deploy to the British Embassy. They entered a time warp: the calendar read 'January 1991', the residence having been deserted since Gulf War I. With the help of Mahdi Alwen Rahim, the Embassy caretaker since 1978, they ensured the buildings were secured for British diplomats.

H-J continued:

> It's all quietened down here for a couple of days before we take over the next town. Hopefully, now most of the war is over we will be replaced by other troops to carry on the task of clearing up, and we will return home in a couple of months.
>
> I've taken a few photos, so I can show you the various places we've been out here. It's not a particularly clean place out here but still interesting, on the rare occasions we are not busy.
>
> I'm not sure how much longer we will be here, probably another month or two. I've lost track of time to some degree, so one day just flows into the next. All my guys are doing well and no one has been hurt, although we've all lost a bit of weight.

On 8 April, Bush and Blair released a joint statement on Iraq's future:

> Coalition military operations are progressing well and will succeed. We will eliminate the threat posed by Iraq's weapons of mass destruction, deliver humanitarian aid and secure the freedom of the Iraqi people. We will create an environment where Iraqis can determine their own fate democratically and peacefully.
>
> The day when Iraqis govern themselves must come quickly. As early as possible, we support the formation of an Iraqi Interim Authority, a transitional administration, run by Iraqis, until a permanent government is established by the people of Iraq. The Interim Authority will be broad-based and fully representative, with members from all Iraq's ethnic groups, regions and diaspora. The Interim Authority will be established first and foremost by the Iraqi people with the help of the members of the Coalition

and working with the Secretary General of the United Nations.

As Coalition Forces advance, civilian Iraqi leaders will emerge who can be part of such an Interim Authority. The Interim Authority will progressively assume more of the functions of government. It will provide a means for Iraqis to participate in the economic and political reconstruction of their country from the outset. Coalition Forces will remain in Iraq as long as necessary to help the Iraqi people to build their own political institutions and reconstruct their country but no longer.

The first British troops to enter Maysan province discovered locals regarded democracy as ungodly: the rule of the people clashed with the sacred rule of Allah. Allah, not people, made laws, and non-believers could not possibly be the equals of believers; democracy also clashed with the tribal system. Government merely required a group of entitled men descended from families of religious lineage to interpret what had been enshrined in the Koran; a Council of Guardians as it was known in Iran. The indigenous population was also unfamiliar with the Arabic translation of democracy, '*dimokraytiyah*', and the closest word they knew to politics, '*siassah*', also referred to the whipping of stray camels – '*sa'es al-kheilsa*', he who brings lost camels back to the caravan. The proximity of Iran was another factor in the locals' support for theocracy – the late Ayatollah Khomeini, who remained a revered figure twenty years after his Islamic Revolution, regarded democracy as 'a form of prostitution'.

Tom could hardly contain himself as he wrote on 13 April:

Good news. We are now in Phase 4 of the war which means it's all chilled out, fighting pretty much stopped, now dealing with policing the towns and humanitarian aid etc, wearing floppy hats and no body armour, thank God!

Phase 4 also means its 21 days planning to get us home and another 21 days to [actually] get us home. So it should be 42 days at the latest, and being RMP we have to guide everyone back so we are going to be one of the last ones to leave. So it will be sometime, end of May, early June, that's for sure but there is not an exact date as yet, but not too long to go!'

On 15 April President Bush convened his National Security Council in Washington, DC. He was looking to recruit four divisions of international troops – one NATO, one from the Gulf States, one Polish and one British – to serve as peacekeepers. This would allow the United States to begin pulling out troops within weeks and by autumn 2003 reduce its commitment from 140,000 to 30,000 service personnel. General Tommy Franks was present and flew into Baghdad the following day to brief his commanders.

Not even by best-case scenario estimates was such a de-scaling of manpower possible – at its current strength the US had insufficient forces to seal Iraq's borders, allowing terrorists to pour into the country. The collapse of Iraq's civil infrastructure had also been unforeseen, as Condoleezza Rice later conceded:

> The concept was that we would defeat the army, but the institutions would hold, everything from the ministries to police forces. Any big historical change is going to be turbulent. There was a lot of planning based on assumptions, based on the intelligence. It is also the case that when the plan meets reality, it's what it didn't think of that really becomes the problem. So the real question is, can you adjust and make the changes necessary?

Retired Major General James Marks gave his opinion:

> We didn't have enough troops. My position is that we lost momentum and that the insurgency was not inevitable. We did not have enough troops to conduct combat patrols in sufficient numbers to gain solid intelligence and paint a good picture of the enemy on the ground. Secondly, we needed more troops to act on the intelligence we generated. They took advantage of our limited numbers.

As post-war planning was devised by the Department of Defence (DOD) rather than the State Department, Donald Rumsfeld was in charge. His model for post-war Iraq was post-Taliban Afghanistan, where stability, or more precisely a level of stability relative to a state at war for thirty years, had been achieved using a fraction of the US troops stationed in Iraq. Thus the ratio of soldiers to population would be tightly controlled. James Dobbins, the US Special Envoy to Afghanistan said, 'Afghanistan offered a much more congenial answer in terms of what would be required in terms of inputs, including troops.'

President Bush posted Jay Garner to Baghdad to be Iraq's civilian administrator. His time was short, as he lamented: 'John Abizaid [Franks' deputy commander and eventual successor] was the only one who really had his head in the post-war game. The Bush administration did not, Condi Rice did not. You could go brief them, but you never saw any initiative come of them. You just kind of got a north and south nod. And it ends with so many tragic things.'

MAYSAN province was a flat, rural backwater roughly the size of East Anglia with its own distinctive customs and culture. Its people were determined these would not be tampered with by Coalition Forces. The main tribes in Maysan were the Al Bou Muhammed, the province's biggest tribe, Al Wehaddat, Banny Malik, Al Bahadl, Al Bou Aboud, Al Bou Eli, Al Bedhaan, Al Fartous, Bayit Menshed, Al Shuganbah, Bayit Nasser Allah and the Al Bou Bekheet. In Arabic these were known as bodies and split into sub-tribes, collections of extended families with marriage between cousins common, known as thighs. There was a continuity to the tribal system, generation after unquestioning generation having maintained indigenous customs. Each tribe was led by a sheikh whose honour depended upon his ability to impose taxes and command obedience to his rulings.

Self-respect was every tribal member's moral imperative and measured more by how others treated him than how he behaved; avoiding shame and the 'blackening of the face' was a constant priority. If a member of Al Shuganbah was told to move his car by a policeman of the same tribe he would, after great protest, drive to another illegal parking area out of the policeman's sight. Both men would believe face (*wajh*) had been saved; the policeman's instruction being followed and the driver parking in a place of his choosing.*

The people of Maysan had high expectations of the Coalition Forces providing humanitarian aid: thousands of propaganda leaflets had proclaimed a bountiful future after the deposition of Saddam Hussein.

On 19 April, 1 PARA moved up to Maysan's capital, Amarah. The city's people had liberated themselves, without the need for or help of Allied forces, as was also the case in Al Adil, Al Uzayr and Majar al-Kabir. Patrols of Amarah found sixty-seven T-55 tanks and fifteen armoured fighting vehicles abandoned by the Iraqi Army. With Brigade HQ already installed in the deserted military base, 1 PARA's companies camped at the airfield on the city's outskirts.

One private soldier established a record for the number of food parcels received in one day: seventeen, all from a supermarket in Barnsley. Private Monkhouse and his mates ate a lot of Mint Imperials. Witnessing absent-mindedness on the part of one's fellow soldiers had a similar effect on morale as the receipt of such food parcels. Corporal Pat Granger, a Territorial Army Para, became lost driving from Sheik Abadi Mosque to the athletics stadium in Amarah – amusing, as Pat was a trainee London taxi driver. The desire to laugh at one particular soldier's misfortune had to be tempered. He was literally blown off a toilet seat and suffered severe burns after dropping a cigarette butt – the excrement below had previously been doused in petrol. The soldiers tasked with burning it off had left to find a match before the unsuspecting man arrived.

With boredom becoming the troops' number one enemy, 8 Platoon found themselves desperate for new things to do. Mark Weadon, the former electrician, won the 'Dushka challenge', a contest for who could hold the heavy machine gun's barrel for the longest time with his arms outstretched in front of him. This was considered an 'ally' feat, making Weadon's taste for Earl Grey tea over 'NATO standard' brews apparently all the more strange. Jock Robbo, the Bravo commander, won the middle-distance running. As 8 Platoon sunbathed – while also guarding US Cobra

---

* An example of tribal behaviour in Majar al-Kabir described to the author on visiting Maysan province.

helicopters – they spotted a building 600 metres away and it was agreed they would race individually to see who could run there and back in the quickest time. 8 Platoon also raided 9 Squadron (RE) at night to pinch the weights and bars the Engineers had sculpted from Iraqi vehicle parts.

Ross was 'gazetted', promoted from 2nd lieutenant to lieutenant, and was no longer a 'one-pip wonder', as the most junior officer's rank was known. There was a chorus of 'Nice one boss' but the tee totaller could not be tempted from abstinence by Jordanian whisky or locally brewed banana gin.

In Support Company, former Bingo caller Del Aspinall came into his own as a quizmaster, while RMP Russ Aston wrote to the Cottage pub, Newhall, Derbyshire:

> Hello all,
>
> I have been working quite hard out here. I've been working with 3 PARA as a sniper, so needless to say I have a lot of souvenirs. Tell Dave I miss him and can't wait for a fucking good session. There have been quite a few firefights over here. We took Basra, I guess you probably saw most of it on the TV. There was quite a lot of resistance by the enemy in and around the area. The Americans have managed to toast some blokes again. They killed one and critically injured two. They're really shit soldiers (all the gear – no idea).
>
> Everything is starting to get back to normal now Baghdad has been taken. Don't know where Saddam is but rumour is he is being harboured in the Russian Embassy, but nobody really knows.
>
> Anyway, let me just say how much I miss your flat beer and ugly women (only joking). I don't know when I'll be home, but yet again the duty rumour is the end of May. So with a bit of luck I'll get the rest of the summer. I really do miss you all and look forward to getting home and seeing you all again. Please take care and I'll see you all again.

At the time when the RMP role was most important, it was announced that the strength of 156 Provost Company was to fall from approximately seventy-five to twenty-five – three sections, A, B and C, each of six men and headquarters staff. Though the reduction was in line with the fall in British troop numbers in Maysan it would place a considerable burden on those staying on. Simon Giddings and Matthew Peck were safe, having deployed in January with the advance party. Those who had served in Afghanistan shortly before Op TELIC were also given dispensations. Tom, alas, had a nervous wait:

> Well, I've heard some dates…4th to the 14th of June, flights
> have been going back which have been moved forward to May 23rd
> to June 4th so there's some good news. Only one problem. They
> want a platoon strength of 25 people to stay behind for an extra
> month. As yet we don't know who those 25 people are, it's possible
> I could be one of them, when I know for certain I will give you a
> ring, but let's hope I'm not one of the ones to get spammed for
> staying behind.

Paul Long felt similarly: 'I know now when I might be home, if I'm lucky and don't get picked to stay behind. I could be home either first two weeks of June arriving either 2nd or 3rd of June, or if I'm unlucky early or mid-July. So I could be home for my birthday.'

AS the temperature rose, so the locals became more violent. When they took on the new arrivals, 1 PARA responded aggressively. One such patrol led to the death of Wa'el Rahim Jabar. After his shooting the duty RMP section was called out, as one Red Cap recalled:

> I was out on patrol one night and this Para shot this lad dead in
> Amarah; they [the Paras] were doing Surge Ops in the village behind
> the stadium. And this fucking flip-flop had come out and brought
> his rifle into the aim position, so this guy dropped to his knee and
> shot him dead. We went out there and dealt with it initially. We
> don't treat it as a contact; we treated it as a crime scene.

Jabar's death was investigated by Amnesty International:

> He was walking along the main street with a Kalashnikov rifle slung

over his right shoulder, accompanied by two friends, Majed Jasem and Mu'taz 'Ati who were unarmed. It was 9.10 pm and dark, so they did not realise that there was a UK military foot patrol, consisting of four paratroopers and no interpreter, in the area. One of the paratroopers began shooting from a distance of about six metres, firing two rounds which struck Wa'el Rahim Jabar in the chest and neck, killing him immediately. The paratrooper reportedly fired without warning.

The Paras insist that Jabar was a criminal who set up illegal road blocks in the area patrolled by C Company. On that night he was seen firing at British soldiers and would have killed the paratrooper who shot him if he'd been quicker to fire. Jabar's friends were also armed, according to British eyewitnesses.

About 10 days later a group of paratroopers visited the home of Daoud Salman Sajet, the victim's maternal uncle, and expressed their condolences about his nephew's death. They stressed however that the soldier had opened fire because the victim was carrying a weapon in public even though the British Army had warned Iraqis not to do this.

FOUR 'To the captives, come out'

'Remember, I'm not that cheerful, it's shit out here. I'll tell you about it when I get home.'   PAUL LONG

'I met the Chief of the General Staff the other day, General Sir Mike Jackson. Don't know if you've heard of him, he's on the telly a lot and on the front pages of newspapers. He's about 65–70 and seemed as senile as they come, worrying isn't it?'   BEN HYDE

AS General Jackson had predicted in February: 'The post-conflict situation will be more demanding and challenging than the conflict itself which could be relatively swift and with low casualties. Then there is the question of rebuilding...It is not just a military process.' British and American forces were seeking to impose order upon a country the size of France and with a population of 22.4 million – a scale of operations not attempted since 1945 and with a fraction of the troop numbers. The RMP were no longer a rear echelon force but, as one of the corps' senior officers put it, at the 'tip of the divisional spear'. Their tasks – in particular the rebuilding of the Iraqi police force – were critical to the achievement of the war's political aims. Thousands of police officers across Basra and Maysan provinces required retraining and rearming; while a process of 'de-Ba'athification' was required to prevent the re-enlistment of Saddam's loyalists.

Concepts of policing by consensus and disarmament were unknown to the civilian population and the locals were like locusts, swarming over abandoned properties and stealing all but the buildings' foundations. The British were powerless to intervene and only wished they could capture such sights on time-delay cameras. It was of greater concern that the Iraqis stole intensive-care equipment from hospitals, and telephone and electricity cables. Yet with the RMP up against such odds, international organisations such as Human Rights Watch (HRW) were highly critical: 'Coalition forces seem to have arrived unprepared to meet their obligations to provide security and justice in the areas under their occupation. They lacked troops trained to provide direct security to the civilian population and military police were scarce and late.'

Tom was frustrated: 'At the moment we are just offering advice to the local police to try and restore some normality to this shitehole of a country.' He was not normally given to swearing; his mood had changed. His mother and father were alarmed. 'I absolutely hate stinking Arabs.'

At least he was getting the tan he wanted:

> The weather is roasting at the moment. Received the shorts, well, spray-on pants! on the 23rd I think. I'll have to go onto the roof to wear them as I'm on camp with 3 PARA and would get ripped to pieces, the RMP lads took the mickey enough. They weren't any proper shorts at all! Well, for the price of them let's hope they work.

With 1 PARA responsible for Amarah, the rest of Maysan province was divided between the 7th Royal Horse Artillery (7 RHA), 3 PARA and 3 Army Air Corps. Hostility towards those whose 'liberation' of Iraq had destroyed its infrastructure was inevitable and patrolling Amarah was similar to Catholic West Belfast in the early 1970s: overtly hostile, with daily shootings and general lawlessness – fortunately for the British, most of the shootings were the Iraqis firing at each other. As even the battalion's older soldiers were only children in the 1970s, the oft-repeated suggestion that they could lean on this experience was a misguided one. Their experiences of Ulster, however difficult, belonged to a more benign era.

The province's most powerful man was Abu Hateem, whom Beckett courted assiduously. Hateem was imperious in his flowing white robes and revelled in the epithet 'Lord of the Marshes'. He was lauded as a resistance fighter against the Ba'athists and, as the leader of Iraqi Hizbollah, commanded 8,000 men. Hateem controlled Amarah with the 'tactit approval of British forces'* and told British officers he would fight them if they stayed too long. It was said that some years earlier Hateem, disguised as an Iraqi general from Baghdad, had travelled to Basra in a Mercedes and summoned a dozen of Saddam's southern commanders to a meeting. They had cowered in their seats as Hateem berated them for their failure to control the area. Hateem then pulled out a revolver from beneath his borrowed uniform and shot them.

7 RHA manned the northern plain between Amarah and Kut. A, B and C Companies, 3 PARA, took the south-eastern sector, from the Route 6 highway to the Iranian border. A Company's 100-square-kilometre area of operations included Qalat Salih and Al Kahla; neither town had water or electricity. Schools and hospitals were closed, medical supplies had run out and there was neither a police force nor any civil infrastructure. The subalterns commanding 2 and 3 Platoons, known to the locals as 'Mr Ed' and 'Mr Gary', were appointed mayors of the towns.

A Company, 3 PARA suffered the Parachute Regiment's first fatality. Private Andrew Kelly, who had deployed on 14 March, five days after his eighteenth birthday, was killed at Camp Sparrow Hawk. Private Kelly, who had only ever wanted to be a Para, died when his weapon discharged as he cleaned it. His colleagues attempted emergency first aid. Kelly's last words to his mother Helen, just days before, had been: 'Don't worry about me, mum. Paras always go to heaven.'

B Company, 3 PARA set up camp at the former Ba'ath Party head-quarters in Al Musharrah and while on patrol captured nine members of the CIA-backed Patriotic Union of Kurdistan (PUK). Armed with US money, which the PUK received as a group opposed to Saddam Hussein, they sought to buy influence in Maysan. Like Majar al-Kabir, it straddled the world's most notorious heroin-trafficking route.

---

* Control of Amarah was delegated to the warlord according to Ministry of Defence documentation (J2 HQ Multi-National Forces (MND), Basra).

Drugs and terror shared a common ground of geography, money and violence. The cash crop had to be protected, hence the proliferation of Dushka and RPGs. Grown in the south-western provinces of Afghanistan, the drug was moved west through Iran, Iraq, Jordan and into Saudi Arabia. Eighty per cent of the heroin in Britain was smuggled from Afghanistan, where, since the fall of the Taliban, opium production had risen from 185 tonnes in 2001 to 3,400 tonnes in 2002. Narcotics were the primary source of income in the country's warfare-decimated economy and in the towns through which they passed in Iran and Iraq.

Despite these mounting problems a sense of calmness exuded from H-J's latest letter. Throughout the war his letters had suggested he was in control of himself and his situation:

> Hello Mum,
> All we are doing now is confiscating weapons from civilians and keeping the peace in the towns and cities. Our replacements can do that seeing as how we have done all the hard work. I hope you are feeling well and I hope there are not too many problems at home. I know that when we return we will have to spend a week in camp, but straight after that, I will come down and see you.

He drew positively on his experiences: 'Because we have moved about quite a lot I have managed to see quite a few of my mates from different units, so that has been good but other than there is not much news. I will write again soon.'

Any personal suffering was mentioned only in the context of hardships imposed upon all – which was remarkable in comparison to his colleagues. The paternal instinct that showed in his relationship with Katie's son Ollie extended to his men: 'I've lost about a stone in weight, but so has everyone. I'm very tanned, and quite healthy, none of my guys have been hurt, so all in all things are OK. We are just a bit bored now. Hopefully it won't be too long before we return to the UK.'

A SPIRIT of conquest permeated President Bush's address on the USS *Abraham Lincoln* on 1 May, the valedictory speech that signalled war's end. To the President, the future looked bright; three days earlier the US-chaired conference of tribal and opposition leaders had agreed to seek to form an interim Iraqi government within a month and the US had also published its 'road map' to peace in the Middle East. Wearing a pilot's jumpsuit reminiscent of his National Guard service, the President was flushed with pride:

> You have shown the world the skill and might of American armed forces. After service in the Afghan and Iraqi theatres of war, after 100,000 miles on the longest carrier deployment in recent history, you are homeward bound. Your families are proud of you, and your nation will welcome you. We are mindful as well that some good men and women are not making the journey home. Every name, every life is a loss to our military, to our nation and to the loved ones who grieve.
>
> And wherever you go, you carry a message of hope, a message that is ancient and ever new. In the words of the prophet Isaiah, 'To the captives, come out; and to the darkness, be free.' Thank you for serving our country and our cause. May God bless you all. And may God continue to bless America.

With the hardest battle being for Muslim hearts and minds, it could be argued such a quotation was tactless. Not all Iraqis saw the Coalition Forces as one homogenous group. As was explained in Amarah: 'You British, you OK. You *abu naji* [father/good man]. American, Bush, no OK.' Thus the former Iraqi Army barracks was named Abu Naji. Such praise was taken lightly: the Arabs had always been smiling assassins – charming one minute, brutal the next. British soldiers muttered, 'They [the Arabs] will break bread with you in the morning and spill your blood in the evening.'

As the President spoke consideration had begun over which members of 156 Provost Company would form the 'stay-behind' party. Despite the Iraqis' behaviour towards women RMPs, some of the female Red Caps were to be selected. For those chosen, home would be a further two months away.

On 1 May Lieutenant Colonel Eddie Forster-Knight became the senior RMP in Iraq, replacing Lieutenant Colonel P. Baillie. His Red Caps' workload in Basra was high: in a single week they responded to 500 reported incidents, including nine murders and two kidnappings, while police stations 1 and 2, as the RMP numbered them, recorded a dead body count of sixteen. The stations were commanded by 2nd Lieutenant Graham Chetwynd, who had only been commissioned into the British Army in December 2002 and had deployed without attending the RMP Police Training School, where he would have learnt the basics of military policing. Chetwynd and his men were frequently shot at, and despite having been in the Gulf for four months, some were yet to be issued desert combat fatigues.

At Abu Naji, Russ was still awaiting issue of desert boots while C Section worked for seventy-two hours without proper sleep, patrolling, manning vehicle checkpoints and training the Iraqi police force. They sought to gain the trust of the Iraqis by cajoling them and adopting a non-aggressive stance. To this end the Red Caps began the practice of leaving their rifles in their vehicles.

Russ's friend, the usually cheerful Ben Hyde, was moved to write to his parents:

> Hello,
> Well another boiling hot day over here and its 11 pm and I couldn't be any wetter if I'd just been in the shower with my clothes on. Two 15-year sergeants signed off to get out of the army today, they are so disgusted with the way our lads in the unit are being treated. They said they had never known anything like it in 15 years. For example we have five checkpoints, one of which I'm now at. Two of them have just been told over the radio to be ready for collection at 0600hrs in the morning, normal collection time is 0830hrs to 0900hrs. When my section commander [H-J] asked if this would affect the collection time of the other 3 call signs he replied, 'The only person who knows that is my boss and he's in bed.' Its alright as long as he gets his sleep, we'll just get up 2 hrs earlier after three

hours sleep and wait to see if we're picked up early or not. Things like this are happening 5 or 6 times daily, its disgraceful, no wonder half of the people from 156 Provo have signed off over here (I can't for another year, more is the pity). Its red hot, you get no food, no sleep, you can't wash properly, everyone wants to go home and you get treated like shit.

There's a brigade function in a couple of weeks, some comedians and bands are coming over to do a show from England. Our OC [Major Bryn Parry-Jones] has decided we can't go but won't tell us why, the hardest-working unit in the brigade by far, but no, the lads getting a couple of hours off for the first time in four months...

By early May around 300 auxiliary policemen had been recruited. The hope was that by June the judicial system would be effective and Major General Peter Wall – Major General Brims' replacement as GOC 1 (UK) Division – could reopen the Al Maqil prison.

RMP PAUL Long delivered bad news:

Hello Mum, Byron and cat,
How are you all, good I hope. Well mum, there are 45 of us flying home on 6th June however I'm not. There is 25 of us having to stay over here for a few more weeks. I'll be back in UK for 14th July, no later than the 17th of July.

Imagining his mother's anxiety, Paul urged positive thoughts:

It's not long now, it will soon go, before you know it we'll be at yours as one happy family. When we come home you'll have your son home safe and sound. I'll be calling you Grandma, not mum, going to be weird. I know you're looking forward to seeing him [Pat had never seen her grandson]. I know what you're like. Me and Gemma won't see Ben all the time we're up there because you'll want to do everything. We can all go for a drink. Can't wait to see you all as I've missed you all so much.

At least Ben would be working with his mates, he told his parents:

> I'm staying in the 16 AAB [Air Assault Brigade] main complex at the
> moment. We are staying here for a night then staying out for a
> couple of nights at various police stations, there's no need for us to
> stay out but that's the Army for you, always the most difficult
> option. I'm working with H-J, Russ, Tom, Si and Paul, so we've got
> a good section. Russ says hello, him and Tom are coming up for a
> weekend during leave, dad you'll be in your element as Tom used
> to be in the Paras, lots of Army chat, so you'll have to come out for
> a few.
>
> Russ is having a bad week, he's got a septic cold sore on his lip
> and he got stung by a scorpion the other day while he was having a
> dump, nice. He's keeping a low profile at the moment because he
> doesn't like anything messing with his precious face.
>
> I've finally decided what car I'm going to get, a Vauxhall Astra
> 2.0l. I think I deserve it, 1,000 quid in the building society then a
> little holiday and piss up with the lads, sort me right out.

Most broke the news about staying on until July via satellite phone. Si did
not tell his father about his Land Rover crash, an accident put down to
sheer exhaustion. Si, who was Staff Sergeant Pullen's driver, had suffered
minor injuries.

Ben was looking forward to attending his girlfriend Sarah's degree
ceremony a few days after his scheduled return date to the UK. Before
then, he had a few more ideas for making up for lost time:

> Mum and Dad,
> I've just finished writing one letter to you, the one I wrote on differ-
> ent days, but I hadn't finished so I thought I'd write again and tell you
> about my list of things I want to do when I get home. Here goes:
>
> Have sex, get drunk, eat steak, have a bath, sleep in a bed, get up
> when I feel like it, have a shit in peace, have a shit on a toilet, use
> proper toilet paper, have sex again, get drunk again, persuade mum to
> buy me the clothes me and the boss ordered from the catalogue about

two months ago…more sex…go to the supermarket…put clean clothes on, not start sweating again 10 seconds after having a wash, watch telly for a week…

In Major Parry-Jones' absence there would be changes in the running of 156 Provo. He had been accused of being 'too timid' and a 'yes man', incapable, it was alleged, of securing the equipment, manpower and weaponry for his provost company. In his defence, it was hard to secure concessions from those who dictated policy in 16 Air Assault Brigade with the RMP so peripheral to airborne operations. As the Officer Commanding 9 Parachute Squadron (RE) would later remark, 'An incessant thirst for action is the trademark of the Airborne soldier.' RMPs did not have this characteristic but were wrongly considered lesser fry.

On 7 February, 16 Air Assault Brigade had declared 'full operational capability' despite the main body of 156 Provo being still in the UK – an announcement indicative of how poorly the RMP were valued. It was all too common for attachments from corps such as the REME, R SIGNALS and RMP to have to fight extremely hard for their corner. Within the brigade the RMP were a '3rd line support' unit, bringing up the rear of the ORBAT. The Red Caps' basic functions, policing the British Army and mentoring the Iraqi police, were extremely trying yet they received little recognition for either.

The migration left Steve Stainton, a staff sergeant, and Lieutenant Richard Phillips in charge. Lieutenant Phillips, a softly spoken Welshman, was almost half H-J's age. He left much of the planning and operational decisions to H-J and Stainton, who held sway over him – a case of experience trumping rank. But in the words of a fellow NCO, 'being a staff sergeant did not hold a torch in the brigade'. That its most senior personnel had returned to the UK put 156 Provo at a disadvantage.

Among the new arrivals was the new company sergeant major, Warrant Officer Matthew 'Bob' Marley, an ex-Close Protection officer with a tough reputation.

PAUL Long was due further disappointment as time spent with US forces had raised his expectations: 'Life should start to get better soon as there is a big camp being built which I move into in two weeks or less. Every other camp that has been established in Iraq has a mobile Burger King and Pizza Hut, so fingers crossed we get it too.' These were luxuries beyond the British Army's capability in Amarah. Some of Paul's wishes would be granted, others not: 'Air conditioned Portakabins, accommodation, showers, cook house, TV, radio, internet, so send me your email address, phone kiosks and laundry service.'

There was a calendar in Paul Long's head. No matter how hard he tried, the pages refused to turn: 'Latest I (rumour) now might be home is by 6th July 03. I hope so, only 50 days or seven weeks + one day, or 1 month and 3 weeks.' However he massaged the figures, there were too many days left to countdown. His imagination filled with the life-enriching pleasures he missed:

Mum, when you said you will cook me a roast and rice pudding. The day I travel up I want one of your home-made large cheese and onion pies, and chips. Tell Byron to start saving up if he is to buy me a drink and go up town (sorry, up the toon, Big Market when we come up) and you Mum a night with a Chinese, are you throwing me a little party? If not, why not, HA, HA! Only joking.

The temperature was rising every day: 'What is the weather like back home? Nice I hope, what, must be 17–20 degrees Celsius, well today its 48–50 degrees Celsius, 99–105 degrees f, very hot, sticky and only just managing to cope.' Paul signed off:

From a very hot, very sweaty, very dirty and very, very bored and p***ed off son Paul.

Joke section: Why do women get married in white? A: Well the dishwasher has to match the fridge and the cooker.

p.s. send my love to Grandma and everyone else.

ON the morning Amarah's main bank reopened, the RMP placed barbed wire around the building and positioned Land Rovers to create a funnel towards the main door sufficiently narrow for the Iraqis to approach in single file, or so the Red Caps thought. The crowd grew agitated and the heavily outnumbered military policemen were pelted with rocks. The doors opened and the crowd charged.

'Step away from the barbed wire!' RMPs urged as the Iraqis climbed over each other.

Land Rover windscreens were shattered, tyres let down and radio antenna pods ripped off the bonnets. As per their training the Red Caps showed restraint, which put their security in jeopardy. It was a warning, as one Red Cap admitted: 'Anyone could have got fucking slotted there.'

ON 14 May Ben wrote:

When the wind blows you can feel it burn your skin as though somebody has a hot hairdryer on you all the time. You might think driving with the windows open would give you a nice breeze but it just makes it worse.

I still can't believe that most of the lads are going home soon, three weeks tomorrow, well today, they will be back in Colchester. I saw Russ [Aston] the other day, first time in about three weeks. He says to say hello and hopes you are both OK.

And the next day:

Well, it's four in the morning on the 15th which means that today I've been here for three months, seems more like three decades. A lot of the lads will be moving down to Kuwait in less than two weeks ready to come home, it's just not on.

Most of the lads are looking forward to going home in a few weeks and the rest of us are looking forward to the hierarchy going home in a few weeks just so we have time to relax for at least five minutes a day. Right, I'm going to write a few more letters. See you in 6–8 weeks.

On 22 May the UN Security Council approved a new resolution granting the United States and Great Britain interim control of Iraq and lifting UN sanctions.

RUSS Aston wrote to his wife and child: 'Dear Anna and Pyklet, I love you both very much and miss you very badly. Well sweetheart, I might be staying until August, it's not one hundred per cent yet but I should know soon.'

Russ and Anna had two dogs. Whiff, a border collie–terrier cross was diabetic and blind. They had raised her and Gypsy, a lurcher, from puppies. Whiff was having treatment: 'I'm glad the dog is getting better. She is going to have to get a job to pay her own way. Maybe Gypsy could go on the game around Newhall.' And the obligatory weather report: 'It's really hot again. It reaches 60 degrees C sometimes; it's so hot you could cook off the rocks. I burnt my feet the other day; my toes were blistered.'

TONY Blair was the first coalition leader to visit post-war Iraq and adopted his well rehearsed 'at ease with the troops' routine. A party from 1 PARA was flown to Basra to meet him. One private soldier asked, 'So Prime Minister, where are you sending us next? Korea or Iran?'

Blair replied, 'Well, er...I'm not too sure.' The PM swiftly moved on. In his official speech he told the massed ranks:

I would like to express to you the pride everyone has in Britain over the magnificent job you have done. The taking of the Al Faw peninsula and then the taking of Basra and the way it was done with the minimum loss of civilian life is famous around the world now.

This was a real war with real bloodshed and real casualties and there were people you will have known who aren't going back home and we grieve for them and we pay respect to them for everything they did and the sacrifice that they made.

The liberation from Saddam is one huge thing – a momentous and mighty outcome for the people of Iraq which you did and of which you can be proud.

He added:

What you did serves as a model of how armed forces anywhere in the world should conduct themselves – you then went on to make something of the country that you had liberated and I think that's a lesson for armed forces the world over.

When people look back on this time and on this conflict
I honestly believe that they will see this as one of the defining
moments of our century and you did it.

On the day of Blair's visit, responsibility for Maysan province shifted
from the whole of 16 Air Assault Brigade to the 1 PARA Battle Group –
3 PARA and 1 Royal Irish were going home. In the realignment of areas of
operation (AOs), 1 PARA's A Company would patrol Amarah, B Company
and Support Company the northern plain between Amarah and Kut, and
C Company, including 8 Platoon, the southern sector including Al Uzayr
and Majar al-Kabir. Each company would have a six-man RMP section
attached to it.

Logically, C Section, consisting of Sergeant Simon Hamilton-Jewell,
Corporal Russ Aston, Corporal Si Miller, Corporal Paul Long, Lance
Corporal Ben Hyde and Lance Corporal Tom Keys, was configured to
work in C Company's sector. C Section's mission was to work alongside
the Iraqi police to ensure:

> Effective police shift systems were adopted, that adequate manning
> levels were maintained and that the Iraqi Police were diplomatically
> introduced to effective police working practices. Refurbishment of
> the police stations was to be carried out in a controlled manner to
> reflect value for money.
>
> The initial plan to semi-permanently base RMP assets in police
> stations, including Majar al-Kabir, was discounted when it was
> decided that only one RMP platoon was to remain and a centralisa-
> tion of RMP assets was required.

The 1 PARA Battle Group also included the 650-strong battalion, an RAF
detachment of two CH-47 Chinook transport helicopters, an Army Air
Corps element with Gazelle and Lynx helicopters, 9 Parachute Squadron
RE, Pathfinders, a Field Surgical Team (FST), Intelligence Corps, D
Squadron, the Household Cavalry Regiment, chefs, logistics personnel
and a Civil Military Cooperation team (CIMIC).

ARRIVING from the UK, WO2 Marley regarded the Red Caps' daily routine as 'slack', with men not shaving every day and apparently falling asleep on duty – a crime punishable by death in some armed forces. The new company sergeant major (CSM) faced resistance when he attempted to raise standards. Asked why they were not shaving daily, his men replied: 'We're too busy. We haven't got time to admin ourselves up; we're not getting enough down time and the hours we're doing are ridiculous. We just can't physically stay awake!'

Marley was mentally and physically fit; his men were anything but after three months in the 'sand pit'. Every RMP should also have been rotated through off- and on-camp duties to lessen the drudgery. But with female Red Caps no longer patrolling, the men had to do more field work. 'The blokes' thought 'the burden' (as they referred to female RMPs) should never have left Colchester, and it had proved a mistake to deploy as many, or any, women – Arab objections towards females in authority were entirely predictable.

Marley had to clamp down on ill-discipline without being too hard; morale was already low and teamwork had given way to one-upmanship. 156 Provost Company had obtained a fridge that, as it ran off a faulty generator, produced cool rather than ice-cold water; but it was a refreshing change from hot water. On VCPs the thought of a cold drink was nirvana. But patrols returned to find their water had been stolen or different name tags put on their bottles.

PRESSURE was increasing on Tony Blair regarding WMD. Their existence and implicit threat had been the reason British forces had deployed – not to enforce regime change – or so the publicly aired argument went. At the G8 Summit in Evian, France, Blair was asked if he stood by the prewar assertion that Saddam Hussein was capable of delivering a weapon of mass destruction at forty-five minutes' notice. He replied:

> I stand absolutely 100 per cent behind the evidence, based on intelligence, that we presented to the people…and I simply say to you that the British intelligence services are among the best and finest in the

world and the idea that Saddam Hussein has for 12 years been obstructing the UN weapons inspectors, has been engaging in this huge battle with the international community, when all along he had actually destroyed these weapons is completely absurd.

So I simply ask people to just have a little patience. There is a process in place and it will take some time to carry out. But when we get the results of it we will put it before people.

Simon Hamilton-Jewell read his mail:

> Dear Simon,
>
> The weather here is very hot, and sometimes rain. The BBC is in a lot of trouble for showing the deaths of the two soldiers who were killed. Everyone is up in arms about the BBC showing it last evening. Did Blair pay a visit to you and your mates? Will you be able to let me know a couple of days before you come home so I can get some things in for your sandwiches etc. Hope to hear from you soon,
>
> Love Mum

He replied:

> Dear Mum,
>
> I hope you are well. Sorry I haven't written for a while but as usual it's been quite busy. We will be home at the beginning of July, so it's not long now. I am looking forward to coming home for a while.
>
> We are the last of the war-fighting troops to return as all the ones here now are doing the peacekeeping job and didn't arrive until after the war. It's a bit of a pain staying here after all the others have gone but not to worry at least it means I get more leave.
>
> I don't know if I told you but I will be on leave until September. I will write again soon so take care.

The RMP were sickened to see Paras getting more down time. Their weightlifting group was called the 'Get Massive Club' and when not on duty the Paras worked out, ate and slept. One 1 PARA officer spent hours running up and down the steps at Amarah athletics stadium with a 40 lb bergen – preparation for United Kingdom Special Forces (UKSF) selection. Colour Sergeant Fordell Luke, a Support Company NCO, was already massive. Weighing over 16 stones he was one of the battalion's largest men. Suitably, he fired the biggest weapons and led a Manoeuvre Support Group (MSG). 'Lukey' had been a recruit instructor at Depot PARA and looked even bigger sitting alongside his rake-thin charges for passing-out photographs. One of his lightest and youngest 'Crows' had been Tom Keys, whose parents Reg and Sally had kept the picture. Lukey looked as if he was acting as ballast for Tom and all those junior soldiers on his row.

There were now fewer 'infanteers' to provide force protection for A, B and C Sections and the Red Caps' sense of collective insecurity was heightened after their individual ammunition allocation was reduced and patrols with Iraqi militia became the norm. The civil defence force abused their powers for personal gain, detaining suspects for five days, rather than the stipulated five hours, before handing them over to British forces. Consequently they were deeply unpopular and subject to attacks. Working alongside them increased the RMPs' vulnerability.

There was now a degree of isolation between 1 PARA and the RMP, with call signs from both units operating within the same AO yet unaware of each other's presence – on at least one occasion 8 Platoon arrived to patrol a village only to find C Section already there, training Iraqi police. Sub-units such as the RMP and the Intelligence Corps were not checking out 'through the Ops Room', i.e. making the Battle Group commanders (and not just their own senior ranks) aware of their movements. By the nature of their role as the British Army's police service, military policemen kept themselves apart. For a peacetime law enforcement body this was essential but on wartime operations it made for poor communications and compromises in security.

SI was delighted; he had his return date and it was less than a month away. On 17 June, his father was at his desk in Newton Aycliffe, County Durham when the telephone rang.

'Hello, mate.'

John, whose sons always called him 'mate', recognised the voice: 'How are you, son? Great to hear from you, how's it going?'

'I'm OK; I've got my flight back! It's on the twelfth of July. I can't wait to get on the plane.'

'That's fantastic.'

'How's our Jon doing? Has he finished his training, [Si's brother was at the RMP Police Training School in Chichester], and has he got his posting?'

'Yes, he's got Hohne.' John knew this British garrison well from his army days. It was no glamour posting. He chuckled. 'It's nothing but tank tracks; awful.'

Si laughed. 'He's just got to make the most of it. Anyway, my flight's on the twelfth.'

'Right. Jon's flying out to Germany on the fourteenth. He's got some leave first so I'll come down and see him then be with you. We can get in a bar, lock ourselves away and get rat-arsed.'

'I can't wait for that.'

'Any other news, son? How's Emma?'

Si had some bad news – he and Emma were supposed to be getting married the following month: 'Well, she's OK.' Simon was hesitant. 'But I want to have a break in my relationship because I want to do a bit more with my friends. I think I am a bit too young to settle down at this time. I will get married some time though.'

John knew from personal experience how his son felt. He was saddened but supportive: 'Take some time out then, son. Give yourselves a bit of space and then see how you both feel.'

'Yes, I'll do that.'

Every phone call was a relief for John; the mere sound of Si's voice a fillip. 'Well, son, you know me and your mum we love you both [Si and Jon] so much and we are so proud of you. Don't be a hero, keep your head down. God speed and come home safe.'

'I love you too, Dad, and can't wait to see you.'

The appearance at Abu Naji of the 1st Battalion, the King's Own

Scottish Borderers advance party reinforced Si's belief that 1 PARA and the RMP would soon be home. Less well received was the reallocation of more weapons and ammunition to the incoming soldiers.

TRACER fire flashed across the night sky as the younger RMPs gathered – a week early – for Tom's birthday party. Late at night it was still hot enough to strip off and the 'happy fire' was like a fireworks display. The Red Caps, the males at least, paraded their tanned, lean bodies around the RMP leisure area, a patch of dusty scrub beneath a canopy of camouflage netting. Si's collar bones protruded and his tattoos were prominent: oriental lettering on his right shoulder, a black panther below and a dragon on his left shoulder blade.

They had been drunk on tiredness; now they swigged Stella Artois – a heady brew after four officially dry months. Most evenings had been spent watching 'hexi TV' (the campfire).

'The burden' ensured Tom received a birthday cake. H-J, who kept a watchful eye on Tom, presented him with another cake made of congealed Mars Bars with a candle on top. Keeping chins up was H-J's forte and with his library of jokes he made an effective cheerleader. Nor did he mind playing the fool, even running around the camp wearing one of Emma Morris's black thongs as an eyepatch.

In the vernacular of military radio communications, H-J was 'on permanent send', he never stopped talking or wisecracking. Most appreciated it and those who did not had to concede its positive side. His relationship with Katie had blossomed while they were apart, and much to his colleagues' envy the long-legged 19-year-old pledged her undying love in 'e-blueys' (slang for emails to the UK) and phone calls. She had also sent ninety letters. H-J would turn 42 in December; two engagements earlier in his life had come to nothing.

Would this be third time lucky?

He teased her: 'I am going to take you to Paris to ask you something.'

'Oh, what would that be?' Katie replied.

'Well, I'll have to speak to your dad first.'

H-J emailed his friend Lee:

Hello mate. Looks like I'm flying back on the 12th July, so I'll be on the piss soon after. Katie will be out with me and no doubt have to carry me home, having been dry for 5 months. I will be on leave until 1st September and will spend most of that time training hard and eating well, with the occasional night on the piss. I have lost 22 lbs (10 kilos or a stone and a half).

I'm pretty skinny, but there isn't an ounce of fat on me. I hope Clare and the little one are well, say hello for me and try and get the fat ginger bloke out on the piss. Got a few photos and some amusing stories to tell; so keep your head down and I will see you soon. H.

C COMPANY, 156 Provo and the CIMIC team conducted house-to-house weapons searches in the village of Abu al-Allaa, near Majar al-Kabir. Sniffer dogs were used, although not inside houses. The mere presence of dogs insulted the Iraqis – whilst some Kuwaitis kept dogs as pets, Iraqis regarded dogs as dirty. A DAF truck also became stuck between buildings, causing minor damage. The escapade left locals feeling shamed and angry.

Their demands were hardly unreasonable: food, water and to live as their culture and religion prescribed. The lack of humanitarian aid had angered them. As Major Hayward, 1 PARA's logistics officer, had been asked soon after entering Iraq, 'Where is the helping?' It still had not reached Majar al-Kabir three months later.

Exposure of the new authority's promises as hollow pledges made political capital for groups opposed to the Coalition Forces. The Supreme Council for the Islamic Revolution in Iraq (SCIRI) advocated an insurgency to win the 'freedom' of Shia Muslims, theocratic rule and closer links with Iran. As opponents of Saddam, the SCIRI had benefited from US and British patronage; now they were becoming the enemy.

The group was led by Ayatollah Mohammed Baqir al-Hakim who, as the son of the former Grand Ayatollah Muhsin al-Hakim, the spiritual leader of Shia Muslims, had unimpeachable religious credentials and led 10,000 fighters. Born in Najaf in 1939, Al Hakim had returned to Iraq in May after twenty-three years of exile in Iran. Maysan's political and tribal leaders flattered him with conspicuous displays of respect; when he arrived at meetings they jumped to their feet and when he spoke they sat in silence.

As Al Hakim told a rally in Nasiriyah: 'Do the Americans accept it if the English govern their country, even though they share a similar culture? How can we accept a foreign government whose language is different than ours, whose skin is different than ours? Oh, brothers, we will fight and fight so that the government we have is independent, that it is Iraqi.'

Younger clerics such as Moqtada al-Sadr disapproved of Al Hakim's negotiations with Allied leaders and his support for the US-appointed Iraqi Governing Council. Al Hakim had many reasons to thank the US; for the past 20 years his opposition to Saddam Hussein had been funded by the CIA. However, its agents would not be there to protect him in August when he was killed by a car bomb. The presence of CIA agents infuriated Beckett, who threatened them with arrest unless they cleared operations in 1 PARA's AO through him.

The battalion detained Islamic fundamentalists who had crossed from Iran with car boots full of AK47s and thousands of unused US $100 bills. The weapons were wrapped in greased paper just as they would have left the factory. The Intelligence Corps interrogated the detainees after the Paras had 'maintained the shock of arrest'. The Intelligence Corps brief had been that prisoners should be transferred feeling harassed so that they could then play the good guys.

On 21 June Major Kemp visited the council of elders in Majar al-Kabir to inform them that 8 Platoon would, from the 22nd, spend three days and nights at the police station. Kemp wanted Lieutenant Kennedy's platoon to establish a permanent presence in order to quell the upsurge of disorder. Kemp had been stoned on a recent visit. The elders were unavailable but Kemp left a message that his men would be arriving the following day with orders to 'smile at people'. 8 Platoon also hoped to collect, but not search for, weapons.

The recent violence had come as a surprise as until recently 8 Platoon had patrolled Majar al-Kabir without incident and the brief from 3 PARA

– the town was included in its area of operations until May – was that the locals were chatty and nosey but unthreatening. The mood swing suggested Islamic fundamentalists, loyal to al-Sadr or al Qaeda, had gained a foothold in the town.

On 22 June the RMP suffered its first casualty. Staff Sergeant Ian Wright of 111 Provost Company was shot in the arm by an Iraqi murder suspect in Basra. The incident took place 200 metres from one of the rebuilt police stations, which at the time was being visited by his OC, Major Nadine Heron. Staff Sergeant Wright's colleague Corporal Williams ran to alert her. 'Sorry to bother you, ma'am, but Staff Wright has just been shot. Can you call a medevac [Medical Evacuation]?'

THE toss of a coin determined whether Alpha rather than Bravo would start the first of the two 36-hour stags on 22 June. Under Ross's command Alpha drove south, taking the DAF and a Land Rover, which they parked outside the police station in Majar al-Kabir. The Toms stripped off for 'tan ops' while the OC went for a lie-down in a shaded room. By mid-afternoon not a single weapon had been handed in.

It was Private 'Grif' Griffiths' turn on 'stag' and he paced across the roof waiting for something to happen. Around the corner from the main street appeared scores of men, some of them armed and chanting: *'La, la Amerika! La, la Amerika!'* They pumped their fists in the air. Grif trotted back to the edge of the roof, looking down at his naked mates.

'Oi, you lot!'

'What?'

'Take a listen to this!'

'La, la Amerika! La, la Amerika!'

Ross ran into the courtyard to see his Toms dressing hurriedly. One of the first windows to be smashed was just inches from where he had been lying; shards of glass now covered the bed and floor. His second-in-command Mark Weadon joined Grif on the roof while Ritchie Clement and Tim May crouched in firing positions at the front door – their orders were not to let anyone pass. Ross reached for his satellite phone – there was no time to waste; even if he got through to Abu Naji immediately it could take half an hour for the QRF to arrive. He also attempted to quell the crowd, speaking to them via the local police.

The stone throwing intensified, smashing every window and hitting 8 Platoon's vehicles, all to the cries of *'La, la, Amerika! La, la Amerika.'*

'It's Lieutenant Kennedy in Majar al-Kabir; crash out the QRF. My call sign requires immediate extract from the police station, over.'

'Roger that, Ross,' said the voice from the Ops Room.

Ross heard 'friendly' gunfire from the roof. He ran upstairs to see Mark Weadon shooting over the Iraqis' heads.

'Cease fire! Now!'

Weadon obeyed Ross's command.

'Don't fire, it'll wind them up!'

Weadon was angry about being 'gripped' (reprimanded) by his platoon commander – such a dressing-down was embarrassing.

Alpha had a Federal riot gun – a baton gun – to deter the Iraqis' advances. Two plastic rounds were fired, one of which bounced off the ground and struck an Iraqi on the head. The QRF arrived – consisting of a column of WMIKs and Scimitar armoured vehicles. A member of the QRF dismounted and attempted to push back the Iraqis by pressing his rifle against them. They tugged at the weapon and had almost prised it from his grasp when Tim May intervened. His punch felled an Iraqi.

Scimitars and WMIKs forced the horde back and Alpha extracted through the cleared space. Abu Hateem persuaded the crowd to disperse then went to discuss the rioting with Beckett. A report of the ambush was written to be presented at the Intelligence Summaries (INTSUMs) attended by representatives of every unit at Abu Naji.

The Paras' level of violence left locals angry, a sentiment the British soldiers were aware of. Non-commissioned officers concurred when a junior Tom said: 'The next time we go into that town we are going to get attacked with weapons.' The attack on 22 June was a warning of further violence if the Paras returned.

On 22 June, Major Kemp, his Company Sergeant Major Grant Naylor and the newly arrived 1 KOSB commander met the town's elders. Kemp's hosts were prone to make ludicrous claims, which he emphatically denied. Local leaders accused him of working with supporters of Saddam Hussein to, as they put it, to 'repress the people and steal the oil'.

In an attempt to placate the elders, Kemp agreed to suspend weapons searches in the rural area surrounding Majar al-Kabir while assurances were also given that none would take place in the town itself.

A document signed by the British party and the Iraqis reflecting the new arrangements was, alas, incoherent and ambiguous:

> The process of searching heavy weapons in Al Majar district to the Security Commission and the foujer [Militia] established inside the district and the province and there is no necessity that the Coalition and its different people be there – and according to the following strategical plan. Searching heavy weapons for two months, before that, a period of a week must be given to inform people to hand their heavy weapons including Dushka, Mortars, heavy cannons, and ground defence weapons against airplanes. We want to see results in 1 month.

Kemp believed he had made it clear that patrols would continue. Surplus weapons were to be handed in, leaving every household two AK47s to guard front and back doors. These weapons were not to be paraded on the street; armed men would be considered a threat and ordered to disarm. The British Army's Rules of Engagement in post-war Iraq were those adopted back in March when soldiers crossed the border: they were entitled to use lethal force. Alpha and Bravo would return on 24 June, to show that British forces were not to be intimidated. If the locals did attack there would be two multiples rather than one to respond.

A brief tour of the town by Bravo, led by Robbo, passed off without incident as the meeting took place.

ILLICIT alcohol flowed in 8 Platoon's den well into the night of 23 June and the early hours – a few soldiers would be nursing hangovers in the morning. Spirits had been bartered for pornography, as one of the Toms remarked, 'They give it all that Allah shite but they're mad for "sex books" [the Iraqi name for pornographic magazines].' Majar al-Kabir was no place to be dehydrated and have a banging headache, and there was some trepidation about returning to the town.

THAT evening H-J and Lieutenant Phillips met to discuss C Section's tasks for the following day, 24 June. The sergeant and his men had to be in Al Uzayr by 1400hrs for a meeting with a senior British officer. On their way they would pass through Majar al-Kabir and Qalat Salih.

FIVE The souk

24 June 2003

0940–1030hrs

THE Iraqi flag hung apologetically from the police station's highest point, a turret overlooking the town and beyond. Lost in a ripple of heat haze to the south, the River Majar parted into the Adil and Wadiya tributaries and the former marshland area began. Majar al-Kabir had been the place wayfarers hired canoes to meet the marshland's lost tribe. But the Madan no longer lived among a sea of reeds. Copies of the *Bradt Travel Guide*, the soldiers' best intelligence resource on Iraq, told of Saddam's ecocide but not the town's quirky notoriety – its reputation for fine *dhakar binta*, teenage male prostitutes hired for dancing and more at weddings.

A narrative was etched into the masonry and strike marks from small arms fire told of the people's contempt for authority. The police station's pitiful appearance suggested it had been hurriedly deserted. The school opposite was stately by comparison, towering over the station like a younger brother whose sudden growth has left an elder sibling in his shadow.

At 0940hrs on June 24 the sound of RMP Wolf Land Rovers stirred the dogs as the lead driver braked over uneven ground. Two more Red Cap wagons appeared in his side mirrors and emblems on each stood out: a black chevron pointing left, identifying the vehicle as belonging to the Coalition Forces, and two numerals and a letter – each vehicle's radio call sign.

The patrol commander debussed. The desert that drove many half mad found H-J at his most sane: 'All in all things are OK,' he had reminded his mother. A positive mental attitude was a vital asset for a senior NCO. He squinted in the sun at the scuffed yellow brickwork. It appeared to have been constructed only because no better use could be found for the materials. The police station stood within an earthen yard where vehicle parts scorched orange by the sun lay abandoned.

Others jumped down; Ben was as tall as H-J but skinnier, Russ more chunky. Russ, the former physical training instructor, was a hero to his friends back home, fitter than they could ever be and always entertaining company. Listening to Metallica's *Enter Sandman* had broken his recent boredom and illness. Ben and Russ had bonded: while Ben mocked Russ's vanity and recent insect bite on his face, Russ described Ben's girlfriend Sarah, who was less than five feet tall, as a 'feisty little rodent'.

They were joined by a smaller man who had cycled from his nearby home. Working as an interpreter was a lucrative sideline to his usual job at the town's sugar factory. He had come to know the RMP well and regarded them as friends. He moved with H-J, Russ and Ben towards the building's entrance, while Tom, Paul and Si stayed with the vehicles where their rifles and body armour were kept. The latter trio would await the drive to Al Uzayr via Qalat Salih – the section's eventual destination before returning to Abu Naji.

C Section had spent too much time on Route 6. Every kilometre gazing at the fissured earth on either side took longer than the last and their enthusiasm for Op TELIC had long since died: 'Remember I'm not that cheerful, it's shit out here', as Paul had told his mother. Their minds and bodies, like their vehicles, had been eroded by unrelenting heat. Paul wrote of home-cooked foods with a fondness usually reserved for old friends. With only a fortnight or so to go he was getting closer to his mother's 'cheese and onion pies and rice pudding'. Tom intended to eat 'like a man on a mission' once he was no longer surrounded by 'stinking Arabs'.

His uncharacteristically explicit comment was temperate compared to other popular terms for Iraq's indigenous people, like 'sand wogs', 'yip-yaps', 'towel-heads', 'flip-flops' and 'crusties'. As the Iraqis demanded so much from Tom and his colleagues, their hostility was understandable.

A skirting board of dirt blurred where the police station walls met the ground, while a painting of a cupola dominated the entrance to the station: its position was apt, for in spite of the police's efforts, laws, when they attempted to enforce them, were but grains of sand beneath the twin pillars of Islam and the tribal system. The British insistence on patrolling Majar al-Kabir without approval of the elders was considered an affront by all tribes, who had united against officialdom and the external threat. It was a matter of shame that their town was controlled by the British and many had been injured while protesting against the occupation two days previously.

8 Platoon call signs Alpha and Bravo had arrived in Majar al-Kabir at 0925hrs and just after 1000hrs had abandoned their foot patrol after Zubaida warned Ross of 'bad men' in the town. There was no way Ross and Robbo could allow the Iraqis to dictate terms altogether – a patrol, either mounted or on foot, had to take place; anything less would have been a potentially fatal sign of weakness. A compromise of a vehicle patrol was reached with Zubaida and at 1010hrs Billy Brown and 'Big Steve' Oellerman drove off from the militia headquarters in their Pinzgauers along the River Majar's western bank.

Having passed through a lightly industrialised area and by two jetties stretching out across the water, Bravo turned left. The bridge looked a temporary structure, as if made from tens of thousands of black matchsticks. This was no conservation area; pastel green, the choice of colour for the low railings, seemed random, as if nobody cared that it clashed with the surroundings. As usual, the sound of the British vehicles had been met with raised voices, but today's youths were more angry than curious. Locals had interpreted yesterday's agreement to mean the British would not only stop searching for weapons but also stay out of the town altogether. Robbo and his men would have been no more conspicuous had they arrived naked.

Dolman was unmoved. Tales of his fighting prowess were whispered among C Company's new intake. With everyone in 1 PARA priding themselves on uncompromising soldiering, it was some feat to be awarded such a deferential sobriquet as 'The Dolmanator'. Epithets, if not of the 'Smudge' Smith, 'Grif' Griffiths variety, were usually mocking: a particularly short soldier in Support Company was known as 'Inch'. 8 Platoon's junior soldiers were Dolman and Robbo's acolytes.

Shadows covered the tradesmen selling fish farmed in the town's reservoir and gaps in the crowd revealed walls decorated with anti-Coalition graffiti and portraits of Shia clerics. There was no space between the Paras and the locals; it was as if the Toms were having multiple visions, the mob seemed so big and the streets so narrow. Buildings pitted with shell fragments seemed to lean towards them. Forever anticipating Saddam's next attack the locals had postponed repairs – such was their aversion to physical labour. Had this excuse not existed they would have found another for they considered such work dishonourable; simple jobs were for simple people. The explorer Wilfred Thesiger recorded that non-urbanites were less proud: 'The desert Arabs had always been a people born to hardship. For them there was no ease or comfort. They took a fierce pride in danger and suffering and never doubted their superiority over villager and townsman.'

Alleyways once bombed by the Sunni-dominated Iraqi Army now rocked to pounding feet and the Paras' security ebbed away the deeper they drove into the souk. It was 1015hrs.

'Cover your arcs.'

Toms nodded and scanned the crowd.

'One through to three, three to six, to nine. Got it?' NCOs spoke deliberately but without shouting, determined to maintain an outward appearance of calm. Armed with GPMGs, Gary Hull and 'Smudge' stared nervously, even though their weapons could turn concrete walls into dust in seconds. Mark Lewis and Serge Lynch felt uneasy about their Light Support Weapons (LSWs), or 'L-S-Trouble-U's' as they were renamed, which were less powerful and awkwardly weighted. Mark and Serge tucked their weapons tighter beneath their shoulders and hunkered down as the Pinzgauers chugged along.

'They're not moving, cocky fuckers,' yelled a colleague.

The Pinzgauers had no armour, no weapons platforms and were smaller than WMIKs and US Humvees.

'Get out of the way!'

The order was ignored. Shorn of combat body armour and helmets – it was considered too hot to wear them – the Paras were less bulky and hence less intimidating.

'Back off...'

It was becoming harder to appear unflustered. 'Come on, move it!'

Iraqis flashed toothless smiles before delivering another volley of rocks.

'Watch that fucker.'

Two months ago the same youths would have shaken their hands, begging them to pass on congratulations to Tony Blair for 'liberating' Iraq.

'Cheeky little twats.'

Faces took on a uniform ugliness as fear tightened its grip. Non-essential thought processes were shut down and the British soldiers no longer noticed peculiar physical features and dress styles.

H-J, RUSS and Ben discussed the security situation and the refurbishment of the police station with the Iraqi police chief, his deputy and a civil engineer. There was little other meaningful activity in the building, where forty to fifty policemen idled away another morning. Dressed in civilian clothes, they hardly looked like an effective law enforcement body. Faced with policing a town with as many weapons as citizens, being confined to the building was their standard operating procedure. In terms of influence their police chief was a pygmy alongside the warlord Abu Hateem.

A canopy of trees provided partial shade over the courtyard's central feature, a well cast in white concrete. It was surrounded by grass and stone walkways. The Iraqi police took little notice of these and their feet had cut dirt paths across the lawn. Empty cells retained the smells and stains of former occupants.

BRAVO'S presence was attracting the most unruly of Majar al-Kabir's people, who channelled contempt for the Coalition's empty promises into every stone thrown.

'For fuck's sake, we're in the shit.'

Rocks bounced off Billy's windscreen. 'It hasn't been this bad before, this is well cheeky.'

'*La, la Amerika. La, la Amerika.* Hide your weapons! We must not let them disarm us.'

Today's riot appeared coordinated.

'*La, la Amerika. La, la Amerika.*'

'I can see fucking towel-heads everywhere.'

'There's hundreds of 'em.'

'This is mega, isn't it? And fuck-all ammo,' snapped one Tom. The stone throwing was constant.

'They've really screwed the nut leaving us with a hundred rounds each.'

'Use the baton gun!'

It was 1020hrs; the crowd was getting louder. Robbo knew his satellite phone would not work in such a built-up area nor while he was on the move.

BACK at the militia headquarters the attack intensified, with hundreds of children hurling rocks at members of the Alpha call sign before scampering away to fetch more from the riverbank. Crouching behind the wagon, Alpha stared back at the youths and pointed with their fingers extended like gun barrels. The multiple was lower on firepower as Mike King, who usually carried a Minimi, had been retasked to the Ops Room.

In 'Sleepy Hollow', men spoke softly into mouthpieces above the low beeping and crackle of radio transmissions. Warrant Officer Matthew 'Bob' Marley sat in the RMP seat while Lieutenant Lawrence Knighton had taken over from 'Bobsleigh Bob' as watch keeper. Captain Todd flitted in and out of the room and chatted to Major Tootal.

Beckett was off-base meeting senior locals. The CO was constantly aware that any machismo on the battalion's part could rebound with disastrous consequences; as he had reminded his men, they were there to stabilise Maysan province, not kill people.

FISTS slammed onto the bonnets of Bravo's vehicles. Seeing the mob's growing confidence and strength, Robbo could remain passive no longer: 'Debus, debus and push them back. We need a cordon around the vehicles, and hold it.'

He pointed, his face tightening with anger. Dolman gave the same order on the other wagon prompting a clanging of boots and rifles against metal as the Toms leapt out. Iraqis clawed at their weapons but were pushed back. 'Attack them, attack them,' the ringleaders shouted. Robbo and Dolman made a mental note who they were.

The Paras put their collective weight into a forward charge. Billy and 'Big Steve' responded by upping the revs and hard metres were won. An open view north presented itself from the end of an alleyway, a possible escape from the labyrinth of lanes. 'Stay calm,' an NCO reminded, 'no flapping.'

Out of sight, men gathered more rocks and rifles. The urban environment played into the attackers' hands.

Those on the second Pinzgauer looked behind them. 'Where's the militia?'

Eyes darted across angry faces but there was no sign of them. The 'friendlies' had bugged out.

'Fucking duck!'

A rock smashed into the lead wagon's windscreen.

'*Allah akhbar!* They've come to rape our women, attack them, attack them! *La, la Amerika, La, la Amerika.*'

It was 1025hrs as Robbo ran back to Dolman's position. As they had identified the mob's leaders, so the Iraqis had recognised them as the British commanders. Incoming masonry marked their coming together for an 'Orders Group'. 'We're in the shite here.'

'You're not wrong.'

'Comms are fucked; we've got to make it back to the militia headquarters and marry up with Alpha.'

'Then exfil.'

'There's hundreds of 'em.'

'We'll have to be more aggressive.'

Both knew from Northern Ireland that using plastic bullets could inflame as well as calm a situation – but with the Iraqis refusing to back off, they had little choice. Armed with the baton gun, Dolman awaited his cue from Robbo. He had seven dildo-shaped missiles to knock down the ringleaders: they had to work; he and the Toms were too lightly armed for a firefight. 'Peacetime munitions scales? Fucking mega!'

'Just keep an eyes on; there's little flip-flops everywhere.'

The baton gun opened like a shotgun. Iraqis eyes locked on Dolman as he slid in the first dummy and snapped shut the weapon; it looked a lot more threatening than an A2. Taking aim with the red dot sight his targets were in range; he was trained to fire directly at them but below the waist. Up to 50 metres the gun would drop a man and cause serious internal injuries comparable to being hit by a golfer's drive at close range. Dolman breathed in deeply, and on exhaling, fired. The round left the chamber with a dull thud amid a plume of white smoke.

The crowd surged, leaping up and down. It was impossible to tell, but it was likely some of them had protested outside the police station two days ago and seen a baton round fired into an Iraqi's head.

'Fuck. It hasn't worked.'

'They're not backing off.'

Robbo spotted another gap.

'John.'

'Yeah?'

'One o'clock, one hundred metres, lay-by.'

'Seen.'

'Mount up there.'

'OK.'

'This is turning to rat shit.'

As the instruction was passed through the multiple a white 4x4 vehicle drove towards Bravo's wagons and blocked the route. A furious Robbo took Joseph with him: 'Tell him to get his vehicle out of the way!'

Joseph explained but the Iraqi shrugged, his attitude mocking Robbo's authority. He was grabbed by the shirt and pressed against the wagon. 'Move!'

Reluctantly, the Iraqi drove away.

The crowd had made up the distance while the argument went on. Stone throwing recommenced as the Toms marched north. Robbo's last card before lethal force was to fire warning shots; but here they were considered inaccurate rounds, not a desperate, last resort. He took personal responsibility, squeezing off his first round with an ear-popping snap. The A2's muzzle flashed and empty casings were spat out at 90 degrees. The tinny sound as they hit the pavement was lost beneath the din. More warning shots were then fired with GPMG and Minimi. At last the Iraqis turned.

'Thank fuck for that,' said one voice.

The street partially cleared, revealing shops that had hurriedly closed. Their owners now sheltered behind the elaborately painted shutters. Iraqis had left to fetch their weapons and would return. As the leader of the 'white tribe' had fired, so would they, and not miss. Iraqis never fired warning shots.

The lull allowed most of Bravo to remount the Pinzgauers while Serge Lynch and Gary Hull stayed with Robbo and Dolman. Eyes were trained on 'The Dolmanator' from a first-floor window and an Iraqi snapped a magazine into his weapon. With the shaven-headed corporal in his sights the local opened fire. Rounds burst the air.

'Fuck!'

'Get down!'

More lead drilled into the road as Dolman dived for cover behind a garden wall. Serge and Gary were also under fire.

'Enemy, first floor!'

'Seen.'

'Se—'

The volume of gunfire echoing off buildings drowned out the next response. At such close range the AK47s seemed incredibly loud. Robbo and Dolman fired at the man in the window.

'Lynch, Hull!' Robbo screamed. The Toms' heads turned towards him.

'Get back on the Pinz and give us [Robbo and Dolman] some covering fire!'

As the sergeant shouted two more gunmen ran from cover and shot at Dolman, still crouched behind the wall. He was showered with secondary fragmentation and stone chippings stung his face.

Serge and Gary opened up with their machine guns. Gunmen went down. It was 1030hrs.

AT the sound of gunfire, H-J, Russ and Ben had exchanged concerned glances and the meeting was suspended. They filed out of the chief's office to the courtyard. The noise had also stirred the resting Iraqi policemen. Curiosity led them to follow the British NCOs to the entrance, but not to lead. From the dark corridor into the shimmering light, they looked out. The town always had the look of war, now it had the sound as well.

The Red Caps were unaware, but there had already been fatalities in the souk. With Iraqi lives lost, it was now *maktub*, 'written', that the locals would exact revenge. As the killers were outsiders the responsibility to settle the blood feud fell not only upon the victims' families and members of their tribe but upon all tribesmen in the town. Every white man in Majar al-Kabir, whether included in Alpha, Bravo or C Section, RMP, now belonged to the 'murderer tribe' – some of its members would have to die for Iraqi honour to be restored.

SIX Four-tonner down

Call sign Alpha, Militia HQ, Majar al-Kabir
1025hrs

'YOU hear that?'

'Yeah.'

'That's not just AK, is it?'

'No, that's us.'

The sound of an A2 was at a higher pitch and on single shot – the Iraqis fired on automatic. Fears of an additional threat, which had precipitated the doubling of 8 Platoon's strength, had proved correct and the size of the crowd had grown every minute. Alpha saw hundreds of people chanting and throwing stones at them.

The locals' anger craved expression but their words were just an inarticulate, unnerving noise to Ross's soldiers.

'You hear that firing?' Ross bent down to address a militia member.

'Sorry?'

'The gunfire!'

'Ah, yes' The 'friendly' hesitated. 'It is happy fire, no problem.'

'Bollocks it is. We can hear our guys firing. Bravo must have been engaged.'

Ross got his men together. 'Mount up.'

'We've got to get down there.'

'That crowd's growing.'

'It's a gang fuck, mate.'

With its alleyways like a rabbit warren, Alpha knew how confined and intimidating the souk could be.

'Come on, let's go.'

'Jump on. Robbo's guys are in contact. There's no comms. We'll have to guess where they are.'

Tim climbed up into the DAF and slammed the driver's door shut as Ross jumped in beside him. 'Right, nobody overreact. Cover your arcs and keep an eyes on for those with weapons.'

'Grif, Ritchie.' The Toms looked up at Weadon. 'Get up in those fire positions.'

On his call they climbed above the cabin, their weapons facing to the front. This was a precarious position but necessary to cover 'Ross the Boss' and Tim below. 'Only fire if you can identify armed targets.'

Grif in particular would have to be careful as he was armed with the GPMG, more suited to sustained fire than sniping.

'Move out!'

The DAF started and Tim found second gear – he never put the wagon in first gear as that increased the chance of stalling on the next gear change. The vehicle rolled forwards, looking more like a float entered in a town carnival than a military vehicle.

'Fuck off, you little bastards!'

'Go!'

'Keep an eyes on.'

On the journey into Majar al-Kabir the Toms had sat relaxed in the cargo hold. Not on this drive.

IRAQIS had chased Bravo through the souk but watched frustrated as the British remounted their vehicles and drove away. The opportunity for revenge had passed, for now at least. Armed with RPGs and AKs they ran north; they would arrive at the crossroads at the same time as Alpha.

'GO!'

'Floor it, Steve.'

'Big Steve' worked clutch and gears as, under fire, the Pinzgauer wheels gripped the tarmac then shot forward. He would be the last to flap: as second-in-command he and Dolman had to look out for the younger, less experienced soldiers.

On the lead Pinzgauer Billy Brown was driving.

'Further on, Billy, keep heading north.'

'Thank fuck we're clear.'

Billy nodded – he had an idea of the route and knew he would hit the central crossroads. Shabby buildings passed by – Majar al-Kabir was one of the scruffiest towns Billy and his mates had visited.

Robbo's plan was to lay up close enough to the militia headquarters to assist Alpha's extraction. Among Robbo's men, Smudge, Gary, Serge and Freddy pawed at their faces, wiping away sweat. They were graduates of a hard school – Depot PARA excelled in breeding 'group identity', a band of men with a shared culture and mutual respect. They were no longer combat virgins and had passed every infantry soldier's ultimate test: their reaction to effective enemy fire. This was a test that most British soldiers never got to take, and one that some failed.

'COME on, you fucker.' Tim May's wagon needed every encouragement. Under a hail of stones the DAF accelerated over the bridge, eventually out of range of stone fire and the chasing pack of youths.

'Where the hell are Robbo's blokes?'

'Fuck knows, they must have extracted.'

'It's gone fucking crazy 'ere today.'

'Watch your arcs. Most of 'em are unarmed but keep an eyes on.'

'If you see a fucking AK, shout.'

FROM the front of the police station the RMPs and their interpreter saw armed men gathering and heard shots at diminishing intervals until they could be heard 'second after second'.

'Get the vehicles inside,' H-J ordered.

His men sprinted to the Land Rovers, from where they collected their rifles.

The police station compound's walls offered little protection, however, and could be scaled easily. Some of the Iraqi police left, promising to investigate the trouble; their probable intention was to escape.

Some of the mob turned towards the RMPs. 'Everything had looked rosy' on the security front according to their departed OC Major Parry-Jones. The scene being played out before the RMP now was far from rosy.

IRAQI messages were being broadcast from loudspeakers: 'Arm yourselves; the British are attacking. Fight for your freedom!'

'Contact right, two o'clock!!' a Tom screamed.

'Fuck!!'

Iraqi targets fell when hit. Tim gulped; he was defenceless and had to carry on driving. 'Christ.'

'Debus, debus,' Ross ordered – it was a standard operating procedure (SOP) to dismount under heavy fire. 'Bomb burst out!'

Weadon rallied his men, knowing an RPG would do for them all. 'Get the fuck out, split left and right!'

Clusters of Toms dispersed; rounds chased Stevie Holland's heels across the road as Chris Coyle and Tim May also ran for cover.

An Iraqi family saw two members of Alpha running towards them: 'No, no, go away!'

'We just want to hide!'

The other Tom saw an empty building about the size of a bus shelter and beckoned his oppo to follow him in.

'No fucking way, it'll get RPGed. This way, here!'

But the family protested. The pair would have to find shelter elsewhere.

Alpha received so much Iraqi fire that those nearest the DAF took cover beneath it. The lorry had come to a halt on the north-east corner of the crossroads. They may have been visible from the police station but no members of the multiple saw the RMPs or the policemen's Land Rovers.

'Under here.'

'Come on, move!'

'Fucking hell!'

Rounds pinged off the tarmac at eye-level as the men lay down.

'Right, do a head count.'

'Number off!'

'Who's here? Who's missing?'

'Yup, yup...Where the fuck's May?'

'May?'

'May?'

'He's not 'ere, boss.'

Tim heard his named called as he crouched on the other side of the road. 'Boss!'

'May, fucking get over here!'

Alpha couldn't go anywhere without their driver – but the enemy fire was too intense for Tim to run across.

'We've got to push them back.'

Jase and Grif hauled themselves clear of the wagon. With the latter armed with the GPMG they would advance directly towards the on-rushing Iraqis.

'Stand by!'

'Go!'

They charged, buying Tim time to run back to the DAF protected by their suppressive fire. He slid beneath the wagon as his colleagues took cover behind a wall. There were further Iraqi fatalities, and their bodies lay prostrate on the road.

'We've got enemy coming from down that road as well,' another soldier barked as he pointed down the main street.

Barry, Stevie and Ritchie pepper-potted* south; gunmen retreated but it was difficult to tell them from bystanders. Alpha's rules of engagement were to fire only at those carrying weapons. When not firing, the gunmen hid their rifles.

'Move!'

'Moving!'

*a method of advancing to or from contact in pairs.

Quick battle orders rang out.

'Not too far, Ritchie!'

The trio found themselves beside an Iraqi police observation post, a concrete mini-tower some 100 metres south of the crossroads. The Iraqis had eluded them by turning left and left again to bring them back up to the police station.

'Back here now!' Weadon yelled.

They carried out a tactical withdrawal.

Eyes turned to Tim. 'What's he doing under there?'

'Fuck knows.'

'Oi, Tim, fucking come out!'

Tim could hear laughter. 'What the fuck?'

'What you doing under there?'

'Ha, ha.'

'Fuck off. I only jumped under here because I saw you lot here.'

'Ha, ha, wanker!'

'What? We were never under there.'

'Yes you fucking were.'

Ross briefed Mark Weadon: 'We're going to remount and extract to the edge of the town. Comms are fucked; we'll have to exfil.'

'OK boss.'

'May,' said Ross, 'get up there and drive!'

'There's no way it'll start.'

'What?'

'It'll have to be jump-started.'

The DAF rarely started first time and the JP8 fuel used by Coalition Forces disagreed with its engine.

'Keep those guys where they are.' Ross pointed to Grif and Jase who would be the last to remount. 'Right, the rest of you, get behind there and fucking push!'

'Stand by...Go!' echoed Weadon.

Tim turned the key in the ignition, put the wagon into second gear and pressed down hard on the clutch. He would have to wait for the Toms to give it a huge push first. *Don't stall on me now*, he thought.

'Come on, for fuck's sake.'

No movement.

'Come on, come on!'

'Come on!'

'Push!'

Inch by inch the DAF's momentum increased, but not enough to start the engine.

Iraqis were getting closer.

'Jesus, start, you bastard!'

'LOOK for a gap.'

Bravo eyed turnings off the main street, north of the crossroads. They had passed the scene of Alpha's contact not more than two minutes before. A suitable exit was located.

'Here we go, mate.'

'Now where the hell are Boss Kennedy's men?'

Billy's Pinzgauer spun left.

'I can't see 'em.'

'Where's the DAF?'

'Must be behind us. They're in contact wherever they are.'

'Did we pass them?'

'I dunno, but one of 'em is giving it some of that GPMG.'

AS Depot PARA instructors were fond of saying, Grif was 'turning rounds into empty cases'. With a bandolier of 7.62 mm lying to his left-hand side he squeezed the trigger, making the belt jump and copper cases dance along the tarmac. They were spat out on the other side of the GPMG.

'Come on, push, push.'

The DAF rolled forwards but was still not moving fast enough to start.

In fierce heat and under enemy fire, Alpha kept on pushing. Only three men stood off – Jase and Grif, who engaged the enemy, and Ross who, as officers are supposed to, observed the scene.

'Come on.'

'Start, you fucker.'

The engine rumbled.

'Yes!'

'Thank fuck!'

Tim pressed hard on the accelerator and engaged the hand brake. On its release the DAF would have enough momentum to shoot forward.

'Back on!' shouted Ross.

Toms jumped aboard.

'Jase, Grif, withdraw!'

Each ensured the other received covering fire as he retreated.

'OK, fucking go, Tim!'

'Floor it, you bastard!'

Hand brake released, the DAF pulled clear. But Tim had only driven 30 metres when two Iraqis fired at him from an alleyway.

'Shit!' His rifle was at his side, but he had no time to reach down and fire it through the window. He had to carry on driving. 'I'm fucked.'

'Enemy right!'

Having been the last to remount, Jase Davidson had assumed the firing position above Tim's cabin. He slotted the first guy as other Toms rained lead on the accomplice: threats neutralised.

'Christ, I thought we were dead!'

'Keep their heads down.'

The DAF sped north under fire.

TWO British targets, Alpha and Bravo, had eluded the Iraqis thus far. One remained. The mob closed in on the police station.

'I need the police to stand here to face them,' H-J told the interpreter, his voice vying against the crowd. The section commander, conscientious by nature, had a crisis to deal with.

The numbers of protesters swelled as the interpreter repeated H-J's command: 'He says bring policemen to stand facing the armed advancing mob.'

The officer summoned his men, who moved forward. To the RMPs' dismay, once the Iraqi police saw the crowd's size and ferocity they retreated into the police station. They kept on running, across the sun-dappled courtyard towards a far corner – so much for the RMPs' efforts to train them. The Iraqi police huddled in a cell and worked to break one of the barred windows. They would squeeze through it to make their escape.

In March, Tom Keys had pondered whether his contribution towards Op TELIC would even result in him leaving Kuwait. Two weeks of conflict then passed before he saw an Iraqi combatant. In April and May he had been, as he told his parents, right at the dud end of the action and as safe as he possibly could be. Paul Long, too, had told his mum that worrying was unnecessary; all he was doing was confiscating weapons and keeping the peace. These tasks were, however, fraught with danger. Even Majar al-Kabir's most peaceful citizens demanded to keep weapons; their argument against confiscation being that, as neither the Coalition Forces nor the Iraqi police were capable of protecting them, they should be able to protect themselves. They also wanted to live free of British interference.

'CONTACT front!'

Enemy were closing on Bravo from both sides of the river.

'All round defence!'

'Where the fuck's his [Ross Kennedy's] multiple?'

'I can't see 'em.'

'There's enemy everywhere.'

'Where? Identify targets.'

'Other side, little bloke, running right, now.'

'Your arc!'

'Seen!'

'Got him.'

'I thought Alpha was over there!'

'I can't see 'em.'

'Me neither.'

'All round defence.' The command was barely audible.

'Enemy moving!'

'Half right!'

The lack of ammunition began to tell: 'Magazine!'

'Covering your arc.'

The Tom kept the weapon in one hand, lifting it to access the empty cartridge, which he dropped down his unbuttoned DPM (Disruptive Pattern Material) shirt. He pulled a fresh magazine from a front webbing pouch and slotted it into the rifle body then closed the fastening to prevent spare ammunition falling out.

'Mag on!'

'Took your time getting it back in, didn't you?'

'What?'

'Watch my strike. Towards them flip-flops there.'

'Fuck off!'

'It's your arc, mate. Leave 'em then.'

THE only position in the Ops Room where the C Company satellite phone could find a signal was on a dusty ledge eight feet above the ground. Corporal Den Starkie, a laid-back Lancastrian, could scarcely hear its strained ring-tone. He worried how many calls had been missed. It was 1037hrs: 'Hello, Ops Room.'

'It's Robbo!'

Den was struck by Robbo's urgency.

'I'm in a contact; put the watch keeper on.'

'OK, Robbo.' Den took the phone from his ear and saw Lieutenant Knighton sat next to the bird table. 'Sir, contact. Take this.'

The Ops Room was sufficiently intimate for Den's message to be heard by many. The 'c' word was a conversation stopper. Knighton leant towards him. Lifting the receiver, he heard gunfire. 'Robbo, it's Lieutenant Knighton.'

The multiple commander was hunched down with AK fire snapping inches from his ears. 'We are in a heavy contact. We've killed several enemy already and we're starting to run low on ammunition. No casualties.'

More incoming fire could be heard.

'We're surrounded. Request immediate QRF, over!'

'Roger that, Robbo. I'm going to get the QRF moving immediately so I'll hand you over to Pat Granger. OK?'

Knighton passed the phone to Pat Granger, 8 Platoon's watch keeper, while he looked for Captain Todd. 'Somebody get the Ops officer?'

A junior soldier trotted out in search of him.

'Where are you, Robbo?' asked Pat. 'Robbo, repeat, where are you?'

'Somewhere near the centre of the town, on the eastern side of the river, north of the souk.'

'Roger that.'

'There's hundreds of guys firing at us. Where's Mr Kennedy?'

'What, Robbo?'

'I said where's Mr Kennedy?!'

'No word from him, Robbo. Isn't the boss with you, over?'

'No. He was at the militia headquarters. We lost comms.'

There was the briefest of silences.

'OK, Robbo, got that. We'll get help to you now, over.'

'This is really urgent. We're in the shite here!'

'Roger that also, Robbo.'

'We'll need an ammo re-sup.'

HAVING driven north up Route TOBRUCK, Alpha were clear of the mob. Relief washed over them: 'Jesus, we were fucked.'

'Too right. Didn't think we'd get out.'

'Stevie mate, rounds were fucking chasing you across the road!'

'The fuckers had me too.'

'Then they all seemed to change mags at the same time.'

'Thank fuck eh? Muppets.'

On the palm-tree-lined road they gazed at the portrait of a senior Shia figure painted onto a white plinth. The face belonged either to Grand Ayatollah Ali Sistani or Moqtada al-Sadr's exiled father; they weren't sure. Elderly men with black turbans and white beards looked much the same. At last they were safe.

'Crap shots, mate. How fucking close?'

'Fucking knew we'd be in a contact the next time we went into Al Majar.'

'That shithole is the worst, man.'

'Fucking obvious, they warned us.'

'Bone, mate, going in there, fucking bone.'

'And a bloody bump start! What about that!'

'Fuck *Black Hawk Down*, that was four-tonner down.'

Ross couldn't hear the snapping from the cabin. Under his instruction Tim drove to the junction with the Main Supply Route – Route 6. The Toms debussed and took up firing positions, exhausted and sweating furiously. Looking back, only the sugar refinery and the fish farm were visible. No Iraqis had followed them.

'What's happened to Robbo's men?'

'Let's get that sitrep in.'

Danny Connolly gave his OC the iridium phone. Ross knelt on one knee and called the Ops Room.

2 KILOMETRES south of Alpha's position, four of the RMPs had taken cover behind their Land Rovers as the crowd saw the other two scale the roof of the police station and plead for calm. But the mob would not be calmed; at least not until a debt to the dead had been repaid. As they had done before dawn, waking those at Abu Naji, they let off rounds. The 'ritual fire', or 'happy fire', acted like a call to arms.

'WHAT'S happening?' Todd appeared on Knighton's shoulder. Taller than the watch keeper, he angled his head down.

'There's a C Company patrol in contact in Majar al-Kabir. It has already killed people. They're split into two multiples. Sergeant Robertson says his is low on ammo.'

'OK, OK.' Todd frowned – he had only been Operations officer for a few weeks.

'Where's Ross?'

'Robbo says he hasn't heard from him. Neither have we. We're trying to establish comms.'

'OK.'

Other Ops Room staff eavesdropped. Messages were relayed. The RAF desk called the helicopter landing site: 'Stand-by the Chinook; contact in Majar al-Kabir.'

The Army Air Corps desk was told to get a Gazelle helicopter ready for immediate departure.

'Let's get the QRF moving,' said Todd. 'We'll need the chalk commander in here for a briefing. Lawrence [Captain Knighton], have you alerted the QRF?'

'Done that.'

'Alert the air.'

'Done that.'

The duty Ops Room runner sprinted over to the QRF tent to relay the message in case the telephone link was down. QRF I, the first team, consisting of a batch of Support Company soldiers, was on two minutes' notice to mount up, fully equipped, and five minutes to leave camp – their meals were brought to them and they rarely left the tent during the day or night. A second batch, QRF II, was on twenty minutes' notice.

'Duty pilot to the Ops Room please, over.'

'Bob' Marley had listened intently. His schedule told him 156 Provo had a six-man patrol passing through Majar al-Kabir on its way south.

He told Todd: 'I have a section going through that town this morning. I can't confirm this information because we've not had comms. They may well be on their way to Qalat Salih by now.'

The Ops Officer nodded. Todd was in a difficult position: how to factor a possible but unconfirmed RMP presence into the rescue mission?

'We'd better get hold of the CO,' another officer suggested.

'And Abu Hateem,' one replied.

'Get the Int Cell onto that. He seems to make things happen around there.'

THE crowd outside the police station had reached frenzy, waving AK47s over their heads and taunting the RMP. By tradition this was where the Iraqis protested: this shabby building, a totem of oppression. There had been numerous attacks on police stations and court houses across southern Iraq since the collapse of the Ba'athist regime, reams of documents relating to outstanding crimes being destroyed.

'RICHARD?'

'Sir.'

Tootal appeared from the Planning Cell, as the office he shared with Todd was somewhat pretentiously called. Todd might have addressed him as 'Stuart' privately, but not in an operational environment with the pressure on.

'Tell me what is happening.'

'Sir, elements of C Coy are involved in a heavy contact in a town south of here, Majar al-Kabir.' Todd pointed to the bird table.

'They've killed a number of enemy,' Tootal's face tightened, 'but none of our guys have been hit.'

'Thank you, Richard.'

Sergeant Jason 'Buck' Rogers strode towards them. 'QRF present.'

Buck was on his third Gulf war: decorated as a United Nations observer during the Iran–Iraq conflict, he had returned with the Royal Navy on Op GRANBY before switching services.

Knighton ran over the basics: 'Buck, there's a C Company call sign in a contact in Majar; they've killed several gunmen. We're unsure of their exact location in the town and they're low on ammo. You'll need to get down there. The Chinook and the Air Corps have been warned off already.'

'OK.'

Todd butted in: 'As soon as the duty Chinook pilot gets here I'll give you both a quick brief.'

'Right.'

'Basically, as long as the Chinook is good to go I am going to send your guys down there on it, to see what you can do. There are hundreds of armed locals around them but they're holding them off.'

Tension gripped the air; staff responded to the situation exactly as they were supposed to, but on auto-pilot, as yet unconscious of the weight of events.

Buck tapped a Para signaller on the shoulder. 'Get comms with my QRF guys now. Scrounge as much ammo as they can off QRF two and anyone else. I'm going to need it for call sign Bravo and us.'

This was the Battle Group's doomsday scenario – two lightly armed multiples outnumbered and trapped in a volatile town and, possibly, an RMP section too. Lives depended on effective communications and men and assets being mustered immediately, but ammunition and medical kit was packed away. It was supposedly too dangerous to allow soldiers to keep their personal morphine phials beyond the war-fighting phase as they might use them in a suicide bid. On an endless tour of Northern Ireland the reasoning might have been sound – but with less than a fortnight before they returned to the UK from Iraq?

Whether soldiers had been permitted to retain their morphine for the last month of the tour had been a perk of rank. In Support Company, the Toms' supplies were recalled while 'lance jacks' and above kept theirs. There was no consistency: 8 Platoon and H-J's section were visiting the same towns and were therefore similarly vulnerable, yet all members of the former kept their morphine, regardless of rank, but the RMPs had relinquished theirs.

SEVEN 'It's our duty to stay'

Field Surgical Team, Abu Naji

1045–1055hrs

'WHAT'S happening?' Gavin McCallum asked.

'Something's gone off, in a town south of here.'

'Really?'

'There might be casualties.'

'OK.' The news surprised him. He had picked up few, if any, anti-Coalition Forces vibes.

'An IRT [Immediate Response Team] is leaving in fifteen minutes.'

'I'll be ready.'

The IRT would be spearheaded by 1 PARA's Regimental Medical Officer Captain Andy 'Doc' West (RAMC), one of the battalion's tallest men and not built for squeezing into helicopters. Corporal Lenny Thorne was similarly preparing to leave the Regimental Aid Post (RAP).

'A "dedicated rover" will take you and your ODA [Operating Department Assistant] to the HLS, Gavin, when you're all set.'

'Yup, just give me a minute.'

McCallum, a RAF anaesthetist, belonged to 3 Corps Support: a tri-service provision of surgeons, doctors, nurses and dentists. His 'grab bag' was pre-packed ready for such emergencies and contained anaesthetics, analgesics (morphine), airway management and canular equipment (needles), dressings and chest drain apparatus. He would also take an oxygen cylinder and monitoring equipment. Immediate support for those on the ground was essential.

'PAT, we're surrounded here! What's happening?'

'OK, Robbo,' said Pat, 'the QRF's on its way.'

'They'd better be; there's enemy all around us. And where's the other call sign?'

'They've extracted, Robbo.'

Those eavesdropping were stunned by the tone of Pat Granger's conversation. Robbo was no flapper; his situation must have been dire.

The duty Chinook pilot breezed into the Ops Room. She was ogled more than most females and considered Abu Naji's most attractive woman – although a taller, blonde physiotherapist ran her close. Todd began his briefing as Major Kemp, Captain Johnno Palmer (second-in-command C Company) and Colour Sergeant Fordell Luke came into view.

'OK, we've got two multiples in contact in Majar al-Kabir; there's been fighting, enemy dead and our guys are heavily outnumbered.'

She scribbled notes, before asking: 'Can I have a drop-off grid [an exact location to land]?'

'No,' said Todd, 'I can't give you one because I don't have their precise locations on the ground.'

'OK.'

'You'll be approaching Majar al-Kabir from the north. There's lots of firing going on. Once you've flown in there I suggest you drop the troops off just short, out of immediate danger.'

She nodded in understanding as Todd turned to Buck. 'Sergeant Rogers, once you've been flown in there, obviously try and give the best support you can to the multiples. It's impossible to say what to do from here.'

'Sure.'

'And there might be RMPs in the town, we're not sure . . . '

'Right,' she turned to Buck, 'let's go.'

Marley waited nervously for news, any news, of H-J's section, but had still heard nothing. He had not heard from H-J since the section commander checked out. As there had been radio silence since then, Marley hoped H-J had left for Qalat Salih.

'SAVE yourselves!' shouted Hassan, the police chief.

'It's our duty to stay,' one of the RMP replied.

Again H-J requested that Hassan's men pacify the crowd.

'No, you should leave with us.'

By now more Iraqi officers had left than remained. This was not out of cowardice – disregard for personal safety was an Iraqi trait and they were raised to endure pain: the Al Bou Muhammed tribe delayed circumcision until a boy's early teens to make it a test of sufferance – but because siding with the British now was tantamount to suicide. The crowd were chanting their names and threatening to kill them for being collaborators.

'We will not run away,' repeated one of the RMPs.

'Please come!' the policeman begged. 'You'll be safe with us if you come...'

'No.' H-J was unmoved.

DANNY Connolly rejoined his Alpha mates, who were still talking animatedly. It was 1050hrs. 'Jesus, I hope we're not going back in there again.'

'Thank fuck we're out.'

'What about Robbo's guys? Could be anywhere.'

'Must have extracted though. Laid up somewhere?'

'But where?'

'Dunno, just hope they're out.'

'Fucking good timing, Jase, with 'em two in the alley.'

'Saved Tim's life.'

'Where is he?'

'What was he doing underneath the DAF when we were behind the wall?'

'Monging it, the bastard.'

'It's like, "Crack on, lads, I'll just lie here."'

'Be fair, he was under fire.'

'But so were we by the wall.'

'Where is he?'

'Oi, Tim, what about you hiding under the wagon?'

'Fuck off. I told you bastards I went under there because that was where you were.'

'Mate, we were returning fire. We were in a firefight.'

As his men cracked jokes, Ross used the satellite phone. He explained to the Ops Room what had happened to his multiple and was briefed on Bravo's predicament.

'Robbo's men are still in the town, Ross,' said the crackling voice.

'Roger that.'

'Reinsert to assist their extraction if possible.'

This was a request, not an order; as the commander on the ground he would play it as he saw it.

'Roger that, we'll do everything we can.'

Facing a test of leadership, he turned to his men. 'We've got to go back in.' He started coolly enough, but inside he was shaking. 'Robbo's guys are still in there . . . '

Thoughts pinged around his cranium: *What if they refuse my order? What do I do then? What if I lose men when we reinsert? What if I can't find Bravo?*

The command sunk in.

'Let's go,' said Weadon.

Those closest to Ross just managed to stifle their naturally nervous reaction to his order. Those standing out of earshot were more expressive. 'We're going back in?'

'What?'

'Oh fuck!'

'Seriously?'

'Oh mega, that is!'

'Get your body armour and helmets on and move,' said Mark.

'What was that before…four-tonner fucking down? You can say that again.'

'Fair one.'

'Fucking DAF will probably break down again.'

'Move it, get your armour on.' Weadon halted the chuntering. 'Get mounted up, now.'

They were even more breathless in the heat for donning their protective kit.

'Combat body warmers!'

'Fuck me, give us that water.'

'After me though.'

'Come on! Give it 'ere, wanker.'

'Mount up.' Weadon intervened.

'Get a fucking grip!'

With all aboard, Tim accelerated away, but too hard for his platoon commander's liking. 'Take it steady.'

He slowed to marching pace.

'Not that fucking steady!'

TOOTAL stared at the map as Todd went on: 'QRF has been briefed; Air has been briefed. The Chinook will be heading down there while the land elements form up at the main gate.'

'Well let's just wait a minute and see who else we might be able to send, Richard, rather than sending in piecemeal.'

Socially awkward he might have been, but Tootal was respected for his organisational skills. What assets did the Battle Group have at its disposal? How would they best be deployed? Would it be more effective to infiltrate by air or land? What were the town's critical features? Areas of dead ground, obstacles, landmarks to aid navigation? Any friendly forces? Though every second counted, haste or assumptions at this juncture could lead to a small, poorly briefed rescue force being sent into as much if not more danger as those already stranded. All these factors had to be considered. He also had to make an appraisal of the enemy: who were they and what were they capable of?

Tootal needed 'eyes and ears' on the ground: 'Get me OC C Coy, please [Kemp].'

BRAVO had debussed and remained under heavy fire as Robbo was updated: 'Alpha extracted to the perimeter of the town under heavy fire, over.'

'Roger that, zero.'

'They will attempt to reinsert to assist your extraction. They have no casualties, over.'

'Roger that.'

'Out.'

Robbo shouted to Billy Brown, 'Get over to that Pinz and get it running...'

'Fuck that!' said Billy – it seemed like a suicide mission.

As they spoke, there was a huge explosion. Bravo stared at the wagon Billy was supposed to run over to.

'Shit!'

An RPG had burst the fuel tank – it was just as well Robbo's command had not been delivered ten seconds earlier.

'How the fuck are we getting out of here now?'

Daggers of fire stabbed upwards as glass shattered. Paintwork melted into a scorching liquid which dripped onto the earth.

'This is really cake and arse stuff now.'

Generally, 'Big Steve' laughed uproariously at misfortunes, but not this one. It seemed a matter of when, not if, the other Pinzgauer would be hit. Some Paras readjusted downwards their percentage chances of survival.

'Another mega day in the Paras, eh?'

'Fucking comms. It's a joke.'

Communications, just for a change, had been the problem; too many buildings blocking the VHF and satellite phone signals. Had they known Alpha had left militia headquarters Bravo would have followed them out of the town.

TO the exaltation of the mob, an RMP Land Rover had been set ablaze. Thick smoke consumed the cabin and billowed through its front windows. The Red Caps' two other wagons were as vulnerable; soon it would not be safe to remain outside. From within the police station they would have to rely on local communications – but no Coalition Forces numbers could be dialled from the Iraqi telephone system.

'You'll be safe with us,' Abbas Baiphy pleaded. He was one of the few Iraqi policemen left in the courtyard.

H-J still refused to take flight, even though the level of danger was such that a retreat would not have been cowardly.

'I need a radio,' H-J told the interpreter. 'Ours has been burned in the Land Rover.' The RMP did not carry 'body-comms'.

'We'll get in touch by phone with the police at Qalat Salih,' said the Iraqi.

'Good,' H-J replied.

'We'll tell them about the grave situation and that we're besieged by a big mob.'

'Then get yourselves in a safe position,' H-J instructed.

The Iraqis ran beneath the entrance's protruding stucco frontage and through the doorway. Inside it was darker and a defunct single strip light, minus its protective cover, hung from the ceiling. Crossing the courtyard the pair found Iraqi police officers escaping – they were pushing each other through a window one after the next before running across the yard to safety.

'LET'S get a larger force, Richard, and send it in as one big packet.'

'Yes, sir.'

Kemp emerged from behind Colour Luke. Lukey was not on QRF duty, but as someone who had commanded many WMIK escorts he was eager to assist.

'Let's send down MSGs [Manoeuvre Support Groups],' Tootal continued. 'What have we got?'

'We're counting,' Lukey replied. 'My guys are getting ready to go.'

'OK.'

'And Chris, I want you to take what you can get from your company, B Company and Support Company, get down there, assess the situation and report back.'

'Roger that.'

Kemp was a phlegmatic, no-frills officer. 'Lukey,' he said, 'tell everyone to form up at the front gate.'

Kemp turned to the Toms acting as Ops Room runners: 'Get into every company's accommodation areas and round everyone up.'

One headed for the scoff house. 'Hey, it's kicked off in Al Majar.'

'What?'

'Where?'

'Seriously, a couple of C Company multiples are in a right gang fuck in Majar al-Kabir.'

'Shit.'

'Chris Camp [Kemp's nickname] wants every swinging dick to go on the QRF.'

'Fucking hell, let's go.'

'It's a fastball, mate; they're leaving any minute.'

Soldiers dropped mugs of tea and stampeded out. After months on the leash this might be their first proper contact.

NOBODY flapped, but those who knew each other well exchanged guarded glances across the Ops Room that said, 'Fuck, our guys could die before we reach them' – and they were not even aware of the RMPs' predicament.

EIGHT 'Any buckshee ammo?'

Junction of Route 6 and the road to Majar al-Kabir (Route TOBRUCK)
1055–1105hrs

THE DAF rumbled south through the avenue of crooked telegraph poles with its human cargo more nervous than before; they were going back into the town where they had almost lost their lives. The Iraqi gunmen would scarcely believe their luck – they would have thought their chance of destroying the DAF and everyone aboard had passed.

Two Toms were in the 'crow's nest', the shooting positions above the cabin, as the remainder crouched in the cargo hold. The town's outskirts came into view, the fish farm, the mosque and the sugar factory all crystallised by sunlight. They waited for the first 'eyes on', the first sight of the enemy scurrying into trenches either side of the road, into doorways and behind cars.

'*La, la Amerika, La, la Amerika.*' The chanting piped through the minarets grew louder; Alpha were around 500 metres from the police station.

'Enemy right.'

'Watch those guys moving.'

'They're not carrying!'

Iraqis ran from the rows of houses.

'Some are!'

'Seen, he is.'

Alpha knew the drill: when the DAF was hit by a burst of enemy fire, debus as soon as possible and take up firing positions on the ground.

'You hear that firing?'

'There's hundreds of 'em.'

'They'll see us any second.'

'They're moving north.'

More gunmen approached the wagon, front and rear, left and right. Bullet holes appeared in the cabin door, an indicator light was smashed and the windscreen cracked.

'Fuck! Contact front!'

'All sides!'

Enemy fire was returned with interest but the Toms could not defend the vehicle or themselves against RPGs, the shoulder-fired grenade launchers. Small arms fire peppered the DAF including, miraculously, rounds which passed through the cabin, through one open window and out the other side.

'RPGs!'

'Oh fuck.'

'Debus!'

'Go!'

Tim was still on board – those on the ground could only pray the missiles missed.

'Get out, mate!'

'Christ! Take that fucker out!'

'Shit, this one's on course.'

'Oh fuck.'

The RPG deflected off a single electricity wire, showering the DAF with fireworks. But the drooping single wire had saved Tim's life, altering the missile's direction and deflecting it towards earth.

'Grif, left, left!' Mark Weadon wanted him to engage enemy targets closing from the sugar factory. Armed with the GPMG, Grif held the multiple's most potent weapon.

'Enemy front! Closing!'

'Yeah.'

'Seen!'

There was so little cover, at best a concrete block or a gutter for Alpha to press their bodies against. Tracer fire missed Stevie Holland by inches as he lay in a ditch while rounds pinged off the masonry protecting other Toms. Tim, now on the ground, had so little cover he was unable to bring his rifle up to a firing position. *This is it, I am dying now,* he thought. The faces of his children flashed before him.

BUCK returned to the QRF tent to find his men milling around two Pinzgauers, awaiting his briefing. He recognised the 'lance jack' running towards him. 'Can I come?'

It was Gaz McMahon, who had just finished his shift in the Ops Room. 'Have you got your kit here?'

There was no time for him to collect it.

'I have.'

'Get in then.'

The multiple had been due to hand over QRF duty at 12 noon, after a 24-hour stag. After four months in the desert these soldiers – from Anti-Tank and Mortar Platoons – looked considerably older than the men their families had said goodbye to. Over Op TELIC some had developed unusual tastes: pipe smoking had taken off in a big way while two soldiers were known as 'Mr Pebbles' and 'Mr Jingles'. Other nicknames were more predictable: Private Murray was 'Ruby' and Lance Corporal Phil Johnson was known as 'Tubs'. Gaz was the only Scot; 1 PARA's 'Jock Mafia' tended to hunt in packs, rarely leaving a stray with the English.

'OK,' Buck began his 'snap orders', 'there's a C Coy call sign under fire in Majar al-Kabir; they're low on ammo and it's a heavy firefight.' Rumours of British losses were spreading. 'They've got dead.'

'Fucking hell!'

'We're getting a Chinook down there so we'll drive to the accommodation block to pick up some extra kit and the GPMG,' Buck made eye contact with Dan Marsh, who would carry the heavy weapon, 'then head up to the HLS.'

'You heard him, let's go,' said Steve Thurtle, the 'full screw' who was Buck's second-in-command.

'Come on!'

'Hey, Dan,' said Gaz, 'let us carry the gun, eh?'

'No way mate, you can have the baton gun!'

'Oh, mega.'

'What about comms?'

'Buck's got a sat phone, Del's got a 352 [VHF radio].'

WITH the second Pinzgauer also now in flames, Bravo's options for extraction were severely limited. They were too deep into Majar al-Kabir to escape on foot so Robbo called on Joseph's local knowledge: 'Find me a way out of here. We need somewhere to hide.'

'OK.'

'We'll have to hole up in a house, or something like that.'

Once inside they would stay hidden until the ARF arrived.

'Buddy up, we're going to fire and manoeuvre then lay low.'

They wiped away sweat and mud from their faces as they listened.

'Watch your distances, keep closed up and make every round count.' Seeing his men were low on ammunition, Robbo added: 'Check mags.'

Bravo moved fast and watchfully, the dusty ground yielding beneath their boots and firing bolts of fatigue up their legs.

'Moving.' One ran forward as his oppo found cover and put down defensive fire. 'Gone firm.'

As their NCOs had taught them, the Toms 'watched their bounds', the maximum distance each could travel without the group becoming separated. 'Two enemy, right, one hundred and fifty metres.'

'Seen.'

'Give it some.'

More Iraqis were killed.

Bravo zig-zagged along cratered streets with the River Majar on their left-hand side.

'Watch your arcs.'

'And your rear.'

'Red Phos' and smoke grenades would have helped Bravo screen their movement but these, like so much of their ammunition and their bayonets, had been withdrawn. The enemy's weight of shot increased as a Dushka came into view – it was the Russian equivalent of a Browning .50 cal and the multiple had no weapon to match it.

Crouched behind a battered car, Dolman felt the ground shake. 'Fucking Dushka,' he cursed.

'All round observation,' an NCO urged, pointing to his eyes with fore and middle fingers.

Every time the Dushka fired the ground shook.

'They're behind us,' Joseph urged.

'For fuck's sake!'

The Iraqis were enjoying the chase. Robbo and a Tom were pinned down by half a dozen gunmen including one armed with an RPG who crawled towards them.

'Just tell me when he's ready to fire that thing,' said Robbo.

'Right.'

'He's in the aim, Sergeant...Now!'

Ignoring his own safety, Robbo stood up from cover and sniped him. The RPG man fell; the Tom was impressed. Naively, the other Iraqis revealed their positions and were hit with accurate, single shots.

Bravo could now advance. 'Go!'

They ran under more fire.

'Move!'

'Moving.'

'Move!'

THE three British elements on the ground, the two multiples from 8 Platoon and C Section, RMP were within 400 metres of each other yet were unable to communicate and were unaware of each other's whereabouts.

Six RMPs faced hundreds of men, mostly armed, all angry and noisy. They carried their AK47s in their right hands, the sword hand, and there remained only one price for the spilling of blood.

'STAFF update.' Tootal's clear, clipped tones rang out.

'ARF is about to leave, sir, with the med team, and the QRF is forming up,' Todd responded, adding, 'Hopefully the Gazelle will establish comms with the multiples and act as re-bro [re-broadcast station, to transmit back to the Ops Room]. We're onto Div [1 (UK) Division in Basra], sir.'

'Thank you, Richard.'

'The CO is en route and we're looking at whether the Americans can provide fast air.'

'Were we expecting a protest in Al Majar today?'

'I don't think so, sir. It was quiet there earlier this morning.'

'Very well, Richard.'

'YOU have that; I can't carry it all,' said Dan, handing over his magazines of 5.56 mm ammunition.

'Cheers, mate.'

The offer of buckshee ammunition was too good to refuse and Dan would be weighed down with 7.62 mm link for the GPMG. He draped the bandolier over his shoulder.

'How much you got there, Dan?'

'Four hundred link, mate, but some of it's rusty.'

The Pinzgauer arrived at the front gate. The ARF would have to run the remainder of the distance from here to the HLS because it was unsafe to leave wagons unattended outside Abu Naji.

'Debus, guys; let's go.'

They ran to where they saw two Chinooks. One's rotors were spinning, while the other's were tied to the ground. The dormant helicopter belonged to the female flight lieutenant who had received the Ops Room briefing, the active Chinook, which had just touched down from Basra, was flown by Wing Commander Guy van den Berg. Neither Chinook had sufficient armour to conduct combat operations.

'This one?'

The ground crew directed Buck's men towards the woman's Chinook.

'Yeah? Sure?'

'Yup.'

Their nerves twitched: little personal admin jobs, ensuring webbing pouches were fastened and spare magazines were accessible were done three times before the men were satisfied.

Steve Thurtle, Buck's ARF second-in-command, gathered the team around him. 'Listen in, lads.' The Toms looked up. 'I don't want anyone doing anything stupid out there; no heroes, nobody trying to win a VC or any of that crap.'

'Yes, Corporal.'

'Just be sensible, stay switched on and look out for your oppos.'

They nodded acknowledgement; if anyone was winged during a mad dash, it would take another two men to pull him clear.

The rescue force wanted to leave immediately but their pilot would not be pressured into haste; all pre-flight procedures would be adhered to.

As she continued, Regimental Quartermaster Sergeant (RQMS) Tim Fleming brought a sandbag full of additional magazines aboard.

Most of the multiple stood by the helicopter ramp, wondering what was causing the delay. 'What are we waiting for?'

'Come on, love!'

She was now speaking to van den Berg.

'What's happening?' he asked her.

'There's been a contact south of here.'

She requested use of van den Berg's Chinook, as his was ready to fly and hers would take more time to prepare for take-off.

'No, I'll take them.'

'OK, sir.'

'My rotors are still turning. Get them to cross-deck into my aircraft.'

'Yes, sir.'

'Where am I going exactly?' asked van den Berg.

'The northern sector of Majar al-Kabir. We haven't got specific details on the locations of the stranded multiples.'

'Roger that.'

'There's probably been casualties. You'll have medics coming with you.'

'OK.'

First aboard, Gavin McCallum, Doc West and their ODAs had pick of the seats, with the odd numbers on the port side and the even numbers on the starboard. McCallum sat to port, about a third of the way in. The air was thick with avgas. Buck's men charged down the landing ramp of the 'chick's' Chinook and across the HLS. The phrase 'screw the nut' entered their minds; the RAF personnel were wasting time. The medics heard a crescendo of banging as the Paras emplaned. Both parties, Paras and medics, were surprised to be sharing the same helicopter, thinking it made more sense for them to infiltrate Majar al-Kabir separately. It seemed that Doc West, Lenny Thorne and McCallum had brought half a hospital with them, there was so much medical kit.

One Tom nudged the man next to him. 'We might need all that later.'

'Don't, mate, just don't.'

'Hey, give us that oil bottle.'

'Wait a second.'

'I don't want a stoppage.'

'Neither do I.'

'Just use a dry cloth.'

'Let's get a move on, for fuck's sake.'

'Come on, guys, get it together.'

'Who's going where?'

'Gaz, get over there.'

'Dan, where are you going?'

'Mick, Del, Cleggy?'

'Yup.'

'All right, I'll sit here.'

'Come on, move up.'

'Ruby there, Pebbles, Jingles, where's Gaz?'

Buck saw him sitting halfway along the port side. 'Sorry, you can't sit there. I need to be there for comms.' Buck pointed to headphones attached by a coiled black cord to the helicopter's internal radio communication system.

Gaz moved across to starboard, sitting with Dan and Tubs on his left, Ruby, Jingles and Del Aspinall on his right. Steve Thurtle, McCallum and RAF Corporal Robbie Cormie sat opposite.

'Up a bit.'

'Where's that oil bottle?'

'I haven't got it, I said.'

'Who has then?'

'Pass it around.'

'You don't need it, for fuck's sake!'

'Bollocks. If I don't oil it, it won't work.'

Buck sat where Gaz had been and put on the headset. The speakers covered his ears and he spoke into the microphone which hung parallel to his jaw line: 'I'm Sergeant Rogers, the chalk commander.'

'OK, Sergeant, Wing Commander van den Berg here.'

'We've got everyone and we're ready to move out.'

'Just to check, we are bound for Majar al-Kabir, correct?'

'Yup, that's about all I know as well.'

As Buck and van den Berg conversed, the chuntering continued between the increasingly nervous soldiers in the cargo hold.

'Why did you bring the baton gun, Gaz?'

'Fuck knows, anyone else want it?'

'No way.'

'Like we'll be firing dummies. This ain't fucking peacekeeping.'

'But one hundred rounds? Fuck all eh?'

'We're supposed to be the fucking QRF.'

'Dan, give us your buckshee ammo.'

'Can't, I've already let it go, mate.'

'Cheers, mucker.'

The Chinook's M-60 rear door gun had been removed since the war-fighting phase had ended. Buck's men reckoned its disappearance had more to do with the RAF's reluctance to clean sand out of it every day than the switch to peacetime weapons scales.

'On landing, we stay tight.'

'What?'

The engines were roaring now. It was difficult to hear: 'On landing...'

'What?'

'Everyone know their fire team?'

'Steve's [Thurtle] six or Sergeant Rogers'?'

'I'm staying with you when we get out of here, mate.'

'OK, Gaz, Dan, Tubs, you're with me.'

'OK, Steve.'

The pilot moved the throttle into the operating position. With the increase in engine noise the hull shook and voices were drowned out.

They would have to scream or use hand signals to communicate from now on.

DRIVEN by a turbine shaft engine, the Chinook's twin rotors accelerated, blasting warm air in all directions. Massive, mushrooming dust clouds suffocated those below and obscured the pilot's view. For a moment the helicopter seemed as likely to drill a hole in the ground as lift off.

Finally, the Chinook rose and tilted forward – translation lift had begun. Buck's men looked down at the gradually sinking HLS and the ground crew still cowering against the backwash. Mechanical sounds drowned out voices but not fears – they wondered if they would ever see Abu Naji again.

THE Army Air Corps' Gazelle helicopter was by now approaching Majar al-Kabir. 'Gaz 1' had been tasked with with locating Alpha and Bravo and acting as an 'aerial re-bro', providing both multiples with a VHF comms link to the Ops Room.

Almost as an aside, Gaz 1's briefing by the Ops Room had mentioned the pilot should 'have a look at the police station [for the RMPs]'.

It was 1105hrs.

NINE 'Lion-hearted Englishmen'

THE interpreter had slipped through a window and crossed the scrub. From the top of the compound's rear wall he turned to see the police station for the last time. He saw the mob had climbed onto the roof and the third RMP Land Rover was driven away.

'Inside,' H-J ordered, as his men once more came under fire. The Red Caps ran towards the doorway. One of them tripped.

LUKEY made eye contact with his men: 'It's Majar al-Kabir again.' He slung his personal kit aboard the lead WMIK and slid into the front passenger's seat.

'Al Majar, Lukey?'

'Yup.'

'Was there early this morning. Weird, man. Scarily quiet, I can tell you.'

'What were you doing there?'

'Routine patrol.'

'OK.'

'Cruised through, wasn't many people around or anything; just the way they looked at us. Really eerie like, you know?'

'This is the second time we've been there this week,' another chirped. 'It took Scimitars to push 'em back from the police station.'

'Aye, they wouldn't go away.'

'Smashing up vehicles.'

'C Company again, is it?'

'Same guys, but two multiples this time.'

'Killed a few crusties apparently but they're still massively out-numbered.'

'Shit.'

Each WMIK would have a three-man crew: a driver, an IC (in command) Wagon who sat in the front passenger seat and fired the GPMG, and a .50 cal gunner who sat behind him. The WMIK crews were also on peacetime munitions scales: 100 rounds for the .50 cal and 400 for the GPMG.

'C'mon, we'd better get a move on.'

'Aye, let's go.'

'They should've taken us with them earlier on.'

'It's not like we're busy.'

'A couple of WMIKs have gone up to Baghdad, but that's it.'

'OK, comms?'

'Channel one.'

'Roger that, Lukey's on channel two.'

'And fuck the one-way system and the speed limits around here. Let's go.'

'Those guys in Baghdad will be gutted to miss this.'

'So will we probably; it's always over by the time we get there.'

'Dunno, this contact sounds fucking heavy. We're going to need more ammunition.'

'Swing by the armoury then.'

Bolstering meagre ammunition supplies would cost them time.

SI Miller instinctively pressed a hand to where he felt sharp pain. Blood stuck to his fingers and dripped onto the floor. He was nauseous, the corridor rose to meet him and he pawed at the wall, marking it with a bloody handprint. Each of his strides was shorter than the last. He had been shot.

'I THINK we're clear,' said one of Robbo's Toms.

'Thank fuck for that.'

'How many rounds you got left?'

'I'm pretty low.'

'I'm sweating my fucking arse off.'

They saw Robbo ahead of them, inspecting a house. There was a large garden and a series of smaller outhouses.

'Fucking hell, we going firm here?'

'Yeah.'

Wanting silence, Robbo gestured towards them. The interpreter was at his shoulder as they heard voices from inside.

'Joseph, I want to use here for cover.' The interpreter looked quizzical, wondering how the local family would react to a dozen revved up paratroopers bursting in. 'You need to explain to the elder he and his family won't be hurt.' Robbo knew how frightened they would be. 'We're going in.'

Joseph nodded. 'Yes, yes.'

'As long as they stay calm they'll be OK.'

'Yes, Mr Robbo, I understand.'

'Good.'

'I tell them.'

The Iraqi family, however, were not keen to harbour the British: 'Get out of my house.'

'OK, it's OK. The British won't hurt you,' said Joseph.

'What is this?'

'*Min fadlak* [please], stay here, stay in this room, don't go outside. It is not safe.'

'Don't shoot, we don't have weapons here.'

'Tell them to get on the floor,' said Robbo.

'Lie on the floor. They are not taking over your house for long. Don't be frightened, just stay here.'

'What is happening?'

'Please, don't try to escape. *Shukran* [thank you],' Joseph pleaded.

'It's for their benefit, Joseph, if they start shooting at us from outside.'

Eyes flashed across the darkened room; the Iraqis looked up anxiously, assuming they were going to be killed.

'I don't understand. Please leave.'

'*Allah, Allah!*'

'Don't be frightened, please, they will not hurt you,' Joseph told them.

'*Shukran.*'

'*Shukran.*'

Some of the Toms tried their basic Arabic: '*Salam alaikum* [peace be upon you]', in various regional twangs. The air was even hotter than outside, and so thick they could almost use their forefingers to write their names in it. Dirt was everywhere, down their backs, in their ears, their mouths.

This was Bravo's first lull since leaving the militia headquarters at 1000hrs. Robbo and Dolman knew lulls were dangerous, giving their Toms a chance to reflect on the precariousness of their situation; this could not be allowed to happen.

'Check all your mags and top up.'

'You, get on him now. Over there!'

The commanders dictated firing positions to groups of Toms. The rear of the building was particularly vulnerable.

'Joseph,' Robbo beckoned.

'Yes, Mr Robbo?'

'You need to pass this on to him.'

The man of the house trembled.

'The British commander, Mr Robbo, now wants you to go outside. Check if there are any gunmen. Please do it, then come back. The British had to abandon vehicles near here; they were being followed.'

'What?'

'Joseph, tell him if he sees gunmen to tell us where they are.'

'Yes, Mr Robbo. Maybe gunmen are near where the British left their vehicles? If you see them come back and tell. Mr Robbo wants to leave the town and the gunmen want to stop him and his men. Then they will leave.'

'Oh no.'

'What do they want you to do?' a relative asked.

'To go outside and look for gunmen!'

Fear and desperation would lengthen the minutes while he was gone. His family prayed harder to Allah.

A TRAIL of blood marked Si's progress around the courtyard. His field dressings were pulled out and his mates ripped his uniform away to expose the wounds. He felt excruciating pain as direct pressure was applied. Morphine phials that would have lessened his suffering lay in a box at Abu Naji. Shell dressings staunched the flow of blood before bandages were wrapped tightly around his left shoulder, right arm, lower back and right thigh. His condition made it essential the QRF reached the RMPs – no vehicles and a severely wounded casualty made it much more difficult for C Section to extract.

'Tom.' H-J signalled him to adopt a firing position on a diagonal axis from the main entrance. Tom crouched, his sight trained on the entrance to the police station. He was the only RMP with experience of a major firefight and during build-up training in Kuwait the 20-year-old had taught infantry skills to his colleagues. Op BARRAS had been an offensive operation, precision planned in advance and brutally executed. On that morning in the jungle Tom had had 600 rounds or more for his GPMG and instructions to destroy everything in his arc of fire. Today he was a policeman and armed as such, with fifty rounds for a rifle. For the last hour he and his fellow RMPs had refrained from engaging the civilian, but armed, crowd – a noble gesture, but one which had lead them now to be trapped.

WING Commander van den Berg brought the Chinook to cruising altitude. His flying time to Majar al-Kabir would be around eight minutes.

Bubble portholes allowed passengers to see in front of, behind and immediately below the Chinook. As Lenny Thorne looked down, the chimneys appeared like chess pawns on a board chequered by irrigation ditches. Across the cargo hold Dan ran the 7.62 mm belt through his hands and Gaz lengthened the strap on the baton gun to fit around his shoulder. Others tightened their webbing: every strap was pulled and adjusted, if only to occupy time during this terrifying flight.

They sat facing each other, their backs to the fuselage walls, six feet between them. Like a team in a locker room minutes before the match of their lives, nobody was comfortable and their heads throbbed with the barrage of mechanical noise. There were spasmodic bursts of shouted conversation,

'We'll bomb burst out.' Buck's instruction was inaudible. 'Steve? We'll bomb burst out.'

Steve Thurtle nodded.

'Two sections.' Another NCO held up his fingers.

'Shaking out, left and right.'

'Make sure every fucker knows where his oppo's going to be on landing.'

'Defo.'

'Coz we'll be firing at everything we can't identity as one of us.'

Heads nodded.

'Drop any legitimate target; it's going to be fucking dusty.'

This was for real.

'There'll be shit flying everywhere.'

'OK, mate. You've got the gun in your section. Get the fucking rounds down. I want it up and running.'

'There's wounded on the ground, you know,' one voice cried.

'What? We've casualties?'

'Weren't you listening? Dead, apparently.'

'Dead? Fuck!'

'Suppose that's why we've got so many medics.'

As information circulated at Abu Naji, assumption was taken as fact. There were as yet no confirmed friendly fatalities or casualties. The Ops Room did not know about Si Miller.

'How many?'

'Don't know.'

'Who?'

'Don't know.'

'That's what they [the medics] said.'

'Right.'

'There's got to be.'

'Where are we landing?'

'Fuck knows.'

'Is there enemy there?'

The other Tom shrugged.

ALPHA were pinned down in trenches to the east of the north–south main street and approximately 500 metres from the police station. It was clear the objective of assisting Bravo was impossible. So Ross's favoured course of action was to keep the enemy at bay until the QRF arrived – he was unaware that this would be delayed by ten minutes because the WMIKs had to 'pol-up' [petrol, oil and lubricant] for extra ammunition.

As US drill sergeants told new arrivals in Vietnam, Charlie's rounds would 'tickle their assholes'; Alpha were having theirs tickled now, and their platoon commander was trapped behind a concrete block. One gunman, aiming towards Ross, was a particularly disciplined shot, letting off single precision rounds towards him with a high-caliber sniper rifle.

AN elderly Iraqi, his face the texture of leather, followed the crowd towards the police station. He saw a dead body.

'How did this happen?' he asked one of the young gunmen.

'He was shot dead by British troops.' [Highly likely to be Alpha.]

'Why?'

'He was shot after he pointed a rifle at them.'

This alarmed the elder. 'And what is happening now?'

The pair had RPGs slung over their shoulders. 'We've attacked the police station.' They pointed to the building. 'There is another battle going on in the town. We are going there now.'

They ran away, tracking those already en route to Bravo's hideaway. The old man shuffled closer to the police station and peered around a wall. He saw a Land Rover on fire and gunmen firing through the front windows of the building.

THE house owner tasked to observe the chasing horde saw them picking at the wreckage of Bravo's vehicles. The Iraqis paced back and forth, confused. *Where had the white devils gone? Where were they hiding?*

He walked back inside and told Robbo, 'They are close, outside and many of them with guns.'

Robbo's men were ready to burst out, whenever their cover was blown. There was no way of telling when that might be; they could even be given away by the family if they screamed. Exhausted, the Toms sat with sweat pouring down their faces and were gripped by a sense of isolation. Desperation seeped in beneath the doors; this house on a nameless street in a godforsaken Iraqi town was their world in miniature; and it was getting smaller as the mob circled.

Conversations were whispered: 'How did we end up here?'

'We got dicked patrolling this town.'

'They've been wound up.'

'How long we been here?'

'When did they [the QRF] get crashed out?'

'They should have rocked up by now.'

'Lying there monging it when the call came in, I bet.'

'Tan ops again. Fuckers.'

'They'd better bring ammo.'

'I mean, what's the fucking drama? Just jump on the heli and go.'

'Wonder if the QRF fucking bothered to pol-up the WMIKs?'

'Slack arse wankers. We're only twenty klicks away.'

'Serge, what you got left?'

'Mag and a half.'

'One.'

'You?'

'Same.'

'John [Dolman].'

'Robbo?'

'Get these guys ready to move out. I'll find out when the Chinook will be here.'

'OK.'

'Chuck us that sat phone.'

PAT Granger stretched. The signal was so weak he had to stick his neck out of the dusty hole in the wall of the Ops Room to hold onto Robbo's call – the sat phone should have been kept outside where its ring-tone would have been more audible and its signal have suffered less from interference. It should also have been manned permanently.

'Pat, we're in a hide; we've got gunmen all around us. We're in deep shit, over!'

'The ARF and the QRF's en route. There's an MSG heading down, Robbo.'

'We've got fuck-all ammo left.'

Johnno Palmer, the C Company second-in-command heard Robbo's report. He signalled to Pat that this was no time for concern about the satellite phone bill. 'We'll keep the line open, Robbo. Have you got comms with Gaz 1 yet?'

'We're trying. We're in a house on the eastern side of the river. There's wasteland to the north of us. There's a crowd outside; we were being RPGed, we had to debus and find a hide. The crowd are milling around the wagons.'

'Roger that. The Chinook will be with you any minute.'

'OK, we'll break out of here and marry up with them. But we can't hold out for long, mate, we're fucking low on ammo, Pat.'

'I hear that Robbo. Stay calm, mate.'

ROBBO divided Bravo into two sections. 'John, [Dolman] if we get overrun, you take five men inside the other building. I'll take the other five to the outhouse. We'll stay there until we're relieved, or...'

Dolman nodded then turned to his Toms. 'Get full mags on now. Top up the rest.'

'Yes, Corporal.'

THE Army Air Corps pilot focused on the crowd moving between the industrial buildings and mudhuts. 'Bravo this is Gaz 1, over.'

A crackle in Dolman's earpiece.

'Roger, this is Bravo,' Dolman replied.

'I am a Gazelle hovering over your position; how can I help you?'

The Toms listened in.

'Has Dolman got comms?'

'Yeah.'

'Thank fuck. With the Chinook?'

'Nah, it's the Gazelle.'

'Right.'

'Shut up, I'm listening.'

'Gaz 1, can you tell us exactly where the mob is?' continued Dolman.

'Closing on your position from all sides, Bravo.'

'Roger that, Gaz 1!'

'The Chinook is approaching.'

'Roger.'

'But you may need to indicate your precise location to the Chinook, over.'

'TWO minutes.'

'Two minutes.'

'Got that? Two minutes.'

'You hear that?'

'Airborne Fury' stirred within Buck's men as they made final preparations.

SI'S colleagues had dressed his wounds and carried him to the far corner of the police station, diagonally opposite the main entrance. His slim body was laid on the ground inside a bathroom doorway. He had suffered multiple gunshot wounds; desperate efforts were made to keep him alive.

The waiting continued.

LEFT A young Simon Hamilton-Jewell and his mother at a funfair in south London.

BELOW Anna, Paygan and Russ Aston at Paygan's christening in Derbyshire. Russ would write from Iraq, 'I love you both very much and miss you very badly.'

LEFT Saturday 11 January 2003, H-J and Tony celebrate their mother Teresa's 80th birthday with a pub lunch in Esher, Surrey. When asked about the war ahead, H-J had responded, 'I'm just looking forward to getting out there. We've got an important job to do.'

TOP Late March 2003. Russ Aston (left) puts his arm around fellow Red Cap Corporal Steve Brown as the pair from 156 Provo cross the border into Iraq from Kuwait. Their war had begun.

ABOVE The combat veteran too young to shave: Tom Keys returns home to a hero's welcome after Op BARRAS in September 2000. The fear is in his father, Reg's, eyes. 'Wouldn't you be safer in another unit, Tom?' he would ask. Tom said he would think about it.

LEFT The pastoral 1
PARA CO Lieutenant
Colonel Tom Beckett
QRH whose quiet voice
did not lend itself to
public speaking. He dis-
played moral courage
on 24 June and silenced
the guns. © *Ministry of
Defence*

BELOW March 2003:
another stirring speech
by the 1 PARA head-
shed. The old sweats
have heard it all before.
© *Ministry of Defence*

TOP The Operations Officer Captain Richard Todd returns from an O Group.

ABOVE Corporal John Dolman (left) and Jock Robbo liaising with local 'friendlies'.

RIGHT Private Jason Davidson, one of the many heroes of 24 June.

LEFT Tim May carries one of 8 Platoon's two LAW 94mm anti-tank weapons.

BELOW Hicksey (centre) and Gaz McMahon enjoy the locals' hospitality during Support Company's visit to post-war Baghdad.

LEFT Gordon 'Jock Robbo' Robertson, 8 Platoon's sergeant, and Tim May, the DAF driver, test the enemy's rifles at a weapons dump in Maysan province.

ABOVE May 2003: Tony Blair adopts his 'at ease with the troops' stance in Basra and is asked, 'Where are you sending us next, Prime Minister, North Korea or Iran?'

RIGHT Major Tootal, who commanded the Operations Room as the crisis in Majar al-Kabir unfolded, in 'hearts and minds' mode earlier on Op TELIC.
© *Ministry of Defence*

BELOW There was a warm welcome for 1 PARA in other parts of southern Iraq earlier on Op TELIC.
© *Ministry of Defence*

ABOVE The Red Caps relax at Tom Keys' (seated, third from right) birthday party held a few days before the tragedy. Next to Tom (centre) is Ben Hyde while behind them and to the right, stand Si Miller and Paul Long.

LEFT Sergeant Jason 'Buck' Rogers, the former Royal Navy man who commanded the ARF flight on 24 June.

BOTTOM March 2003: a WMIK sets off from Camp Pegasus, Kuwait. The driver has covered his face to protect him from the sand.
© *Ministry of Defence*

TOP Steve Brown (left) Russ Aston, Tom Keys and (right) Simon Hamilton-Jewell on patrol. Russ was yet to be issued a pair of desert boots. The female Red Cap is Si Miller's girlfriend Emma Morris.

ABOVE Outside the police station in Majar al-Kabir on 22 June, two days before the tragedy. An Iraqi mob disperses after a riot more prolonged and intense than the Board of Inquiry's report into the Red Caps' deaths would lead their families and the public to believe.

LEFT From left: Paul Long, Joanne Richardson and Tom Keys on operations in post-war Iraq. The mood among RMPs is relaxed, as Tom wrote, 'Fighting pretty much stopped. Wearing floppy hats and no body armour. Thank God!'

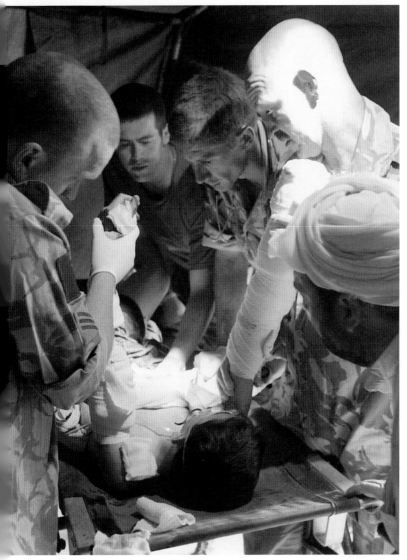

LEFT Regimental Medical Officer Andy West (centre right) and Corporal Lenny Thorne (right) both of whom were on the Chinook on 24 June, treat an Iraqi child. © *Ministry of Defence*

Captain Danny Matthews MC, OC Patrols Platoon, directs movements around the bird table from beneath his floppy hat. Matthews and his platoon joined the QRF in Majar al-Kabir on the tragic day. © *Ministry of Defence*

The process of Searching heavy Weapons
in Al Majjar district to the Security Commission
and the Foujes established inside the district
and the province, and there is no necessity
that the Coalition and its different
people be there . and according to the
following strategical plan.
- ~~Search~~ Searching heavy weapons for
two months, before that, a period of a
week must be given to inform people
to hand their ~~weapons~~ heavy weapons
including [Doshka, Mortars, heavy Cannons
and ground defence weapons against airplanes] etc
~~I~~ ve Want to see results in 1 month. ~~qf~~ o
~~I cl~~

Had this document, signed the day before the tragedy, been more
coherent, the lives of over 100 Iraqis and the six RMPs may have
been spared.

ABOVE A view of central Majar al-Kabir.

RIGHT The sun-dappled courtyard inside the police station at Majar al-Kabir. © *Ministry of Defence*

BELOW The fated Chinook takes off from Abu Naji bound for Majar al-Kabir on 24 June. It would return with 100 bullet holes through its fuselage and carrying seven wounded men.

LEFT After the battle, Bravo patrol the area close to where they hid from the mob. This photograph was taken from aboard a WMIK poised to provide covering fire.

ABOVE With the blood stains of their wounded colleagues on their uniforms, the survivors of the Chinook attack joined the QRF and returned to the town. As they told an NCO, 'We are going back down and that's non-negotiable.' From left: Denny, Marsh, Tune, Clegg, Aspinall and Jones.

LEFT Thousand yard stares: Danny Connolly (seated) and Mark Weadon in the immediate aftermath of the battle. Minutes before they had been under sustained enemy fire. The indomitable John Dolman issues orders from behind them.

TOP AND ABOVE
Members of 8 Platoon
before and after the
battle. Both pictures
were taken at Abu
Naji. Jock Robbo
stands immediately
to the right of the
wreckage.

RIGHT The wreckage
of one of 8 Platoon's
Pinzgauers. Both were
destroyed by the Iraqis.
This photograph was
taken the following
day. © *AP Photo/*
Saurabh Das

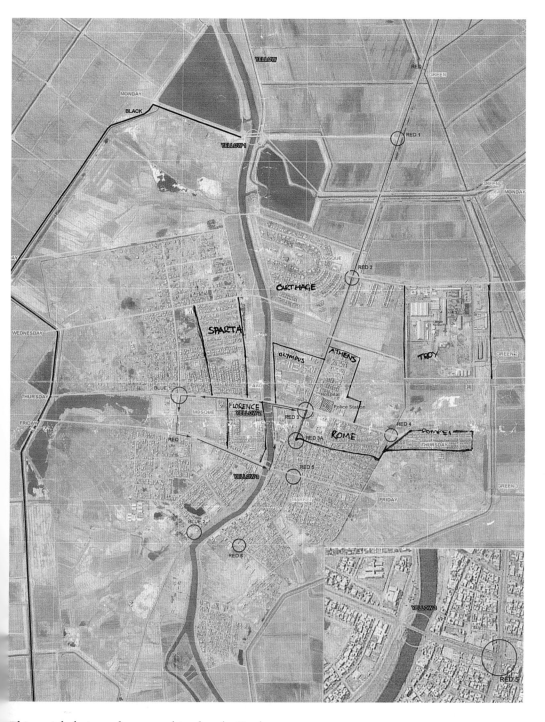

This aerial photograph was used to plan the Battle
Group's reinsertion into the town on Saturday 28 June.
The sugar factory is marked as 'Troy', the area where
Bravo were surrounded as 'Olympus'.

LEFT At his son's funeral, Reg Keys said, 'Five years ago we gave the army a rather shy, introverted young 16-year-old boy. Sadly, what we see before us today is not how we expected the army to return him to us. The day Tom was killed along with his five brave friends he was just four days short of his 21st birthday.'

RIGHT Paul Long's mother Pat said that when her son died part of her died too. His last letter from Iraq had been signed, 'from a very hot, very sweaty, very bored and pissed-off son.'

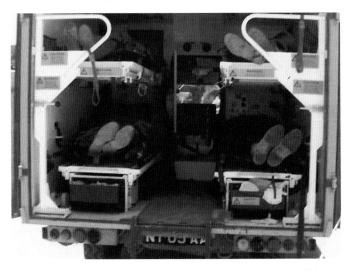

The soles of their desert boots are stained with their own blood: four of the murdered Red Caps are loaded onto an ambulance and driven back to Abu Naji from Majar al-Kabir. The other two lie in another ambulance parked in front.

WITH a last raking stride, Beckett marched into the Ops Room; the ruler returning to find his Battle Group in crisis. As eyes turned towards him he acknowledged those present and headed for the bird table. A picture of what was developing in Majar al-Kabir, or at least something akin to it, manifested itself in his mind's eye, but with his jaw clenched he remained impassive. He spoke briefly to Tootal, and let him carry on. Tootal did so as if the idea of authority being wrested from him had not crossed his mind.

It was the correct decision to let Tootal continue running the operation – there was not enough time to provide the CO with a sufficiently thorough briefing for him to take over and Tootal's plan was already being rolled out. Beckett would be driven to Major Kemp's Incident Command Post (ICP) on the northern outskirts of Majar al-Kabir.

7 PLATOON (C Company) had been stood to and mustered at the HLS. They would emplane the 'chick's' Chinook after Lieutenant Rick Lewin's briefing. They sniggered unsympathetically as a cigarette shook between Lewin's fingers. Once aboard, they found Tim Fleming's sandbag of extra magazines, but 7 Platoon were not its intended recipients. The ammo should have been cross-decked and received by Buck's men.

'STOP, stop shooting.'

The youth turned in surprise at the old man's request and as Arab custom dictated, he listened. In this strictly patriarchal society, he was considered wise.

'Please, stop shooting.'

The gunmen did so.

'Thank you.'

He moved from one young man to the next outside the police station. 'Stop shooting, stop shooting.' Remarkably the old man pacified the mob and began to address them: 'I am going to go inside, so do not shoot.'

He shuffled inside the doorway, with its Arabic script adorning the entrance and his shadow long in the sunlight. Turning left, he passed

Si's bloody handprint and saw Tom's rifle tracing his every step. 'Please don't shoot.'

Gesturing, the RMP granted him passage. He walked on, beyond Tom, to the entrance to a concealed set of rooms where Si lay motionless. H-J stood behind him, protecting the wounded 21-year old.

SWEAT oozed like salty dripping from their roasted bodies, making Bravo blink. 'Where the fuck's that Chinook?'

Seconds passed like minutes.

'You can hear a Chinook from miles off. They're probably still at Abu Naji, wankers.'

'Don't they know the fucking score?'

'Be ready to fucking move and slot any fucker between you and that fucking helicopter! Got it?' an NCO ordered, silencing the chunterers.

'Come on!'

'You ready?'

'Yeah!'

But where was that Chinook?

THE Chinook dipped violently, throwing all its passengers forwards.

'Fuck me, what was that?'

This was a mere appetiser of what was to follow. The ARF recovered their positions if not their composure as the loadie got comms with the pilot. Van den Berg's message understood, he took out the A4 pad more commonly used for passing on regular in-flight instructions such as to fasten seatbelts and wrote: 'RPG.'

They gulped, they weren't even over Majar al-Kabir yet. The pilot had dropped the Chinook to steer a path beneath the missile. Van den Berg was ready for his first pass as those behind him felt their stomachs plunge. As the Chinook descended again it felt like they were dropping down a mine shaft.

Their arrival sparked mayhem on the ground. 'Fucking hell,' said one of Buck's men catching first sight of the town, 'it's Mogadishu down there.' Through a porthole he saw men climbing frantically onto the tops of buildings and opening fire.

'Look at 'em having a good hose,' shouted Gaz.

Lenny looked again.

'Fuck's sake! It's like *Black Hawk Down*.'

Another of Buck's men peered out of the port side and saw fire and plumes of black smoke. This may have come from one of Bravo's Pinzgauers but was as likely to have been one of the RMP Land Rovers ablaze at the police station. As he believed only Alpha and Bravo were on the ground, he did not think anything of what he had seen.

Had H-J's section been carrying smoke grenades one could have been set off to alert the ARF.

'CAN you hear that?' said one of Bravo.

'That's definitely the Chinook.'

'Definitely!'

'At fucking last!'

Its arrival was also a blessed relief for Alpha. Enemy gunmen adjusted their sights towards the sky and as it thundered overhead, turned to chase it.

'Bravo, this is Gaz 1. The Chinook has made an initial pass of your location. You will need to confirm your position, over.'

Dolman broke off comms to tell Robbo. The look on their faces was identical, both men knowing the consequences of revealing their whereabouts.

LIFE drained from Si Miller as he drifted in and out of consciousness. He could, perhaps should, have been a professional footballer, if not with his local heroes Sunderland AFC, then Cambridge United – but his father could only afford to drive him hundreds of miles south so often to a club with a minimal budget for youth players. So he stayed on Wearside, with its industrial and seafaring heritage. Sunderland was often a place referred to in the past tense, such had been its industrial decline. In 1992, to mark the fortieth year of her reign, Her Majesty the Queen had bestowed on it city status. Two years later Wearmouth became the last of Sunderland's collieries to close, ending hundreds of years of mining.

'Go in the RMP, son; it'll give you a trade,' had been John's wise words. He had thought joining the infantry might restrict his son's employment prospects after military service. Si started basic training at Winchester in January 2000 and specialist RMP training in Chichester – 'Chi' in Red Cap speak. His brother had joined him as an RMP as he had settled into life in 156 Provo.

At 21 years old, Si was young for an RMP full corporal, and he had thrived on the challenges presented by Op TELIC.

Serving in Iraq had also made Si realise, 'how precious life is' and he was going to make the most of it when he came home. He had ended his last letter: 'Well, I'll say bye now and remember, don't worry. I'm keeping well and will be home soon.'

Two thousand five hundred miles away, Si's father sat in his office at Angels Close, Newton Aycliffe. John Miller had woken early this morning to sunlight breaking through his bedroom window and eaten breakfast with Marilyn. It was his wife's day off from Sainsbury's so she would go to the gym and walk Bonnie, the West Highland terrier they had raised from a ball of fluff. Tuesday, 24 June was another serene morning during Britain's heatwave and John's day promised to be routine; he had no clients to visit but lots of paperwork and emails to answer. Traffic on his journey south from Usworth had been mercifully light and he had arrived in good time.

He had been at work for an hour when a friend had asked to borrow his company car to drive to Leeds. Like his son he now had no way of leaving his place of work.

TEN Lead magnet

1115–1135hrs

BUFFETING forced the Chinook passengers to clutch backs of seats and each other to remain upright. They heard the engine grinding and rotor blades slapping the air – it would be a relief to land.

'One minute!'

'One minute!'

'Let's do it!'

AT the house, Robbo removed the mini-flares from the rubber-sealed packaging and fitted the necessary pieces. Releasing the trigger would send red light 12 metres into the air. He ran outside and let the first one off; it would only burn for fifteen seconds, nothing like as effective as a smoke grenade. *Had the pilot seen it? Had the crowd seen it?*

Robbo heard more AK47 fire at close range as he fired the second.

Alpha watched the helicopter's final descent and gunmen running to where they guessed it was going to land, but there was nothing Alpha could do to assist Bravo nor those aboard the Chinook. They still knew nothing of the RMPs' plight.

AFTER a tight turn, van den Berg decelerated and his helicopter began its rear-end first approach.

The fear factor rocketed as the dust cloud rose, blocking out all movement on the ground from their view. The Chinook splayed, stuttering 20 metres off the ground. Paras crouched on the edges of their seats, half-standing.

Phil Johnson, aka Tubs, would be first to disembark. Next on the ramp was Steve, the chalk second-in-command. Dan stood with 'the gun' slung low around his shoulders, his left hand clinging to its underside and his right hand on the trigger. Gaz, his number two on the gun, was immediately behind him. The psyched-up Scot with the Fallschirm-jaeger* tattoo across his back would feed link into the GPMG. Behind them were Ruby, Del and the rest of the blokes, all of whom had chosen to wear single breast plates rather than front and back; two was safer but, they reckoned, too heavy.

Iraqis opened fire before turning their backs against the twin-turbine blast. The first burst of small arms made circular holes in the port side. Seeing holes, Buck thought a safety catch had flipped causing somebody to have an ND (Negligent Discharge). He rose angrily. 'Who the fuck's had an...Aargh!'

Another incoming round tore into his inner thigh. 'Aargh, no! Shit!'

A second, heavier burst of fire began, with more AKs engaging than before. Rounds shredded through the Chinook's armourless skin. More holes.

'Down, get down.'

'Aargh, fuck!'

They dived for the floor, lying face down on their weapons, eyes closed and holding their breath. Not everyone got down in time as rounds ricocheted around the metal frame. The second attack lasted five seconds but seemed longer.

Harnessed into his chair van den Berg manhandled the helicopter hard right. The battle was between him and the gunmen as the next RPG flashed skywards. He banked the Chinook to avoid it, in doing so almost flying into electricity power lines. Then van den Berg climbed, raising

---

* The Fallschirmjaeger were the German paratroopers of World War Two. Their influence still pervades the culture of British airborne forces. *See* Glossary.

the pitch of the rotors to a higher, strained tone, like a car's wheels screeching around a fast bend.

There was a brief, eerie silence in the cargo hold before the first groans. 'Have I been hit?' In some cases it was impossible to tell. The last thing any of the Paras wanted to do was claim a wound only to find they were untouched.

'Medic...Medic!'

'Who's hit?'

'I am.'

'I think I am.'

'My leg. Medic here!'

'Medic, medic.'

Buck pressed his hand into his crotch and the gaping hole where flesh should have been – sensations of flames searing his skin and blood dampening his trousers followed. He willed himself to think: *The mission, the mission, got to land, got to help the blokes on the ground.* A mass of bodies tumbled about him, tossed by the helicopter's sudden jolts.

Jingles emerged from the floor with his hand cupped over his eye. Feeling no pain, he gave a thumbs up signal. 'I'm OK.' He lowered his hand from his face. 'Jesus!'

'You're not OK, mate.'

His oppo watched as one side of Jingles' face collapsed.

Tubs cried out: 'I'm hit, I'm hit.'

'Where, whereabouts?'

'In my leg.'

'OK, get his trousers off; get that webbing out of the way.'

His colleagues groped at the fabric.

'Fuck, come on.'

'Use this.'

A knife tore the material. There was no wound or blood on his legs.

'You're all right Tubs; you haven't been hit.'

'I have, I have; I can feel it...'

'OK, lift 'im.'

It took two men.

'Fuck, you 'ave.'

 On his seat, there was a pool of blood.

'OK, mate, we'll get it dressed. Just have to find it first.'

'Aargh, fuck. Morphine, morphine!'

 Only NCOs had the drug; uninjured Toms searched the medics' grab bags for phials.

'Get a line in him!'

Meanwhile, Doc West and Del Aspinall treated Pebbles' head wound. He sat lifeless, his helmet keeping his skull together.

Van den Berg had narrowly avoided three RPGs but 100 holes had drilled into his helicopter's belly and fuselage. Having reached a safer altitude the wing commander and his crew conferred over numbers of wounded and their severity – seven including two head injuries. He decided on his course of action and in military flying, as in civil aviation, the pilot had the final word.

Buck had suggested the helicopter land to allow the uninjured to assist Alpha and Bravo. His request was rejected as the Chinook had taken too much fire and might be unable to lift off.

BRAVO were weary and fear had settled in their stomachs; it had been crushing to listen to the sound of the Chinook tapering off and more intense AK fire. Robbo dialled the Ops Room to ask of the Chinook – Tootal and Toddy were awaiting confirmation of its status.

'Enemy closing to the rear, Sergeant.'

Private 'Smudge' Smith, one of Robbo's gunners, had heard a local trying to break in through the back of the house. Robbo turned to hear gunfire peppering the walls.

They were now engaged in what soldiers jokily called 'fish' (fighting in someone's house) and there were two immediate tactical considerations: Bravo's lack of ammunition and the enemy's proximity; they were closer now, having seen the mini-flares.

'Get on that back door.'

A Tom rushed forward and through a gap saw Iraqis climbing over a crumbling wall. 'Enemy front.'

'Straight ahead, mate.'

Coolly, he engaged with head and body shots. 'And behind 'im.'

'There, twelve o'clock.'

As one assailant was thwarted, another took his place.

THE police station's walls were pockmarked; every window had been shot out and bloodstains streaked across its stone floors. Tired of the elder's interference, the mob charged across the courtyard, hurdling the railings as the trees shot skeletal patterns of shade across their paths. Fearful for him, the elder ushered Tom Keys back from his firing position towards where his colleagues were huddled.

The kindly Iraqi peered past H-J into the storage room where tables and cabinets had been stacked into a makeshift barrier and documents were scattered on the floor in front of Paul, Ben and Russ.

As a character, Russ could have been played by a young Albert Finney; there was much of the loveable rogue Arthur Seaton from *Saturday Night and Sunday Morning* about him. He was a fighter by nature and according to friends, 'as crafty as a shit-house rat'. Over recent weeks the tale of Russ's war had been told by his face; his eyes had lost their natural shine. Today it was told by a trail of blood leading from the bathroom next door; the Iraqis had winged Russ with a long-range shot.

The top half of Si's clothing had been stripped for his wounds to be treated and there was a field dressing over the left-hand side of his face – having kept up his field admin he was clean shaven. The elder looked down to where he lay and reckoned him to be dead.

The elder's presence was now critical to the RMPs' survival. He was thrust into the role of mediator. Mediators were essential in a society in which conflicts were so commonplace. It was easier, however, when both sides were Arab; then appeals could be made to the overriding interests of their tribes and clans. Relatives of some of those killed in the souk, including one man who claimed his brother had been shot dead, demanded that the blood feud be settled in the traditional way, with the blood of the 'murderer tribe' being spilt. The police station was turned into a macabre court room, the two sides appealing for different outcomes to an intermediary.

The ringleaders remained intent on the 'killing for killing's sake' that Russ had described in a phone call to Glenice. Her son was not a killer by nature. He was the son of a roadworks inspector and like his colleagues, an English everyman. A member of Her Majesty's forces, yes, but a killer?

The ringleaders were tiring of the prevarication: 'You have to leave,' they told the elder.

'Please no, why? This is unnecessary.' He was determined to find a peaceful resolution.

'You have to leave because we want to kill the soldiers.'

'But the trouble is not to do with them; it is not of their making.'

He saw the RMPs as innocent bystanders not involved in the contacts involving Alpha and Bravo.

'If you do not leave, you will be killed as well.'

'THE ARF is returning to base location.' The Air desk relayed van den Berg's message. 'There are seven casualties. The ETA is five minutes.'

Beckett and Tootal were unmoved; this was no time to flap.

'OK, we'll need medics to muster at the A and E department. Every available pair of hands.'

'Yup, I'll get the word out.'

'Are Div on Ptarmigan [a secure area communications system linking the Ops Room to the British divisional headquarters]?'

'Yes, we've got comms with Div.'

'Where's our fast air?'

'Struggling for Cobra – but they are seeing what else they can spare us in this airspace.'

'We'll need FACs [Forward Air Controllers] on the ground.'

'Any PF [Pathfinders] en route?'

'There's a PF corporal on the QRF who's [FAC] trained.'

'How many MSGs are free?'

'Counting.'

A critical decision was whether or not to deploy the second Chinook. If it suffered a similar fate to the first, the Battle Group would be left without a transport helicopter to take Buck, Jingles, Pebbles and the other casualties to 202 Field Hospital near Basra. 7 Platoon were adamant it should fly them to within safe landing distance of Majar al-Kabir. They could have advanced to contact from there as the Chinook made a safe return to Abu Naji. Tootal was adamant the town was unsafe for air infiltration and the second Chinook would remain on the HLS.

A now desperate Robbo asked, 'What happened to the Chinook?'

'Badly shot up, with heavy casualties. The pilot aborted and is heading back.'

'We are surrounded here!' A firefight could be heard. 'When's the QRF due?'

'Could be another twenty minutes, Robbo.'

'My guys have hardly any ammunition left. Are there any other air assets en route?'

The man on the C Company net knew he could not give false hope: 'We're still hopeful of some fast air, Robbo.'

'We're running out of time here...What else can I say?'

NEGOTIATIONS continued in the corridor as Tom joined Ben, Paul and Russ. Si's body lay close by. The Red Caps had known before how quickly the locals' tempers could be inflamed – on the reopening of the bank in Amarah they behaved like wild men – but that incident paled in comparison to today.

Today's mood was of sheer vengeance and it was appropriate to have the infidels at their mercy in the police station – it being a relic of Saddam's oppression and where the new external rulers had chosen to take occupancy. No matter that it was not the RMP who had fired on them before, they belonged to the same tribe and that would suffice. They all belonged to the 'murderer tribe'.

Hundreds had joined the uprising and their chants reverberated across this most unforgiving of towns. They were sung most loudly at the police

station, where the Red Caps could only hope the threats were exagger-
ations, a characteristic of Arab behaviour being to issue threats but not
translate them into actions. The more blood-chilling the threat, the less
likely it was to be carried out, so it was said. Most of these men, however,
were Marsh Arabs, a particularly arrogant, intensely proud people who
would rather die than be shamed. A failure to avenge the acts in the souk
would, the mob's leaders explained, be a betrayal of their companions;
which was unthinkable.

*Where's the QRF? They must know we're here! H-J told our head
shed we were stopping in Majar al-Kabir. They'll be here any minute,
surely...*

'WATCH that wall!'
    'More coming through!'
    'Got 'im.'
    'On your right!'
    Bravo's targets fell when hit. But the Iraqis were getting closer.
    'Conserve your ammo!' an NCO reminded; 'we can't stay here much
longer.'
    'What's your ammo stat?'
    'It's all bad news. Down to my last mag, bruv!'
    'Bravo, this is Gaz 1, more enemy closing on your position.'
    'Roger that, Gaz 1!'
    Iraqi bodies piled up around the perimeter of the house.
    'Moving, eleven o'clock!'
    'Yup, 'im there, entering your arc!'
    'Seen.'
    'He's closing!'
    'Yup, got him.'
    'Single shots, mate, single shots!'
    Robbo and Joseph crouched together with only the thickness of a wall
separating them from the pounding outside. The mob kept up the chanting.
    Robbo was curious: 'What are they singing?'

Joseph listened. 'Mr Robbo, they are singing that they want to chop your testicles off.'

'You see those guys there?' 'Big Steve' Oellerman pointed to two Iraqis outside: they were armed but looked 'wilco'. It seemed ages since they had seen locals who didn't want to kill them. 'They're militia?' he asked hopefully.

Robbo watched them too and was encouraged. 'They're taking our side at last. Maybe?'

The pair approached, waving a white piece of cloth.

'Come here.' Robbo gestured. 'Keep your sights on them.'

The men walked closer. Just as Robbo felt relief they raised their weapons. Robbo opened fire, dropping one of them. His accomplice escaped.

'Bastards.'

There were more crushing noises at the back of the house.

'When's the ammo re-sup?' one of Dolman's men asked.

Dolman didn't know what to say.

AS the Chinook headed towards Abu Naji, the cargo hold had been transformed into a field surgery and its walls and floor were splattered with blood. Of the medics, only Gavin McCallum had been hit. He was running on adrenalin, treating the more seriously injured and ignoring the pain after a round had sliced through his right calf. Initially it had felt like being smacked with a baseball bat, and then it began to burn. Now it was numb.

He could hear Buck's men executing their medical drills: exposing their colleagues' wounded areas, compressing bullet entry areas and getting drips up. None of the young guys flapped. This was just as well; with so many wounded men filling the cargo hold, it was impossible for the medics to prioritise as they would have hoped – breathing, bleeding, breaks. They moved from patient to patient as best they could but in the main concentrated on those closest to them.

'I've found that wound, Tubs,' said Del.

'Yeah,' Tubs replied drowsily. He was slipping deeper into shock as haemorrhaging reduced the blood supply to his brain.

'It wasn't in your leg, was it?'

His mates had removed his body armour and ripped open his shirt. *Fuck, his stomach looks more like an arsehole.* The round had entered through his front and left his body near the coccyx.

'You're going to be all right, mate.'

'Yeah?' Nausea overwhelmed him.

'Course you are. How you feeling?'

Tubs didn't answer.

The others made eye contact. The patient was saying less and they could not afford to let him slip into unconsciousness. 'Right, we're going to put this dressing on.'

'OK.'

'You've got to shout if it hurts, mate.'

'We've got to turn you and cut your trousers off first. And your webbing.'

'But there's not far to go, mate. We'll be on the ground in about five minutes.'

The pallor of his skin changed.

'Check his pulse.'

'We're going to give you a morphine jab, mate, make you feel a bit better.'

But who had morphine?

'Here, use mine,' said Gaz. Why he or any other 'lance jack' should have had phials when the Toms were denied them was ridiculous. Gaz pulled the syringe from his webbing and handed it to Del Aspinall. It seemed tiny in his hand as he removed it from its plastic housing. Either end was a coloured nipple, one red, one yellow. His mind pictured the drill for injecting morphine: *Just take it out of the packaging and inject it in your leg, or the patient's leg.* But which nipple was the morphine injected from? *Fuck, I can't remember, yellow or red, red or yellow. Fuck! Red!*

Wrong. Del injected morphine into his own thumb. 'Fuck! Give me another one.'

Lenny climbed over the bodies, which lay at peculiar angles according to where they had been hit. Some were on the floor with their mates kneeling behind them to cradle their heads – one man's oppo perched on the ramp, in danger of falling out of the helicopter. It was 1130hrs.

ON the HLS, 7 Platoon were apoplectic: 'Why the fuck are we still here?'
'We're fuck-all use.'
'Screw the nut, Beckett, you hat bastard. Let us go down there.'
'That's what you get with hats like him and Tootal.'
'Robbo's multiple could be dead.'
'This is a joke.'
'Sums up Ex TELIC, doesn't it?'
'What's the hold-up? Nothing wrong with the Chinook is there?'
'Nah, just those lazy fuckers in the Ops Room.'

AT Majar al-Kabir hospital medical staff began counting Iraqi casualties. Witnesses claimed the British had caused the fighting, shooting their friends without warning.
'There are British soldiers at the police station as well,' one told Dr Fasal.
'Yes?'
Dr Fasal opted against going there immediately, instead calling for an ambulance from Amarah to assist in casualty evacuation.

THE ringleaders reiterated their threat to kill the elder unless he left. H-J stood in the doorway, his colleagues behind him and Si's body at his feet. The RMPs' fears could barely be contained.
Tom Keys had hoped to be home in time for his birthday, while his mother counted down the days before his return by the number of break-fasts her son still had to eat in Iraq. The section's youngest member, he was four days short of his twenty-first birthday and cards had already arrived in Bala. Ben Hyde, too, was ready for home. The only consola-tion for being part of the final twenty-five had been that some of his

closest friends had also been 'dicked'. Two of them, Tom and Russ, were with him now.

Paul had signed off a last note, 'from a very hot, very sweaty, very dirty and very, very bored and p***ed off son. Love and miss you all.' His letters were always amusing. His brother had liked the photo Paul sent of him leaning against a Land Rover, wearing sunglasses. Byron reckoned he looked like the Hollywood actor Val Kilmer; not everyone spotted the resemblance. Had it not been for receiving his mother's food parcels – shoe boxes stuffed with Cadbury's Flake, Mars and Milky Way – Paul would have felt even worse. Predictably the chocolate had melted, but it made a sweet drink. The next time she sent jellies, which he gave to the Iraqi children.

Pat Long had been alarmed to hear gunfire when her son called her from Abu Naji via satellite phone – he had to explain 'happy fire'. After joining the RMP in 1999, Op TELIC was Paul's first operational tour. He was a qualified radio operator – but as he had discovered today, radios did not always work. His mother Pat had her usual breakfast: a cup of tea and a cigarette, before collecting her £76 income support at the Post Office. Around the time her son was confined at the police station, she was on her way to the beach at Cullercoats. Sitting on a bus, she pondered what her son might be doing.

TENSION in the Ops Room was palpable and the temperature rose as US forces said there were no Cobra helicopter gunships close enough to Majar al-Kabir to provide support. The best option was for two F-15 jets to make a detour over the town en route back to base. But the planes were low on fuel and their time above the target would be strictly limited.

Beckett and Tootal had not lost a single man through Op TELIC's preparation, war-fighting and peace-support phases – just days before they were to return home, they now faced the heaviest British combat loss for many, many years.

'Can somebody warn off 202 Field Hospital.'

'Will do.'

'Depending on their health states the ARF casualties will be transferred as soon as possible.'

'There are two with head wounds, sir. One of whom is in danger of slipping into a coma.'

'There's an ambulance on its way to Al Majar also.'

'Div are waiting on the line.'

'We'll update them later; we're too busy now.'

Via the Ptarmigan radio network, the most senior officers 'in theatre' listened to developments. 1 (UK) Division was commanded by Major General Peter Wall. The events threatened to have severe ramifications in Iraq and, politically, in the UK. Inevitably, his staff would have to alert Permanent Joint Headquarters (PJHQ) in Northwood, Middlesex, from where messages would be relayed to the Ministry of Defence and Downing Street.

ELEVEN 'Go, Freddy, go!'

FROM his cockpit the pilot of Gaz 1 could, in theory, see the flow of battle. There were various skirmishes, with Bravo engaged around the house and Alpha north of the police station. He must have been too pre-occupied maintaining communications with Bravo to see the riot at the police station itself. It seemed the crowd near Robbo's position had thinned out – many having left to chase the Chinook or join those sur-rounding the RMPs.

'My section will lead, John [Dolman]. We'll find cover, somewhere,' instructed Robbo.

The Toms nodded. Dolman's men would stay behind in the house and put down suppressing fire to facilitate Robbo's escape. Once the multiple commander's men had made it to an area of dead ground Dolman's section would make their own bid for freedom.

'Get ready to move.'

'Check your ammo stats. We're all low.'

They were.

'We can't put down much suppressive fire. Every round's got to find a target.'

Robbo took his first steps as those behind him scanned their arcs. Tail End Charlie covered the rear.

'Go.'

'Move.'

'Moving.'

They executed a fire and manoeuvre, ('pepper-potting'). Fire and manoeuvre was a basic Depot drill: one soldier fired while the other made ground. Joseph's combat experience during the Iran–Iraq War now paid off; every member of the multiple was impressed by his coolness under fire. If he helped Bravo to escape from Majar al-Kabir, the soldiers would happily give him every dollar they had.

Iraqi gunfire was sudden, its aim erratic. Rounds pinged off metal telegraph posts and buildings.

'Down!'

'Enemy right. Behind that corner.'

'What? Not seen.'

'Watch my strike.'

Suffering heavy casualties seemed only to encourage the Iraqis' efforts.

'There's more of 'em!'

'It's fucking cheeky this, isn't it?'

'Yeah.'

'How many rounds you got left?'

'Ten?' The Tom tapped his magazine.

'Where are we?'

'Fuck knows, but you've got the river there.'

'Good reference for the QRF?'

'If they ever rock up.'

An NCO pumped his fist up and down and patted his head, signalling the pair should close the gap between him and them.

'Go, go on, I'll cover you.'

''Ave a look.'

'Go on, go!'

'OK, OK.'

The first Tom moved watchfully beside a wall topped with barbed wire, his heels kicking up the dust. Suspecting enemy movement he found cover, ducking behind a telegraph pole. Unfortunately, the base had a lattice design. If the Iraqis got lucky they could hit him – although a direct hit would not be down to accuracy, so few of the locals could fire with precision. He crouched on one knee in the gutter and swept his A2 sight across what appeared to be an empty street junction. Seconds passed. Out of fear that his oppo and he would get detached from the rest of their section, he waved his mate towards him.

'Move!'

'Moving!'

'Down there.'

'Jump.'

'Christ.'

'Jesus, we can't fucking stay here.'

With the last pair of Toms having closed the gap, Robbo's men dived into an irrigation ditch full of polluted water. They pressed their bodies against the bank and when they got wet their radios cut out

'They're closing.'

THE Chinook hovered over the hospital.

'Hold on, mate. Just a few metres.'

'I've got you.'

The loadmaster signalled the helicopter had touched down.

'OK, let's get some stretchers here.'

'Go! Fucking move it!'

The first helpers ran through the dust and stared in disbelief at the blood-red floors and walls.

Scraps of voices emerged. 'Give us a hand with him!'

Men had to scream to be heard above the 'wokka wokka' noise of the rotors.

'We need stretchers and at least three men on each. Get some more blokes!'

The wounded had glazed eyes and were delirious on morphine – 'yellow' had made them mellow. Areas of clotted blood were caked in dust.

'Shirts off, cover their wounds! Lay them across!'

There weren't enough men to lift them. Others walked by the helicopter, oblivious to what was happening.

'You!'

One turned.

'Yeah, you.'

'What?'

'Fucking on me [Come here] now! We've got wounded blokes here.'

Bystanders took photographs.

'Put your fucking camera away!'

'I'm just taking a pic of the heli. I haven't seen it land here before.'

'This ain't a fucking RTA [road traffic accident], twat. Make yourself useful.'

A few Iraqis hired for manual labour seemed to find the situation amusing. Paras not involved in stretcher bearing ran over and ensured they stopped laughing.

'Hey, mate, is my cock still there?' asked a wounded man.

'What?'

He had to shout over the noise of the Chinook: 'I said is my cock still there?'

'How should I know?'

'Well have a fucking look.'

The stretcher bearer pulled back the man's blood-drenched DPMs. 'It's still there.'

'Thank fuck.'

'But you've got two arseholes and two belly-buttons.'

'At least I've got a cock.'

'You've been shot in the arse though!'

'No. It's my upper leg and lower back. Not my arse.'

'Nah, mate, you've been shot in the arse. Your mates are gonna love that!'

'Come on, we still need more stretchers.'

'This bloke's heavy; another hand on here please.' It was a long 200 metres to the Abu Naji hospital.

'Swap round; you get on the front.'

WITH every minute that passed it seemed all the more ridiculous to 7 Platoon that they were sitting on the HLS.

'For fuck's sake, I just don't get this.'

'Are we gonna be sitting here all day?'

A member of the ground crew delivered bad news. 'That Chinook that's just come in...'

'Yeah?'

'Full of wounded.'

'Oh Christ.'

'Probably why you lot are still here.'

'Well they could still drop us short and let us tab in.'

'Yeah, that's no excuse.'

'How many casualties? I thought they were only getting dropped off?'

'What's it going to take for them,' said another, pointing towards the Ops Room, 'to send us in?'

IT was 1138hrs. Major Kemp and Grant Naylor had established the incident command post and Lukey's WMIK column sped south into Majar al-Kabir.

'Look left!'

'There's one of the call signs.' The leading WMIK driver pointed, seeing men from Alpha.

'They're our guys.'

Rounds pinged off their WMIK.

'Shit!'

'Contact front!'

'Muzzle flashes; you see 'em?'

'From that building.'

The AK fire was from an isolated concrete building set back 50 metres to the right of the main street.

'OK, hold up. Don't get any closer.'

Lukey got on the radio: 'Vehicle commanders to the front!'

'Ginge' Harvey, Dave Hilditch and Gordon Wilson dismounted. Lukey crouched waiting, needing the back of a WMIK to shield his massive frame. Unbeknown to him, one of his Depot Para protégés, Tom Keys, was 500 metres south. Weight of enemy fire meant Lukey could not get any closer, at least not before reinforcements arrived – so much for the QRF arriving as 'one big packet rather than piecemeal' as Tootal had intended. The IC wagons huddled together to receive their orders.

'Holy fuck,' said Lukey as enemy rounds came in. He pointed to the waste ground. 'Let's move over there.'

'Roger that!'

'Go!'

Ginge had the shortest journey back to his WMIK. John Healy and Carlo were waiting. 'That way, after the lead wagon.'

The driver nodded.

Dave Hilditch mounted the wagon behind. 'Fade right, Martin, onto that scrub.'

His driver nodded while their Geordie gunner 'Hicksy' primed the .50 cal. With just 100 rounds he wanted to make every one count.

'Straight ahead, white building. Engage!'

Hicksy's weight of fire tested the wagon's suspension and within seconds the building crumbled. There was no way any enemy inside or close by could have survived.

'Cease fire, Hicksy.'

'Locate and engage targets on the left flank.'

'Fire coming from those buildings.'

'Locate?'

'Half left...three hundred metres.'

'OK.'

Enemy fire continued but Hicksy seemed oblivious to it. The gunner was often ribbed about his weight – he was still chubby after four months in the desert – but his commitment now, in battle, was inspirational. He continued firing, disregarding his own safety.

'Give it some, Hicksy!'

Across the scrub, more gunners pumped away on .50 cals. This was the opportunity they had waited years for, to fire their weapons in combat.

'Right, that's enough.'

Spent shells flew into the air and littered the crusty ground.

'Look, in those ditches. Eleven o'clock.'

'Who's that?'

'I think they're C Company call signs.'

'Don't fire at them!'

ONCE Dolman's men had caught up with Robbo's group, the two sections of Bravo clambered from the irrigation ditch, their boots sticking in the mud. More Iraqis blocked their path.

'Enemy front!'

Robbo's men were quicker.

'They're fucking crazy.'

Each time one Iraqi gunman was slotted, another sprinted forwards. The Toms were down to their last half mags and none of them had a bayonet to fix.

'Head towards that building.'

With the sounds of WMIKs and Scimitars competing with Iraqi Dushka, RPGs and AKs, Robbo's quick battle orders were barely audible. The enemy had megaphones.

'What's he shouting?' Robbo asked Joseph as he pointed to a man standing on the back of a pick-up truck.

'Mr Robbo, he says people must fight because the Coalition wants to search the women and occupy the town.'

The insurgents had tapped into the general discontent over weapons searches, lack of humanitarian aid and interference in their lives. Coalition Forces had ignored the locals' pleas: *Thank you for your help in ridding us of Saddam, now let us get on with our lives; don't try to tell us how to lead them.* Mountains of aid supplies had remained in Basra when the need was as great if not greater in isolated towns such as Majar al-Kabir.

'ARF has landed, sir.'

'Thank you.'

This was Tootal's stage and he was a more confident performer than his CO. The pair now concluded the time had come for every fighting soldier to be sent down – including Beckett. *The penny's dropped. Finally Beckett and Tootal are acting like proper Parachute Regiment commanders!* thought many in earshot who approved of a full assault on the town.

It was probably too late.

'How are we doing with the fast air?'

'Div has got us that fast air. The F-15 are approaching.'

'Get me that PF corporal. Have you got comms with him?'

'I can't reach him.'

'Try the pilot, we need someone who's FAC trained on the ground.'

'He's on the net [Ptarmigan].'

'OK, speak to him will you.'

The US pilot spoke with a Southern drawl: 'Roger, this is Jet Jockey, over. I am over Al Majar; how can I help you?'

'Well, what have you got on board?'

'How about a couple of thousand-pound bombs?'

'Marvellous.'

'Where do you want them, son?'

'Wait out, sir. I have got to establish comms with our FAC.' The radio operator switched channels.

'Any luck with PF?'

'Nope, no comms.'

'OK, put me through to Gaz 1.'

Without an FAC the US pilot could not engage enemy targets; the threat of hitting British soldiers on the ground was too great.

'Gaz 1?'

'Roger, over.'

'This is Zero [Ops Room call sign]; are you FAC trained?'

'No, I am not FAC trained.'

'Wait out.'

Again, the radio operator switched channels. 'Jet Jockey this is Zero, over?'

'Roger, Zero.'

'I have not got comms with our FAC.'

'Roger.'

'Therefore I cannot give you permission to deliver ordnance, sir. We do not have the exact locations of our call signs on the ground.'

'Well, son,' the pilot reflected, 'we have only got five minutes of fuel to loiter. I tell you what, how about we fly by very low and fast?'

'Yup, sounds good.'

THE Household Cavalry Regiment, having earlier declined to enter the town because of the RPG threat, had now assumed positions within firing distance of the Iraqis and Bravo. It was 1140hrs. Watching their strikes, Robbo feared a 'blue on blue'. Having fought off the Iraqis for so long it would have been even more sickening to lose men to 'friendly' fire.

Alpha observed the scene from positions of relative security.

'Thank fuck the QRF's here,' said one.

'Not too soon eh?'

'They took long enough all right.'

'Nice of them to rock up at all.'

'Just do us a favour and don't fire that fifty cal at me.'

'INCOMING!'

The WMIKs were not making best use of their range advantage.

John Healy, a Tom firing a heavy machine gun on a WMIK, felt a strange sensation in his side. 'Oh fuck, I think I've been shot!' He ducked beneath his turret to check for wounds. 'No, I'm fine. Nothing there.'

Returning to his firing position the pain returned. 'Oh no, I 'ave been.'

He gazed down at the expanding patches of blood on his DPMs.

'Man down.'

'Get him into dead ground.'

He was treated in a covered position behind his wagon by Dave, Ginge and Carlo.

'Where's his dressings?'

He was 'pissing' blood from his left side as the first shell dressing was swallowed by the wound.

'Direct pressure.'

'Get that dressing on!'

'Yup, here you go.'

'I'll be all right; it's not a drama.'

'How you feeling, John?'

'OK, OK...'

'Well, let me give you morphine.'

'Nah, nah, don't bother. It's not a drama.'

'Are you sure?'

'Yeah, yeah, I'll be OK. Don't you dare take my weapon from me!'

'OK, John.'

'Seriously, man, I want to keep my weapon.'

PATIENCE and understanding were the Red Caps' buzzwords. Their way, rightly or wrongly, was to encourage law and order by example rather than force. So here they were, some of the Battle Group's most vulnerable members, alone in a filthy storage room at the back of a police station, two months after the conflict had officially ended. Only the deference of the mob to the elder was keeping them alive. He had granted them a stay of execution, and an opportunity for the Battle Group to realise their whereabouts and rescue them.

They must know we're in Majar, and we're policemen for God's sake. Where else would we be but at the police station! They'll come; they must come...

As a child, H-J had been abandoned by his father. He must have felt abandoned now, as the elder was pushed aside.

THE state of health of the helicopter casualties could be guessed by the size of the huddle around them – the most seriously wounded could not be seen for hospital staff. One casualty, Pebbles, gave particular cause for concern. His mates grimaced.

'Can you guys stay around here?' asked a doctor.

'Sure.'

'We'll probably need your help loading him and a few more of your blokes back onto the helicopter.'

'How's he doing?' The Para nodded at Pebbles.

'Touch and go.'

'That good?'

'But there's not much we can do here for him. He's got to go to Basra, once he's stabilised.'

'Right.'

His mates wondered if he was well enough.

'He's got to go; we're not sufficiently equipped here.'

The RAF ground crew surveyed the holes in the Chinook, varying in size according to the weapon and calibre of rounds.

'Dushka,' shouted one, pointing to one of the larger circles.

'Yup…more AK here.'

'And here.'

They walked around the battered Chinook, screaming against the engine noise.

'Look at this one!'

They crouched near the cockpit.

'How much has that missed the gearbox by?'

Had the round struck the gearbox the helicopter would have crashed, in all likelihood killing all the passengers and crew. Instead it had passed through a three-inch gap.

'Fucking hell, wouldn't want to be on the next crew that flies in this.'

F-15 Eagles arced through the sky and engine noise echoed across the plains. Both had air-cooled 20 mm cannon with rotating barrels delivering 4,000–6,000 rounds per minute. A gentle squeeze of the electronic trigger would have neutralised the enemy threat, but also inflicted mass casualties. With no FAC on the ground, the aircraft guns would remain silent.

The arrival of the planes raised spirits on the QRF, as although they were winning their engagements Bravo and Alpha were still in contact. The Paras anticipated low thundering passes by the pilots and accurate cannon fire finishing off Iraqi resistance. The jets swooped.

'Here they come!'

'Go on!'

But at their lowest point of flight over the town all the planes fired was chaff.

'That's shite!'

'Fuck all use.'

'Some threat. That's not going to have any impact is it?'

The result was temporary breathing space.

The jets made their second pass across the city from east to west, passing over the police station, the crossroads and the River Majar before soaring away.

The enemy remained.

'OK?'

'Ready.'

'One, two, three, lift!'

The trio took Pebbles' full weight and shuffled out of the Accident and Emergency ward, walking past Steve Thurtle, who stared as if it might be the last time he saw his mate. 'We were just days from going home.'

'Yeah.'

'Just fucking days. Now we've got seven wounded and he's probably going to die.'

'I heard you got shot in the arse!'

'No, it was my upper leg and lower back.'

The AK round had taken off a chunk of Pebbles' skull. While three carried the patient's stretcher, another three medical staff held the drips and monitoring equipment that were keeping him alive. Pebbles would be flown to Basra in van den Berg's Chinook – a journey fraught with risk given the amount of lead it had swallowed.

Buck was also helped aboard. Morphine made him smile and he had had a lucky escape: the round into his thigh had missed his femoral artery by millimetres.

EVEN after firing his remaining mini-flares, Robbo was unsure whether the QRF were aware of his position, while Bravo's ammunition state was only sufficient for one more fighting withdrawal. The next 'bound' would have to take them to safety.

Freddy crouched close to his multiple commander. Robbo scribbled instructions for the HCR regarding his position on a piece of paper and handed it to him. 'Drop your webbing and run across there.'

His words were as heavy as a depth charge. Freddy's expression suggested he knew he was going to die. His multiple commander was not supremely confident he would make it either – this was not a command given lightly.

If Freddy was shot, with luck the HCR crews would see his fall. Successful or otherwise his actions would be a remarkable self-sacrifice.

'We'll put down as much supporting fire…' said Robbo.

Freddy knew his mates did not have many rounds left. Those who didn't want to be taken alive would save the last one.

'Go on, Freddy.'

'Good on you, mate.'

There wasn't much to say to make this easier. To Robbo's relief, his order was obeyed.

'Go, Freddy, go.'

'Fucking hell, mate.'

Every round the multiple fired in Freddy's cause would have to score a kill. It was 1145hrs. He set off.

'Run, mate, run.'

All Iraqi and British eyes were on him. His mates had never seen Freddy run so fast; he was whippet-like in build and speed.

'Fucking go on!'

Freddy zig-zagged across the ground to make himself a more elusive target. But this was featureless terrain. The Iraqis fired. Every local head that moved from one of the ditches was sniped by the multiple.

Don't fall. Faster, faster, just don't fall.

Across the ground he went, through gravel and dirt.

Not much further. Fuck, I can't breathe.

There was no tape or winning post, only a row of British armoured vehicles. If Freddy made it, he had, like a gladiator, won his freedom. The Scimitars were getting closer but appeared to be bolting up and down as he covered the uneven ground.

'Go on.'

He made it.

DR FASAL left the hospital and walked to the police station.

TWELVE 'Chickenshit' Beckett

BEFORE today, bad teeth rather than good or bad soldiering had distinguished Freddy from his mates. Breathless, he delivered his multiple commander's note allowing the Scimitars to engage the Iraqis without endangering Bravo with their fire. Although they felt safer, Robbo and Dolman remained guarded against a moment's complacency.

'Get ready to move.'

'Stay switched on.'

Bravo withdrew through Alpha's positions as the HCR's light tanks continued to fire.

It seemed to Alpha that it had taken too much encouragement to entice the HCR into the town when Bravo's fate had looked most grave – the Scimitar commanders had ignored Mark Weadon's earlier requests for them to advance down the main high street.

Dr Fasal's visit to the police station was brief. Wanting to speak to the British commander, he now drove his ambulance towards the column of WMIKs parked on the road heading north, towards Route 6. The QRF, which by this time included men from all 1 PARA's rifle companies, was still engaged in heavy fighting. Locals died valiantly but pointlessly as one suicidal charge towards the British after another was ended by machine guns.

Sergeant McCann's team had debussed into a street battle and one of its snipers became isolated having come under fire as the section crossed a road. He took cover behind a derelict fountain with enemy closing in and pinning him down with AK47 fire. As 7.62 mm rounds pinged off the cement wellhead, his mates mocked his failure to keep up.

One WMIK crew spotted an Iraqi cycling towards them with an RPG balanced on his shoulder. With his left hand on the handlebars and his right balancing the weapon, he cut a pathetic figure. Any sense of comedy evaporated when he called for children to accompany him and they complied.

'Look at that sly fucker.'

'Cheeky rag-head bastard.'

'What a wanker.'

The Iraqi peddled with increased vigour, considering his human shield impregnable. This was a tactical miscalculation: whoever he brought with him, he could not be allowed to threaten the Fire Support Base (FSB). He was a condemned man and they, doomed boys.

'Well?'

The blokes grimaced, genuinely dismayed.

'What a c**t.'

'We ain't got any choice.'

Onward he rode. No more stalling, children or no children. Their deaths did not cause celebration; the WMIK crew members were mute.

THE air was loud with Browning and GPMG fire as Tootal and Kemp spoke again: 'Bravo are accounted for.'

'And Alpha?'

'With the QRF. Do you want me to plan the withdrawal?'

'Wait out, Chris.' A wave of relief brushed over everyone except 'Bob' Marley, as Tootal addressed his men: 'The known call signs on the ground have been accounted for. Is there anyone else I need to worry about?'

'I still have not heard from my guys; they might be in the town...' Marley seemed embarrassed. 'I still can't be sure...'

Tootal asked Kemp if he could push further south towards the police station while Gaz 1 would sweep over the town again.

THERE was now at least one RMP with the QRF: Lieutenant Richard Phillips. He had left Abu Naji as soon as he could after hearing about the contact involving Bravo, and knew C Section were due to have passed through Majar al-Kabir, hopefully before the trouble started. In Phillips' mind nobody knew Majar al-Kabir better than H-J, the NCO who was nearly old enough to be his father. Gunfire echoed around him as he waited for news.

'I'VE got a guy here [Dr Fasal], sir, who says there are four British hostages at the police station, over.' It was 1200hrs.

'Roger that, Chris,' replied Tootal.

The doctor accepted Major Kemp's request for him to facilitate their release. Radio messages were passed to ensure none of the QRF call signs put Dr Fasal under fire.

THE best had been done to clean van den Berg's helicopter, but the blood-stains and sickly aroma lingered as the wounded were lifted aboard. Each would be accompanied by a medic. There were still questions asked over its worthiness to fly.

Having carried the wounded to the Chinook, the ARF survivors joined the 'clusterfuck' of men, the last dregs of the QRF still hoping to see some action in Majar al-Kabir but not having left Abu Naji yet. They were more scared before their second infil than they had been before the first.

But there was only so much room for sentiment. They had a premature 'dead man's auction' as their colleagues from the helicopter still clung to life. To them, it did not matter who the additional ammunition or the body armour plates had belonged to last; it was about being practical; Jingles and Pebbles would have done exactly the same thing. Certain primitive feelings filled their minds; they were all determined to exact revenge upon those who had wounded their friends, or failing that, other members of the enemy – just as the Iraqis were at the police station.

One of the RAF crew described being shot at as 'a detached, interesting experience'. While the Paras did not necessarily disagree, their sentiments were stronger and were expressed in basic Anglo-Saxon.

'Are you all right to go back down?' an NCO asked, seeing their blooded uniforms and dead eyes.

'We're fucking going back down – and that's non-negotiable.'

There would be enough paratroopers on the road to Majar al-Kabir to cordon the town and conduct any operations within that boundary as the CO dictated. This was a British as well as an Iraqi blood feud now.

DR FASAL returned to Major Kemp's position to inform him he had seen three dead British soldiers at the police station. Kemp repeated this to Tootal. There was confusion in the Ops Room, with the figure of three Coalition dead seeming incorrect. Private conversations were held out of Tootal and Marley's earshot: 'Three, why three? Who are they?'

'Don't know, they think they might be RMP.'

'What?'

'Yeah.'

'What are they doing there? I didn't even know they were there.'

'Neither did I. I don't think he [Tootal] did either.'

'I thought it was our blokes who were in the shit?'

'They were, but they're accounted for. This RMP section must have been there at the same time.'

'What were they doing there?'

'Just visiting its police station.'

'Shit, it's looking bad.'

Meanwhile, Warrant Officer Marley spoke with Pat Granger: 'I'm still rather worried about one of my call signs. I might have a patrol going through that town; they're on route to Al Uzayr. I haven't got comms with them.'

'Right.'

'Can you get a TACSAT [Tactical Satellite] message to the British base at Al Uzayr requesting that Sergeant Hamilton-Jewell radios in when he gets there?'

'We'll do that.'

The atmosphere was heavy with portent as Tootal asked: 'Chris [Kemp], can you confirm at the police station? We are missing six RMPs here, repeat six RMPs.'

'Roger that. There is still a very heavy contact in progress here though.'

With Iraqis still swarming about the streets, advancing a WMIK column towards the police station risked heavy British casualties. Dr Fasal said he would go back to the police station – the QRF would stay where it was. It was 1230hrs.

ALPHA and Bravo drove towards the QRF command post in an Iraqi truck 'borrowed' for the purpose – the DAF having been abandoned where Ross's multiple had debussed. There was a surprise for Tim when Grant Naylor, the company sergeant major, called him over: 'May, I want you to walk back into the town behind that [he pointed to a Scimitar] and drive the DAF back here.'

'It won't start.'

'Well, he'll [the Scimitar] drive up behind you and push if you need it.'

The DAF's starting problems came as no surprise to Robbo's men when Alpha explained. Once Tim returned, Alpha and Bravo climbed aboard. Dolman stood by the tailgate, his sleeves rolled up, still directing individuals, pointing out details, as if today was just another day. Mark Weadon clutched the DAF's metal frame and stared, just stared.

With the multiples reunited, Robbo spared a word for Freddy, the man he might have condemned to death. There had been so many gallant acts today that it might have been unfair to place him above the others. In Robbo's opinion, his actions had been worthy of a Mention in Dispatches at least. Freddy played down his role, insisting he had only done what any of his mates would have done, if ordered. He didn't want to be different, to be a hero. He was happy belonging to the 'Toms Liberation Front' – the TLF – which drank illicitly, ridiculed Tootal and chased gangs of 'rag-heads' around Amarah. Such nonsense had made the war bearable. None of them had been in a proper contact before, let alone killed anyone. Today, each multiple had accounted for twenty to thirty Iraqis dead, with many more wounded. The QRF had accounted for at least as many.

KEMP spoke to Tootal. 'Sir, we have just had it confirmed. There are six dead at the police station.'

This was the biggest single loss of British troops to hostile forces since the Falklands.

Those around 'Bob' Marley were clueless as to what to say. Trite comments like 'Hard luck, mate' seemed pointless.

Dr Fasal would collect the bodies; Lieutenant Phillips would identify them. They were *his* men; he was their commander, responsible for their actions and security. Losing the whole of C Section was beyond comprehension. A little over three hours ago, Phillips had seen H-J; he had known where his men were going and what they were going to do. *How could this have happened?* And to H-J's section? H-J knew Majar al-Kabir better than him, or anyone else. *Had there been any intelligence warning of a specific threat there today?* No; protests usually took place on Saturdays.

The most tragic event in the corps' modern history had happened on his watch – he would have to inform Major Parry-Jones. The OC was in for a shock; his assessment had been that the security situation had stabilised, the Iraqi police force was starting to come together and the area was fairly quiet.

THE message 'Six dead RMPs' was broadcast on the PRR radio net. Alpha were stunned, having been no more than 100 metres from the police station.

'What were they doing there?'
'I haven't a clue. You?'
'They were at the police station?'
'Apparently, that's what's being said.'

'Fuck.'

'I'm gutted.'

'We were just there, on that fucking crossroads!'

'Fucking hell.'

'Who was it; we've got to know those guys, haven't we?'

Looking north, they saw the Battle Group's fighting strength poised to storm the town.

'What's the plan?'

'Let's get back in there.'

'The whole fucking battalion's up there.'

'Fastball all right.'

'The rag-heads have killed six of our blokes. Fuck it, man, just get a re-sup and let's crack on.'

'This is what we've been waiting for.'

'They're our blokes.'

'Some of them were good blokes, too.'

AT 1250HRS Dr Fasal returned to the ICP with H-J, Paul and Russ's bodies. They were lifted onto the ground. Those standing nearby could not help but stare. The RMPs had not just been executed, but anointed with lead, with thirty or more wounds to their heads and bodies.

Dr Fasal returned with Si, Ben and Tom. Whoever shot the six men had wanted not only to kill, but also to humiliate them; at least one had been shot near his sexual organs. The others had been hit with rifle butts and stamped on. Blankets were placed over them yet even when just their lower legs and feet could be seen they were a galling sight; the soles of their desert boots had changed in colour from sand-yellow to poppy-red. Perhaps these were men they, 8 Platoon and the QRF, had passed that morning en route to the wash areas or scoff house.

Eventually two British ambulances arrived and the bodies were carried inside. They sank into folded-down bunk beds and were strapped down.

That six Red Caps, six 'Monkeys' even, had been killed as opposed to six paratroopers, was irrelevant. They were members of the same

Battle Group, sharing the scoff house and suffering under the same sun. Feelings ran high, not just with Toms, but officers as well. All that remained was for Beckett and Tootal to let them cross the start line. The CO, however, was unequivocal: all vehicles were to extract and return to Abu Naji. His order, once repeated on the net, met with a predictable response.

'We've just lost six of our guys.'

'What a fucking hat.'

'Runaway Beckett!'

'Chickenshit Beckett!'

AFTER three hours of fighting, stillness fell over Majar al-Kabir, where towards 100 people had died, six of them British. Despite the body count being so heavily in their favour, the Coalition call signs left disappointed they had been denied the chance to exact revenge for the loss of their colleagues.

8 Platoon were treated to bottles of cold water on their return to camp. Relief, however, was short-lived.

'The OC wants everyone in the scoff house now. You've all got to write reports on what happened.'

'Oh right, where's he?'

'In the Ops Room, briefing Tootal. He's coming over in a minute.'

They slumped against the tables exhausted as their mates from other platoons fired questions. Steve Oellerman shook his head. 'I'm telling you guys, I thought I was a goner, man. I thought that was it.'

KEMP arrived and sheets of A4 paper were distributed.

'OK, well done for getting out of there. Now, from the start of the day I need every one of you to write down what you remember, what happened to you in your own words, every detail.'

Afterwards they returned to their accommodation and crashed out, elated but exhausted. Word spread that Freddy might be written up for a gallantry award; the Toms knew they couldn't all be decorated but if Freddy and perhaps Jase Davidson as well could be and not just the commanders, they would take great satisfaction. Ross, Robbo and 'The Dolmanator' were racing certainties for medals.

WHEN the RMP interpreter returned to the police station the armed mob was still there. But there was no sign of the 'lion-hearted Englishmen', as he called them, or his bicycle. He made a note to himself to seek compensation.

AS the head shed wanted to control the passage of information into the public domain, satellite phones reserved for 'compassionate use' were confiscated. This meant nobody in 8 Platoon, the Chinook survivors or in 156 Provo could tell their relatives they were safe. The names of the deceased were passed to 1 (UK) Division HQ and on to the Ministry of Defence – the race was on to inform the six RMP families before the first media reports.

The MoD lost. The news was broadcast that six men from the 1 PARA Battle Group had been killed in Maysan province. In response the Ministry announced:

> There have been two incidents today near Amarah. We very much regret to confirm that in one incident six British personnel have been killed. Arrangements are in hand to inform their next of kin. In the second incident, troops from 1 PARA patrolling south of Amarah came under fire. The patrol took one casualty and two vehicles were destroyed.
>
> In response to the incident an RAF Chinook helicopter carrying a quick reaction force came under fire as it landed. Seven personnel on board the helicopter were wounded, three of them seriously. All were extracted by helicopter and are receiving treatment.
>
> The Ministry of Defence is investigating the incidents, including whether or not they are related. The government will provide more information when we can but we ask the media to respect that the priority is ensuring that next of kin are informed as quickly as possible.

The British commander in Iraq, Major General Peter Wall, made arrangements to fly up to Abu Naji. Lieutenant General Reith, the former 1 PARA CO, now Joint Commander of Operations at PJHQ, ordered a full inquiry. The Prime Minister was informed and Downing Street released a statement:

> The Prime Minister was informed of this during lunchtime today and heard the news with great sadness and it goes without saying that he believes those who died have died with honour doing a very worthwhile job, serving their country with great distinction. We believe it happened this morning and the Defence Secretary will update the House of Commons as soon as possible.

Paul Keetch, the Liberal Democrat defence spokesman, said:

> This is a reminder that British troops remain in a war zone doing a difficult and dangerous job. Our thoughts must be with the families of those killed and injured. Al Amarah had been considered very peaceful and when I visited the Paras there last month they reported that relations with the local people were very good.

Jingles and Pebbles were flown from Basra to a US Mobile Army Surgical Hospital (MASH) in Kuwait.

JOHN Miller glanced at his watch – 4 p.m. on a hot afternoon that didn't want to end. He hadn't heard the news. His office phone rang; it was Marilyn.

'Hi, Maz, how are you?'

'Fine, love, you?'

'Aye, OK. How's your day been?'

'Yes, went to the gym, did a good work-out and then had a sauna.'

'Great.'

Marilyn was puzzled. 'Have you been home today?' she asked.

'No, love, why?'

'It's just the French doors are open into the living room.'

The last person to leave always closed them to keep the dog downstairs.

'I'm sure I shut them before I went out, Maz. I haven't been out of the office today.'

'Oh...'

'I can't leave here because someone has got my car for the day. I'm not expecting him to be back until five p.m.'

'Strange, then,' said Marilyn.

She gazed through the lounge window as a silver saloon cruised by.

'There's a car pulled up at the top of our drive.'

A man and a woman in the car were checking door numbers.

'They've got out now; they're coming down our drive. I'll just see what they want.'

'OK.'

John waited, half-listening to his wife's small footsteps across the wooden floor. Maz opened the door.

John heard her scream.

He sat upright. Was Maz being attacked? 'Maz, Maz!'

She screamed again. 'My son! My son!'

Oh, thank God! The relief. John thought Si was home.

How typical of him to not tell us when he was coming and surprise us!

'My son! My son! You cannot take my son!'

Marilyn screamed again.

What's going on? Si? Si? I thought he was home? I don't understand.

'No, no! Not my son!'

'Maz? Maz?' John stood. All he could hear was his wife's screams. 'Maz? Maz?'

John put the phone down. He felt dizzy, sick. *I've got to get home, got to see Maz. Where are my car keys?* John ran into the car park. No car. He couldn't get away. He ran inside.

'Gavin, Gavin?'

'Yes, John, what is it?'

'Where's your car?'

'What is it? John, what's the matter?'

'I think my son has been killed.'

Everybody stared; they knew Si was in Iraq.

'Can I borrow your car; I've got to get home?'

'Of course you can,' Gavin replied. 'Do you want me to come with you?'

'No, no, just give us the keys.'

It felt like a dream sequence...*What's going on? Is this real? Got to ring home...I'll speak to Maz; she'll be fine and wondering why on earth I'm having such thoughts. Yeah, I'm just going mad today. Everything will be fine; I'm imagining all this.*

The phone was answered but John couldn't tell by whom. He could only hear screaming: 'My son, my son, no! You can't take my son!'

Then: 'Mr Miller?'

'Yes?'

'Mr Miller, my name is Major Steve Bolder. We have just heard about your son.'

'What about my son? Is it the worst?'

'I am afraid it is.'

John ended the call and put his mobile phone on the front passenger seat. Traffic on the A1 was heavier than on his journey to work. He dodged cars and drove as fast as he could. *What about Jon* [Si's brother]? *I've got to tell Jon. But do I do it now or later? No, I've got to ring him now before he hears it any other way. I'm his father; he should hear it from me.*

'Come on, move!' he shouted at the cars in front. His mobile rang. His eyes jumped to the screen. *Oh, God!* He wouldn't have to call him. News had reached the RMP Training School, Chichester.

'Hello, son.'

'Don't tell me, Dad. I know already that six RMPs have been killed in Iraq today.'

'I never heard that, Jon [He hadn't, John only knew about Si]. I didn't know.' John was livid with himself for not listening to news bulletins through the afternoon – *Damn it, if I had done my son would still be alive.*

'Jon, are you all right, son? Where are you?'

'Dad, I'm in my room.'

'Are you sitting down?'

'Dad, don't take the piss. Don't, Dad, don't.'

'Jon, I would not do that to you, son...'

EATING fish and chips on the seafront, Pat Long had pondered whether her son Paul was getting enough to eat, lack of food being one of his most common complaints.

'I'm so excited about him coming home,' Pat had said. 'It's his birthday soon.'

'Oh yes,' her mother replied enthusiastically.

'We're going to have a barbecue.'

Pat pushed her mother's wheelchair along the promenade before they caught the ferry back to South Shields. They said goodbye. Pat would complete her journey home by bus. Pat sat on the first seat on the right-hand side of the bus for the twenty-five-minute journey home. A ring-tone played the melody to Linkin Park's 'In the End'. It was Pat's phone; her son Byron had programmed the song in.

'Hello, Pat?'

She recognised Gemma's [Paul's wife's] voice.

'Hello, Gemma...'

'Pat, I have had the Army in touch with me...'

'Are you trying to tell me my son is dead?'

Pat screamed. The bus stopped and she had to be helped off. A lady who was sitting behind her when Gemma called walked her home. They stopped at Pat's neighbours, Karl and Sonya. Karl phoned a military number: 'I have got a lady here in the house who has just had a phone call to say her son has been killed in Iraq. Can you confirm this?'

'We will check and call you back.'

JOHN Miller didn't hear his son's reply, just a thud. Jon had collapsed. John didn't recognise the next voice.

'Hello, who's that? What's going on?'

'This is Jon's father. Can you get the OC for Jon? Straight away?'

John then explained what had happened.

'Sure, I'll get him and I'll get him to call you.'

'And make sure Jon is all right.'

'Yes, I'll stop with him.'

John's next thoughts were for Dorothy, his sister.

'Hello?'

'Dorothy, it's John.'

'Oh John.' Dorothy sounded shocked.

Perhaps she already knew? thought John.

'Oh John, I've heard on the news: some RMPs have been killed in Iraq. Are you OK?'

'Dorothy...our Simon is one of them.'

'Oh my God!'

They cried together for a few seconds before John said, 'Dorothy, Dorothy, I'll have to go. I've got to get home.'

The front door was open when John arrived home. He ran into the front room; Marilyn was staring, her fists clenched, face whitened. 'Tell me they have made a mistake! Tell me! Tell me!'

She screamed again. John held her – *God, however dreadful I feel, I must, I must stay strong for Maz.* She would need medical assistance. John thanked the TA officers, who promised to return tomorrow. Jon insisted on travelling alone from Kent up to Newcastle. He wanted to grieve for the younger brother he had laughed with, cried with, drank with and even followed into the Royal Military Police.

H-J'S brother Tony hardly ever listened to news bulletins on Radio 4. But with the time approaching 6 p.m. as he drove to Eastbourne, he did so. The lead item was the deaths of six British RMPs in Iraq. Naturally, he assumed the worst. His speed climbed; he felt like being home.

His mobile phone rang; it was H-J's friend of twenty years, Mike Francis, in tears. 'It's Mike, can I pass you on to the army liaison officer?'

An avalanche of thoughts and emotions descended: *They must be wrong. Mum, what about Mum?* Eighty-year-old Teresa, who hadn't seen her son since her birthday party in January, was at home in Thames Ditton. *Mum, what about Mum? I need to be with her!* The army representative agreed to Tony's request not to inform Teresa until he arrived. But he would need to get there fast.

'How long will you be?'

'Max…an hour and a half.'

Tony found it difficult to comprehend: *Tell me I have not had this phone call! 'The war is over,' or so we've been told. What's going on? This is not happening.*

Tony rang his wife. 'Get your shoes on, Eileen; we've got to get to Mum's.'

'It's H-J, isn't it?'

Eileen was waiting on the doorstep. Tony stayed in the car.

'I don't think I am going to enjoy this ride, am I?' said Eileen.

Tony was a former rally driver.

Just before 7 p.m., the army rang Tony. 'Can we please go to your mother's flat and tell her? We have to meet a deadline with the television and newspapers.'

Their other deadline was with the Secretary of State for Defence. Geoff Hoon was due to give a statement about the deaths in the House of Commons. Reluctantly, Tony agreed.

They arrived in Thames Ditton to find Teresa sitting in her armchair. 'What shall we do?' she said. While younger family members and friends were overwhelmed, she was calm. Teresa wept quietly, and hid her tears. As a child, she had grown accustomed to deaths in the family.

'MR DEPUTY Speaker, I regret that I have to make a statement about two serious incidents involving British forces that took place in Iraq today.'

Just before 8 p.m., the chamber was busier than usual with members eager to hear the Secretary of State's address. Mr Hoon continued:

One incident occurred at about 7.30 this morning UK time, 10.30 local time. It involved members of the 1st Battalion the Parachute Regiment, who were conducting a routine patrol in the town of Al Majar al-Kabir, about 25 kilometres south of the town of Al Amarah, in the province of Al Maysan. The two vehicles in which they were travelling were attacked with rocket-propelled grenades, heavy machine guns and rifle fire from a large number of Iraqi gunmen. British troops returned fire and called for assistance from other UK forces.

A quick reaction force – including Scimitar vehicles, additional troops and a Chinook CH-47 helicopter – was dispatched to the scene to provide assistance. It also came under fire. A total of eight British personnel sustained injuries, one on the ground and seven in the helicopter. The casualties were taken initially to 202 Field Hospital, south-west of Basra. Two of them have since been transferred to a United States field hospital in Kuwait to receive specialist treatment for very serious injuries. The other six are being treated in 202 Field Hospital.

Separately, the bodies of six British personnel, who appear to have been killed in another incident, were recovered from Al Majar al-Kabir at about midday UK time. Those personnel were members of the Royal Military Police and had been engaged in training the local Iraqi police. Initial information suggests that they may have been involved in an incident at the police station in Al Majar al-Kabir.

I regret that at this stage I am unable to provide any further details. British commanders are obviously investigating the situation as a matter of urgency.

We are in the process of informing the next of kin of all those who have been killed or injured. I know that the House will want to join me in sending our condolences to these families. Our thoughts are with them at this dreadful time.

We are investigating whether there is any connection between the two incidents. British commanders in theatre are assessing the situation and have been in contact with local leaders. It would not be right to speculate further at this stage. I would certainly caution against reaching any wider conclusions about the overall security situation in southern Iraq, particularly in the United Kingdom's area of responsibility. Coalition forces have worked hard to secure Iraq in the aftermath of decisive combat operations. They will not be deflected from their efforts by the enemies of peace.

Hoon's shadow, the Conservative Defence spokesman, Bernard Jenkin, replied:

> The House will be grateful for the trouble that the Secretary of State has taken to keep us informed. There is very little that anyone can add at this stage to the statement that he has made. This is clearly a tragedy for those involved, and the whole House will join the Secretary of State in expressing our deepest sympathies for those who were bereaved through, or injured in, the attacks. I can assure him that we agree that the next of kin must be the immediate priority.
>
> As he also said, it is too early to tell whether this signals a general worsening of the security situation in Iraq or is part of a pattern. In due course, the following questions will be asked.
>
> Were the attacks co-ordinated, and if so which organisation was behind them? Are we dealing with remnants of the regime, or were the attacks co-ordinated from outside Iraq?
>
> We have the best-trained and best-equipped troops to deal with threats such as this. This is a setback for them, but one that they will take in their stride. They will not be deflected from their mission to bring peace and security to the Iraqi people, and nor should we. All that I ask of the Secretary of State is that he give them all that they need to conduct operations as safely as possible, because that is no less than our armed forces so richly deserve.

'I am grateful to the honourable gentleman for his observations,' Mr Hoon replied, 'and particularly for his thoughts on the families, who will be suffering severely this evening. I know that the whole House will join him in the observations that he has made.'

For the Liberal Democrats, Paul Keetch added:

> May I, too, begin by thanking the Secretary of State for coming to the House so quickly. He kept us fully informed during the conflict, and he is right to come here this evening.
>
> May I also echo the tributes that have been paid to our armed forces, and pass on condolences from the Liberal Democrat benches to the families and comrades of those who have lost their lives, and to the regiments. We also wish a full recovery to all those who have been injured. Our thoughts are with them and their families.
>
> These events show above all that we can never take the work of our armed forces for granted. The job that they are doing in Iraq is difficult and dangerous, and it is far from over. They continue to perform their task with great courage. Our thoughts are with them tonight.

Tam Dalyell was an opponent of the war. 'In these awful and tragic circumstances, is not part of the unpalatable truth that, whether we like it or not, the British forces, like the Americans, are perceived as less of a liberating force and more of an occupying army? In the circumstances, should we not make an urgent approach to the United Nations?'

Hoon replied: 'Clearly, there has been a UN resolution in recent times, and it is important that we identify precisely who was responsible for the attacks before reaching such conclusions.'

Annabelle Ewing said: 'May I add my condolences and those of my Scottish National Party and Plaid Cymru colleagues.

'Our thoughts are also with the families of the soldiers killed and injured in Iraq today. I urge the Secretary of State to do all he can to ensure that the families receive all possible support. As the Member for Perth, where the Black Watch has its regimental headquarters, I also urge him to do all he can to ensure that the necessary level of protection is afforded to our soldiers on the ground in Iraq.'

Hoon replied: 'I can certainly give those assurances.'

Nigel Dodds then asked: 'What is the position in respect of contact with local leaders on the ground in southern Iraq and what level of co-operation are British forces on the ground receiving?'

'As far as local leaders are concerned, we have enjoyed an extremely good relationship across southern Iraq. Indeed, the information about the six deaths at the police station came from local people,' replied Hoon.

Gwyn Prosser next said: 'The men of the 1st Battalion the Parachute Regiment are based in my Dover constituency. They were due to start coming home next week. Can my right honourable friend say whether these incidents have changed those arrangements, and what practical arrangements are in hand to allow families and friends of people still serving overseas to make direct contact with the Ministry?'

Hoon answered: 'I am not aware of any plans to change the arrangements for the return [in the event, the tragedy would delay 1 PARA's departure], though the overall security position obviously has to be kept under review in the light of these dreadful incidents.'

Alice Mahon, another opponent of the war, said:

May I join others in expressing my deep sympathy to the relatives of the dead.

I have mixed feelings tonight. A young relative of mine just returned home from Basra today, so I feel awful about what has happened. I repeat what was said by my honourable friend the Member for Linlithgow (Mr Dalyell): is it not time to call in the United Nations to help? We daily see American soldiers killed and other incidents for which we all feel horror. Is it not time that the whole world came together to do something about security and really help Iraq? If we are serious about helping the Iraqi people, we should secure the involvement of the United Nations. It is clear that there is hostility towards the Coalition.

SHORTLY before midnight on Tuesday, 24 June the white beams of the Intercity 125 flooded Newcastle Central with light. Two men hugged on the platform; one had lost a brother, the other, a son. Both had lost his best mate.

THIRTEEN Honour and Truth

Honour among Arabs is often described as being 'more important than facts', a phrase which implies a general tendency to deny truths which may be self-evident to Westerners, for the consequences of not doing so would be a loss of honour.

BRITISH ARMY LITERATURE TO TROOPS

OTHERWISE contradictory accounts of the fighting, which were given to the international media on 25 June, concurred over who was to blame.

'The British brought it upon themselves with their searches,' insisted the chief of police.

'They wanted to frighten us and show us what strong people they are,' agreed Jawad Shtaway, one of the many eye witnesses who provided testimony.

'We are Muslims. We do not accept any foreigner in our land except as a guest. The same thing will happen again,' said Mohammed Hassan, a nurse at the hospital.

'If they are going to start searching homes again then the same disaster will happen to the British. We are Muslims, we are Shia. We take our orders from our leaders in Najaf and from Iran. We cannot accept the British here,' said Mohammed Sahi.

'They [the local men] did not want to hand over their weapons; they wanted to hide them. The people in Majar considered their weapons to be their weapons, like your army would. So nobody can take them away,' explained Sheikh Shejar, head of the Al Shuganbah tribe.

'We thought we had an agreement,' claimed militia leader Ahmed Zubaida, pointing to the agreement made with Major Kemp and reading aloud the line, "There is no necessity that the Coalition and its different people be there [the district of Majar al-Kabir]." What were we supposed to do? Praise the British for entering our homes? We asked them [the Paras] to go but they didn't listen.

'I argued with the British for a long time,' Zubaida continued. 'In the end we agreed that they would stay in their vehicles and stop the searches.'

But Majar al-Kabir had never been searched and neither Alpha nor Bravo had any intention to search houses, merely to conduct patrols.

'There was a patrol in the market,' said Sheikh Kadhum al-Fraijy, another tribal leader, 'and the people started throwing stones at them [Bravo]. The children were pulling at the soldiers' arms and trying to grab their weapons.'

'The market was very crowded,' said Ahmed Younis. 'I threw myself onto the ground and shouted to everybody to run away or get down. The shooting lasted for about five minutes [until Bravo remounted and drove towards the FAWJ] but there were bullets going everywhere. They were firing on automatic. I couldn't believe it when they started shooting.'

'The Iraqi side fired first,' added Sheikh Shejar. 'Later they went to the police station and attacked there. The mob wanted to shelter at the police station and use it as a base to attack the British.'

'Hundreds of people protested in front of the police station,' said Salah Mohammed. Salam al-Wahele agreed: 'I was among the crowd [at the police station]. I had heard the shots and wanted to see what was happening. I saw people who had guns and were firing on the British. There were more than four hundred there.'

Who had fired first, the RMPs or the Iraqis? Had the RMPs fired at all? Their Iraqi interpreter insisted they had not, and it would have been against RMP standard operating procedures for Sergeant Hamilton-Jewell's section to initiate a firefight with a crowd of protestors. However, the interpretor left his account open to question by his repeated references to 'five' rather than six RMPs being present. The problem that the Special Investigation Branch faced at the outset of its inquiry was obvious: the only British witnesses to the events at the police station were dead. Local testimonies, from eye-witnesses and those passing on what they had heard, were of dubious authenticity.

'Shots were fired,' said Sheikh Kadhum al-Fraijy. 'The military police came out from the police station. One of their bullets came out accidentally. One person was killed and the family of this person heard about it. They went to the police station to avenge the killing of their brother. The RMP did fire at the police station.'

After the Red Caps had 'taken their light weapons to defend themselves', there was 'continuous shooting', according to their interpreter, who added, 'the shots became nearer in single and consecutively.' But he did not say who fired.

'The RMP did fire, killing at least one,' insisted Sheikh Shejar.

'The soldiers fired shots and the people fired back. Then they attacked the building,' according to Salah Mohammed.

The RMP interpreter also remembered a 'deafening bomb' as one of the Land Rovers was 'set into a blaze and thick smoke'. The RMP were 'left alone outside their building near their wagons'.

Having called the police in Qalat Salih to warn them about the 'grave situation' and the 'big mob', the 'British advised me not to worry about them, but to take care of myself and get in a safer place.' He had not argued with them over this.

'We said we would protect them and that they should come with us,' said Abbas Bairphy, one of the last Iraqi policemen to leave the RMPs. 'We knew that we would be killed too because the people thought we were collaborators. But they refused to come with us. He [H-J] said his own radio had been burned when their vehicle had been set on fire. But I had no radio. I felt bad that they would not come with us. I said, you must come or you will die.'

'I am so ashamed we left them,' said police trainee Salam Mohammed.

'They told us to save ourselves though they refused to run away. There was no way they could escape.'

Zubaida claimed he had walked to the police station and sought to negotiate a peaceful settlement, as the elder had done: 'We guaranteed their safety.' According to him, however, the RMPs had refused to hand over their weapons, which was their side of the bargain.

But not according to Salam al-Wahele: 'They had surrendered and had given their weapons to the militiamen. I led a sergeant [H-J] to a side room and said he could escape by a window but he said he didn't want to go and leave the other men behind. He left me there and went back to the room where all the other men were shot. They may have been killed by their own weapons I think, or AK47s.'

'They were murdered in cold blood,' added Salam Mohammed. 'The British were shot in the head several times. The executioners were standing right in front of them.'

Dr Firas Fasal recalled seeing H-J: 'He was in the doorway and it looked like he was trying to protect the others. I was just doing my job; I was trying to bring peace. Often I think if I had got to them sooner, I might have brought them life.'

'I didn't think they would be killed,' said Ali al-Ateya, who worked at the hospital. 'When I returned there with my doctor friends, I saw the bodies in the room. The men were dressed with their desert uniforms except their helmets – those had been removed and were strewn about the floor. One of the bodies was upright against a wall, others were lying about the floor in different positions. Each one had been shot in the head more than once. The blood was still warm and wet, as though the killings had only just happened.'

Firas was one of the few to express remorse: 'It was a tragedy. No one here is happy about what happened. I told the British soldiers the people who killed your men are animals and not all the people of Majar al-Kabir are like that. It does not mean that all the people here hate the British.'

So were the killers from outside the town?

'They were local people, part of the community,' said Sheikh Shejar. Majar al-Kabir would not give them up lightly. To do so would be dishonourable, as would acknowledging defeat in the skirmishes against 1 PARA. Locals claimed just four men had been killed. Such economy with the truth played well at Abu Naji, where the head shed knew a high Iraqi death toll was politically unpalatable.

THE six had been cleaned and placed in body bags. They would be kept in cold storage until a transport aircraft was available to fly them home.

The families were told: 'The aim is to return casualties as soon as is practicable, whilst maintaining the dignity and reverence accorded to those individuals who have died on operations.'

The repatriation mission was titled Op KEIR 8.

The orders and instructions for Op KEIR 8 directed the activity of a number of organisations, but the detailed planning and timings are determined by a range of factors including, the current operational situation, the number of casualties involved and the co-ordination of a range of tasks.

The timings of any repatriation will always be a balance between the need to complete the necessary action as soon as possible and the establishment of realistic timelines but we do always bear the feelings of the families involved in mind and are conscious of their desire to have their loved ones returned to them as soon as possible.

At the heart of all activity is the absolute importance of setting an arrival time in UK that can be met and provide relatives with the certainty that their loved ones will return on the planned day of their repatriation.

Russ's parents and wife Anna paid tribute: 'Russ was a very handsome man, loved by everyone who knew him. He was such a kind and special person with a smashing sense of humour; he could get on with anyone he met. He was a doting father who had lots and lots of friends. When he walked into a room he filled it with his height and presence.'

Ben's father John said: 'The red beret was all he ever wanted. It was his life, so he gave his life doing the job he loved most. All he ever wanted was to be a military policeman and he worked very hard to become one. He was very career-minded, with bags of potential and had been recommended for early promotion.'

Tom's mother Sally said her son 'didn't really' want to be in Iraq: 'He didn't say too much, not half of what went on out there, but we're so proud of everything he achieved. We're just in shock at the moment. He was trying to train the Iraqis to police themselves but he felt he was wasting his time. They were always fighting among themselves.'

Tom's brother Richard remembered: 'When I was preparing to join the army [he was a serving Royal Engineer], Thomas would drag me out on fitness runs.'

At the home of 16 Air Assault Brigade, Colchester's MP, Bob Russell, said:

> This is the darkest day Colchester Garrison has experienced in almost 60 years. The town, where the civilian population has as many former servicemen and women as those currently serving in the army, is in shock. The relief of their safe return [3 PARA and the majority of 156 Provo] has turned to disbelief at what has now happened. Our thoughts and prayers go to the families of those who have lost their lives.

OC Major Parry-Jones said:

> The loss of six soldiers from such a small, tight-knit unit clearly comes as a dreadful shock to us all, not only the friends and families of those killed, but also all those in the Royal Military Police who knew and worked with them. From the oldest, aged 41, to the youngest, aged 20, these soldiers had between them a wealth of operational experience and distinguished service. You will understand that the circumstances surrounding this dreadful incident are still being investigated. We ask our men and women to risk the ultimate sacrifice in the service of their country and it is the sad truth that sometimes that sacrifice comes to pass.

Colonel John Baber, regimental secretary of the RMP Association added:

This is without doubt the blackest day in the history of our long and distinguished regiment. The RMP is only a very small regiment of 2,000 soldiers scattered throughout the world so these deaths have hit us very hard indeed. Our thoughts and prayers are with the family and friends of the dead and with our brothers in arms overseas. The families of our brave colleagues will have every support we can give them at this terrible time.

Attendance was voluntary, yet over 300 gathered for a service of remembrance at Abu Naji. Afterwards, Staff Sergeant Andy Stainton, second-in-command of the RMP platoon, wrote to Ben's family:

156 Provo Coy, Op TELIC, 25th June 03,

Dear Mr and Mrs Hyde,
I am the platoon staff sergeant working in Iraq with which Ben was part of. I want to convey my condolences and let you know that the rest of the platoon is thinking of you at this dreadful time. The guys are still shocked at what happened. To lose one person on an operation is one thing – but to lose six in a firefight is pretty unbearable.

Ben was a character. He had a dry sense of humour and a likeable personality. Despite being junior in his years and service his self confidence made him stand out from other members of the platoon. He would undoubtedly have done well in the Corps and was due promotion to full Corporal.

It is difficult finding words to comprehend but Ben died fighting for his comrades, the guys that he worked hard and played hard with for the past few years. I will miss Ben as will the rest of the platoon and anyone else in the Corps who knows him. Yesterday was a sad and tragic day for the Corps of the Military Police. Our thoughts are with you two and Sarah at this devastating time.

All the very best,
Andy

Beckett had been among the mourners at the remembrance service. Already a lightning rod for his troops' anger, his decision not to address them before, during or after the ceremony caused further dismay. They had hoped for a positive, personal message from their commander; a suggestion that their efforts were appreciated and that he, like them, was suffering for the loss of six colleagues.

The Bishop of Chichester, the Right Reverend John Hind, led 800 mourners in Chichester, home of the RMP Regimental Headquarters.

He said, 'The event was a poignant reminder of the cost of peace-making, peacekeeping and community building. In this world, nothing comes except at a price and those six young deaths are part of the price that is being paid for the reconstruction of a country that has already suffered so much.'

Books of remembrance were opened and Katie wrote of H-J:

Hammy my love, the time we had together was so special, something I'll never forget. I just wish we could have had longer together. I love you so much babe, I always will, I knew what you were going to ask me and that would have made me the happiest woman alive. As written in your blueys I am always thinking of you and always will.

Forever love, your gorgeous babe Katie xxx

Reg Keys had begun his own investigation into Tom's death. 'It would appear that they sent these six young men into a police station to do a job in a hostile country with hostile elements with very, very little support around them. To think that they could get trapped with no immediate support to call upon is of some concern to me,' he said.

Three official investigations had begun: the 1 PARA internal inquest, the SIB murder inquiry, and the report by Colonel Capewell for Lieutenant General John Reith at PJHQ. Alpha and Bravo were interviewed by the SIB. Statements were signed and sealed in plastic evidence bags. An SIB detective, interviewed by the author, claimed Beckett, when confronted by the investigation team at Abu Naji, had refused to provide a statement, telling them he would do so once his battalion had returned to Dover. This is not as sinister as it sounds – he had a crisis situation to manage: the threat of an uprising across the whole of Maysan province.

ALL those wounded on the Chinook survived and were airlifted to the Centre for Defence Medicine at the Queen Elizabeth Hospital in Selly Oak, Birmingham. Pebbles and Jingles, the pair who suffered head wounds, had been fortunate to survive. Buck, Tubs and Steve Thurtle lost substantial quantities of blood and owed their lives to the immediate medical treatment they received as the bullet-riddled helicopter returned to Abu Naji.

With no British presence in the town, the crime scene was destroyed by fire and the killers were given the opportunity to escape. Beckett's priority, for better or worse, was the restoration of peace across the province, not catching the murderers. There had already been riots in Amarah in protest at the battle in Majar al-Kabir. He was therefore adamant that any military reprisals would increase the likelihood of such a rebellion. After spending so long with tribal leaders and warlords, he was convinced all the benefits of rebuilding schools, restoring power supplies, distributing aid and general good work stood to be wiped out by further unrest. His command's toil since the end of the war would be for nothing and they would hand the KOSB a province in turmoil.

To make peace, 1 PARA's senior officers met the council of elders and there was a leaflet drop. 'We will not punish anyone since this would be the method of Saddam Hussein. We will return to set up good relations with you because our concern is to build a peaceful Iraq. Do not let rumours ruin our good relations.'

While General Wall supported Beckett's 'softly, softly' approach, this played less well in London – Downing Street, United Kingdom Special Forces (UKSF) and MI6 had a different agenda.

An SAS squadron commander flew into Abu Naji for talks. The SAS major, a former Parachute Regiment officer, disliked Beckett and to the latter's chagrin proposed a new course of action: 'turned' Iraqis would be inserted into Majar al-Kabir to ascertain the killers' identities and whereabouts. Acting on their information the targets would receive surprise visits by SAS snatch squads, with 1 PARA providing back-up.

Beckett is said to have told the squadron commander: 'I cannot support this. The lives of British soldiers are at stake [i.e. the KOSB].'

Which met with the rejoinder: 'What about the British soldiers who are lying there dead?'

Beckett was insistent: 'This has got to go through Div [General Wall]. Div has got to clear this.'

'I don't work for Div. I work for Tony Blair; take it up with him!'

The Director of Special Forces (DSF) was in direct communication with Downing Street. The DSF's instructions were to capture those who killed the RMP, immediately.

'I've got to consider the bigger picture,' said Beckett. 'The KOSB will have to clear up the mess.'

'Well, we want to go in there and kick some fucking arse – and it's going to happen.'

It did.

With his division on a collision course with Whitehall, Major General Wall released this statement:

> I would like to begin by offering my sincere condolences to the families of the soldiers who lost their lives in the incident which took place on 24 June in Al Majar al-Kabir. Also, to reassure the families, friends and colleagues of those injured that they are in the very best of hands, and receiving the most expert care here in theatre.
>
> In the wake of those events, we have been building a more detailed picture of what took place, and working in conjunction with local leaders. We have received excellent cooperation from members of the Al Amarah authorities and the town council of Al Majar, who met with our local commanders yesterday morning. A number of them went to the town on the day itself to try to restore order, and we have valued their support. They have expressed their confidence in our forces and the continuing strength of the cooperation between the people of Maysan province and the Coalition. We will continue to cooperate with them closely on the way ahead.
>
> We need to establish what took place in order to ensure that the

right follow-up action is taken. I can assure you that we will do our utmost to ensure that those responsible are held to account. This will be done in cooperation with the Iraqi authorities, and we have asked the town council for its assistance.

I am aware of different versions of events leading up to the deaths of the Royal Military Police personnel which have been reported in the media. You will understand that it would be wholly inappropriate for me to make any detailed comments about this incident while we are still trying to establish the facts. The fact that there were no British survivors makes this particularly difficult.

I can say that a six-man RMP patrol left 1 PARA's base location in Al Amarah bound for Al Uzayr. On the way there, the patrol intended to drop in on a number of the local police stations in order to liaise with the local police force. The route that they planned to take was initially to Majar al-Kabir, where they intended to stay until approximately 1100, and then onwards to Qalat Salih. Their purpose was to advise the local police force on policing matters and monitor their progress. This was part of the excellent work the RMP has been doing, and continues to do, across the UK area of operations to re-establish the Iraqi police force.

Following the incident which resulted in their deaths, members of the local Maysan Province Guard Service placed the bodies of the six into local ambulances which were subsequently driven to the 1 PARA Incident Control Point which had been set up close in response to the ongoing incidents.

On the other incident involving the platoon from 1 PARA, I would like to take this opportunity to offer my praise for the professionalism and courage displayed by all those involved.

His praise of 1 PARA was significant as newspapers were reporting that Beckett's men were partially culpable. An account in the *Daily Telegraph* (26 June) stated: 'By about 11am the Paras managed to extricate themselves [in fact, both multiples were still under heavy fire]. But they seem to have forgotten about the six soldiers from the Royal Military Police, who must have heard the shooting as turmoil gripped the town.' Similarly, the *Observer* (29 June) claimed: 'On the outskirts of the city at least a dozen armoured vehicles, including light tanks and around 100 men had arrived from the Paras' base 10 miles away. But for reasons yet to be explained they stood by as another tragedy unfolded.'

Major General Wall continued:

> They [8 Platoon] had intended to conduct a routine joint patrol in the town working with the local militia. When the crowd turned against them, they fought a determined and protracted action to extricate themselves from a precarious situation. I would also like to pay particular tribute to the helicopter pilot and crew of the Chinook sent to provide reinforcements and ammunition, and to the medical team on board. Their actions undoubtedly prevented further loss of life and involved considerable risk to themselves.
>
> The crowd violence appears to have stemmed from a misunderstanding. The townspeople expected searches for weapons to be conducted by our patrols. That was not our intent, and this had been explained to the town council at a formal meeting earlier in the week, when the strength of their resentment to weapons searches had become clear.
>
> The situation in Basrah province and throughout the rest of Maysan province remains calm today. We continue our important work to support the reconstruction of Iraq.

AN SAS operation went ahead, but was aborted amid acrimony. In its aftermath there were tales of inadequate briefings, communications failing between the units, counter accusations and suggestions of an SAS call sign being left on the ground without any back-up. A number of Iraqis were roughed up, but nobody seemed sure whether or not these were the murder suspects. Rumours spread around Abu Naji that the SAS had disguised themselves as RMPs in a bid to gain the locals' sympathy during the intelligence-gathering phase of the op.

Another incident in August, after 1 PARA's departure, would lead to a KOSB commander, Major Stuart Irvine, apologising to the town and paying compensation.

He wrote:

A small group of Coalition Forces were not from Camp Abu Bajir [Naji], nor were they soldiers stationed in Majar. Eleven townspeople were arrested and treated very badly. All were arrested without reason.

The incident happened because we are trying to bring those people who killed our six military police colleagues to justice. The Coalition offers its humblest apologies for the error.

ON Saturday, 28 June 1 PARA 'officially' returned to Majar al-Kabir. Cobra gunships flew overhead and the battalion was accompanied by armoured units from Basra. They toured the route driven by Bravo four days earlier in WMIKs and Scimitars. Beckett believed relations had to be re-established and to the dismay of his critics within the battle group shook hands with the town's leaders.

Beckett had lost the support of a swathe of his men – at the 'open forums' held at company level soldiers asked their OCs: 'Sir, why is the CO so gutless? Why didn't he say anything at the church parade? Why didn't we go back into the town and get the ringleaders?'

What could the OCs say? Privately they may have agreed with their men, but the public forum was for the Toms, not for them to air personal opinions. They had to toe the battalion line: 'Yes, that is true, but that's just the way it is. It's happened; get over it.'

IT was sunset on Tuesday, 1 July; a week had passed since the tragedy. The tail of the C-17 cast a shadow in the shape of a crucifix across the runway and a guard of honour stood motionless at Basra airport.

Padre Stephen Robins, his silk stole fluttering, recited:

Sergeant Simon Hamilton-Jewell, Corporal Paul Long, Corporal

Russ Aston, Corporal Simon Miller, Lance Corporal Thomas Keys and Lance Corporal Ben Hyde.

We give thanks for their lives and we commend them to God our merciful redeemer and we commit their bodies to their journey home. And we comfort one another in our grief.

Almighty God, by whose grace we are called to positions of responsibility and trust, bless we pray thee all members of the Royal Military Police, inspire them to courage and wisdom, courtesy and faithfulness, grant them a true knowledge of thy will that they may guide their comrades aright.

Those who wondered whether Beckett had been emotionally engaged at the Abu Naji service would have had no such doubts here. He was as moved as the RMP commanding officer in Iraq, Lieutenant Colonel Eddie Forster-Knight, who told those gathered:

The events of Tuesday 24th June in Al Majar al-Kabir are a tragedy. On that day, six brave and talented Military Policemen from 156 Provost Coy, who were at that time part of 1st Regiment, lost their lives. They lost their lives fulfilling their ambitions as professional soldiers and Military Policemen. They had fought through and survived the war and then engaged in the difficult task of re-establishing law and order in southern Iraq. They had pitted their training and skills against every conceivable situation during this operation, and none had been found wanting.

Why then did these men stand their ground at that police station in the face of such overwhelming odds on that fateful morning? The truth is we shall probably never know, but there is a bond and a unique loyalty between soldiers, which is difficult to measure. They understood the basic code that governs our work – the values of duty, honour and self-sacrifice. Their duty was to assist with the regeneration of the Iraqi police – to re-establish law and order – to bring peace and hope to a brutalised and suppressed society – it is for those reasons that I believe they stayed there together. They conducted their duty in a brave and honourable manner without fear or favour, dealing with everybody as equals and placing their own lives at risk on a daily basis. Tragically they paid the ultimate sacrifice for their actions – they laid down their lives while in the service of their country. We are fortunate as a nation to have such men – men whose courage and self-sacrifice has allowed others to enjoy their liberty and freedom.

I know that all members of the Royal Military Police, both past and present, are immensely proud of what these men have achieved. But, their loss has left emptiness in our lives. We will mourn their passing – they were our friends, our comrades and most importantly part of our family – a family that has suffered a traumatic loss, but one that will remember their heroic deeds and the great credit they have bestowed upon us all. In time, we will all be the stronger for their actions.

I know that this is a terrible ordeal for their loved ones. Words can never make up for the loss that you have suffered. But the thoughts and prayers of all those in the Royal Military Police are with you at this time. Rest assured also, that we will not be deflected from our duty. We are continuing as a Regiment with our work to re-establish law and order in southern Iraq. We will not forget the sacrifice made by your loved ones – we owe it to them to continue with their work.

We will always remember: Simon Hamilton-Jewell, Corporal Paul Long, Corporal Russell Aston, Corporal Simon Miller, Lance Corporal Thomas Keys and Lance Corporal Ben Hyde.

A piper sounded the 'Last Post' as the coffins, draped in the Union Jack, were carried up a ramp and placed inside the cocoon.

It was dark now and the aircraft's lights shone like candles.

FOURTEEN 'You're home now, son'

Order of Ceremony

0900 Relatives, friends and Service representatives arrive at Assembly Point.

1030 RAF Brize Norton coaches arrive at Assembly Point.

1140 Arrive at Main Terminal to await arrival of aircraft.

1150 Aircraft Lands.

1200 Aircraft arrives at Main Terminal.

Transfer coffins to hearses in order of precedence.

Light Lunch.

RAF Brize Norton coaches depart for Assembly Point.

Relatives, friends and Service representatives depart.

IN MEMORIAM

Adjutant General's Corps
(Royal Military Police)

Sergeant S. A. Hamilton-Jewell

Corporal R. Aston

Corporal P. G. Long

Corporal S. Miller

Lance Corporal T. R. Keys

Lance Corporal B. J. Hyde

WE WILL REMEMBER THEM.

CHAIRS faced the runway and ropes marked off the families' reception area. They sat there in clusters, staring in disbelief at the Order of Ceremony booklets, and were joined by Geoff Hoon and General Sir Mike Jackson, the Chief of the General Staff. The band of the Coldstream Guards awaited their cue. The Duchess of Gloucester, Deputy Colonel-in-Chief of the Adjutant General's Corps, of which the RMP is part, represented the Royal Family.

Grey skies over Oxfordshire were broken and the families saw the RAF transport plane carrying their sons, husbands, brothers and fathers.

'You're home now, son, you're home now,' cried John and Marilyn Miller beneath the aircraft noise.

To Beethoven's 'Marcia Funebrae', Sergeant Simon Hamilton-Jewell was carried first from the cargo hold with a Union Jack draped over his coffin. Members of C Section followed, as they did on 24 June and in order of seniority.

Sally Keys caught first sight of Tom carried aloft. There were no more breakfasts to be eaten; her son was finally home and his coffin was taken to RAF Brize Norton's chapel of rest, where Reg filed past him, breathless. Their other son Richard couldn't bring himself to look.

The six were driven to the mortuary at the John Radcliffe Hospital, Oxford, and a coroner's hearing was opened and adjourned pending military investigations and criminal charges.

The newspapers on 2 July reported Geoff Hoon's pledge made in a House of Commons written statement: 'We will do all we can to establish the facts, and to hold to account those responsible.' The headline on the *Guardian* exclaimed, 'Soldiers' killers will be found, vows Straw', and the Press Association filed, 'Earlier today, Mr Straw said British forces "are not going to forget" their promise to find the men's killers. Speaking as he flew into Baghdad, he described the deaths as "extremely concerning" but "relatively isolated" and pledged such actions would not drive coalition forces out of the country.'

For prosecutions to follow, as much evidence as possible had to be gathered. It was regrettable therefore that when Dr Nicholas Hunt's team removed H-J from his black, zip-up body bag they saw his body had already been stripped and scrubbed. Though some forensics had eventually been found in the burned-out storage room, who was to know what had been tarnished or removed while the crime scene was left unprotected? Some Iraqi witnesses were also too scared to talk to the SIB and the delicacy of the relationship between Coalition Forces and the locals meant they could not be pressurised into producing suspects for questioning. A factor in this equation was the size of the Iraqi death toll on 24 June.

H-J was weighed at 83 kgs and measured at 177 cms tall, with all measurements in regard to the positions of his wounds being taken from the level of his left heel. He was found to be clean-shaved, with light brown, closely cropped hair and short sideburns. Field dressings had been wrapped around two wounds to his right arm and one on each thigh. Dr Hunt traced the passage of rounds through his body and documented twenty-seven separate entry and exit wounds. From these he concluded H-J had received a minimum of fourteen shots from a high-velocity weapon or weapons, most likely AK47s – the theory that he had been shot with a British rifle, possibly his own, would be discounted. There were also many 'blunt impact injuries'.

It was impossible to calculate how long H-J had survived after the first shot but it did seem those responsible had taken their time to make his a prolonged, ritualistic killing, stamping on him with rifle butts and feet either before or after they had anointed his body with lead. The infidel at their mercy received none, and particular attention was paid to his groin.

Si Miller suffered similarly. He had thirty-one gunshot wounds, with the fatal shots concentrated on his head and chest. John chose not to see his son's body, deciding Si wouldn't have wanted his dad to see him in such a state. His mother Marilyn said she had to.

As a former paramedic, Reg Keys dissected every one of Dr Hunt's findings. By cruel coincidence his son, too, had received thirty-one wounds, the single most lethal being a gunshot to Tom's head. The entrance wounds to his left leg indicated it 'must have been completely flexed at the time of infliction'. Reg contorted his body to take up a similar crouching position on one knee. To him it seemed Tom would have fired from this stance. Dr Hunt's next comment shocked him. 'This, when taken in combination with the apparent ligature mark around the left ankle raises the possibility of forced restraint.'

Images of Tom hanging from the police station's ceiling flashed before him. Although the ligature mark had actually been caused by a strapping administered for Tom's ankle injury at Abu Naji, nobody told Reg and the nightmares continued.

With his son's body returned to a chapel of rest near the family home, Reg wanted a last drink with Tom. He dressed him in his service uniform and poured Jack Daniels onto his pallid lips. These were precious final moments. A chill breeze swept off the mountains as he was laid to rest at

St John's Church, Barmouth. Captain James Hibbert, one of Tom's RMP officers, who had returned to UK before the Majar al-Kabir tragedy, read a eulogy:

> Tom joined 156 Pro Coy in January 2002 to 1 PARA's dismay. He transferred to the RMP to fulfil a strong desire to take up the challenges of police work. We were delighted to receive him, in fact, from the moment he first expressed a desire to join us every effort was made to get our hands on him as quickly as possible. I recall the note made by his interviewing officer who described Tom as: 'Confident, articulate, fit and robust, he is precisely the kind of VT who will succeed in RMP. I recommend that his transfer be progressed as quickly as possible. He impressed.'
>
> Tom was an impressive guy – quietly self assured, frankly honest, fiercely loyal and ultimately strong. As a soldier and a policeman he was the consummate professional; he gave his all in everything he did and worked hard to get the job done no matter how menial the task. He wore his Para wings with quiet pride and adored the camaraderie that can only be found in the army. He was universally admired and respected by all ranks – the lads would always refer to him as a 'top bloke', the girls as 'an absolute darling'. Tom prided himself on being incredibly fit and a great sportsman, he was in every sense a man's man, the epitome of youth.
>
> I recall one of the lads, Ben Hyde, saying that no matter what happens in life nothing can be as bad as getting punched by Tom! I can also remember stepping out of the office wondering who on earth was destroying the punch bag in the gym? Had Lennox Lewis decided to pay us a visit? No, it was simply Tom literally shaking the walls as he worked out.
>
> I admired him, he was always a guy who you'd make time for because you knew that he'd always make time for you.
>
> Conditions in Iraq were dire and Tom worked longer hours than he ever thought possible. He had an inner strength, which enabled him to win his own personal battle with the heat, the food and the

flies. Prior to deploying Tom helped out by taking the guys through infantry tactics and drills, others simply drew strength from his Coy. Working with Tom gave you the warm, satisfying feeling that the job was being done well first time, every time. Tom had an impact on each of our lives and with a wry smile we will all remember him in different ways. Personally, I've never met a guy who could eat as much as Tom – the human dustbin. Tom planned to take a holiday to America on returning home; I would have liked to capture the look on his face as he drove a Harley or a Dodge Charger through Marlboro Country.

I would have been honoured to give him his second strip for promotion to Corporal. I will miss him. Now that it's time to put Tom to rest, remember that we can all be proud to have had him in our lives. The world was a better place with him as part of it.

Reg thanked everyone for coming and added:

Five years ago we gave the army a rather shy, introverted young sixteen-year-old boy. Sadly what we see here before us today is not how we expected the army to return him to us. The day Tom was killed along with his five brave friends he was just four days short of his twenty-first birthday. Birthday cards that had prematurely started to arrive for Tom still remain unopened. Wounds from the pain of loss are still too raw to undertake such a task.

Reg built a memorial garden next to his house, planting a cherry tree for each of the six and burying Tom's football boots under one of them.

ALL the six received plaudits with H-J's mother and brother pleased to receive a letter from Lieutenant General John Kiszely MC, the British Army's Commander of Regional Forces:

Dear Mrs Hamilton-Jewell,
I was shocked and deeply saddened to hear of the death on active service of your son Simon. He was my bodyguard in Sarajevo in 2001 for four months. I got to know Simon very well over that time. It

will come as no surprise to you to hear that he did the job superbly, nor that he was completely dedicated and professional in everything that he did and was held in high regard by everyone. I very much enjoyed his company and much admired and liked him. I was horrified to hear of the manner of his death, but I was not surprised by the heroism he displayed. It was very much in his character.

I offer you my deepest sympathy, although I know that nothing can ease the pain and grief you will be feeling right now. I feel privileged to have known Simon – and I know that all of his friends and colleagues will be feeling the same. You are therefore in the thoughts and prayers of many people who knew him well as well as the many people who have heard of him since his tragic death.

Yours sincerely,

John Kiszely

Major Parry-Jones also wrote to them:

I personally had the privilege of working alongside Simon as his Officer Commanding throughout most of the conflict and subsequent operations in Iraq. Throughout his time he was a brave, conscientious and very professional Senior Non-Commissioned Officer who relished the opportunity to help liberate and rebuild Iraq and dealt with all the hardships with characteristic dry humour. He put the welfare of his section to the forefront of all of his activities and was extremely proud to serve as a military policeman alongside some of his former colleagues in the Parachute Regiment [H-J was attached to 1 PARA in Northern Ireland] and 16 Air Assault Brigade.

Simon Hamilton-Jewell was a larger than life character, universally popular amongst all of his colleagues in Colchester and his tragic loss is felt by all ranks.

Lieutenant Colonel Eddie Forster-Knight, RMP, agreed:

Simon was an excellent soldier and military policeman – highly motivated, dedicated and utterly professional in his approach. He had handled himself with great credit during the whole operation and was a fine leader of his section, where he was extremely well respected by all with whom he served.

At a service of thanksgiving and remembrance held at Colchester Garrison Church, Warrant Officer Matthew 'Bob' Marley paid tribute:

> They really came into their own during the peace support operations that followed the war-fighting. The start state for their efforts made daunting reading: a police force [Iraqi] that at best was discredited and mistrusted. I saw 'the Team' [H-J's section] working in the southern area of the Maysan province, take a pragmatic approach, concentrating on what they could change. Corporate identity was given to the new Iraqi Police recruits by the team's provision of identity cards, equipment and basic uniforms. Perhaps the most impressive however was the way in which they gave the new police confidence to actually go out and do the job. Throughout the approach, the fact that the team would always show the Iraqi officers how to do something on the ground was their strongest asset. The corps' motto, *Exemplo Ducemus* [By example we lead], was never so much in evidence.

AS 1 PARA waited to emplane, some of 8 Platoon noticed Beckett alone in the departure lounge at Basra Airport. It made a fitting image: the commander whose moral courage had led him to retreat when those around him wanted revenge, standing in exile.

With the RMPs confirmed dead and all other British personnel accounted for, the popular decision would have been to let the WMIKs and Scimitars sweep through Majar al-Kabir and for the rifle companies to search every house until the killers were found. Privately – but only privately – many realised 'Chickenshit Beckett' had found himself in a 'lose–lose' situation. With the stability of Maysan province hanging in the balance, he had showed noble restraint, in doing so making himself a pariah. As one of the QRF said, 'He would have ended up sacked if he'd let us in there that day.'

It would be a long last year as CO without his second-in-command

Major Tootal, who was promoted to lieutenant colonel and left, as described by *Pegasus* (the journal of the Parachute Regiment and Airborne Forces), 'after 3 years with 1 PARA to write yet another paper at university before becoming MA to the ACGS [Military Assistant to the Assistant Chief of the General Staff].' OC C Company Major Kemp was also promoted and left for the German Army's staff college.

Robbo and 'The Dolmanator' returned to Iraq soon after, having resigned from 1 PARA to join a private security firm. Both were decorated, the Ayrshire man becoming the Parachute Regiment's first recipient of the Conspicuous Gallantry Cross (CGC) while Dolman received a Mention in Dispatches (MiD). It was while working for the Kroll security company in January 2005 that John Dolman was killed in Baghdad. A suicide bomber attacked his convoy causing Dolman's death and the deaths of his client and another Kroll bodyguard. Dolman was buried in Northern Ireland. His platoon commander Lieutenant Kennedy also received a MiD, but for other reasons now feared for his future as a British Army officer.

Robbo's citation read:

Throughout this action, Robertson displayed bravery and leadership of the highest order. He consistently placed himself in extreme danger with no concern for his personal safety. His cool-headedness and tactical skill were inspirational. Despite overwhelming odds, during a sustained firefight lasting over two hours in a built-up area, he managed to extract his entire multiple to safety without serious injury or loss of life.

Subsequent intelligence reports indicated that somewhere between 50 and 100 fighters armed with AK47 rifles, 12.7mm heavy machine guns [Dushka] and rocket-propelled grenades engaged Robertson's thirteen-man multiple. To Robertson and the multiple's credit, local sources reported that the enemy was exceptionally impressed by the tactical conduct of the multiple and the accuracy of its marksmanship.

Disappointingly there was no decoration for Freddy Ellis, although Jase Davidson received a CO's commendation. Three official gallantry awards were a meagre reward. There had always been a political dimension to awards and none were given to H-J's section – perhaps it was considered inexpedient to allow more. All the RMPs would receive were their posthumous Op TELIC campaign medals, awarded to any soldier, sailor, airman or embedded journalist who put in seven days' continuous service in Iraq or Kuwait during the war-fighting phase.

Russ's father Mike Aston said, 'The decision to ignore these lads is stupid and highly insensitive. It would seem that people are much keener to pretend the whole thing never happened than honour the memory of six very brave men.'

Tony Fisher, who changed his name to Hamilton-Jewell and started wearing his half-brother's dog-tags, agreed:

> If army procedures had been followed properly on that day my brother would still be alive. Knowing they aren't even going to honour their ultimate sacrifice with even the smallest medals for them is unforgivable. They just want to brush the whole thing under the carpet.
>
> The Ministry of Defence has told us they can't get medals because there were no British witnesses to what happened. But there have been cases in the past where bravery awards have been given without British witnesses.

The relationship between the families and the Ministry of Defence broke down after they were told there was neither a record of the C Company desk in the Ops Room being informed of the patrol's movements into the area of Majar al-Kabir on 24 June nor any evidence of the patrol communicating by radio with anyone after they had left the Ops Room; both were breaches of their standard operating procedures (SOPs).

But new information cast doubt on the Ministry of Defence's story when one of the families received an email from an SIB investigator:

> We said at the briefing that there was no evidence the patrol booked out with C Coy. Subsequent to this the RMP Ops Warrant

Officer [Bob Marley] has now provided a further statement in which he added that he saw Sgt H-J spend some time at the C Coy desk, although he did not hear/see what he did. We also now have confirmation that Sgt H-J booked out with C Coy that morning, confirming the police stations he would be visiting, including Al Majar al-Kabir, but timings were not provided or requested. The details were recorded on a whiteboard used by the C Coy daily record but no hard copy records were maintained.

Was there a cover-up? The families demanded access to the confidential Board of Inquiry (BoI) hearings after reading a headline in the *Observer*, 'Redcaps tragedy: MoD will blame the dead.'

Mike Aston said: 'It's the easiest thing in the world to blame the dead men who can't defend themselves. They are trying to cover up the simple fact that they got my son killed.'

Tony Hamilton-Jewell added: 'They are blaming the dead because it's the best way to protect the living.'

Overall, the army was doing a good job of appearing incompetent as well as deceptive. Many personal effects belonging to the six – which had been labelled and packed individually into boxes at Abu Naji on the day they died – had still not been returned. The families were told:

These [personal effects] are presently being collated by the SIB. It is uncertain exactly what each individual soldier was carrying on him at the time of death and there is a probability that some items may have been removed from the deceased immediately after they died. Not knowing exactly what personnel were originally carrying/wearing makes it extremely difficult to achieve a precise and complete record and naturally will take longer than usual. Those items that were on the deceased when they were repatriated are currently held by the SIB for forensic purposes and will continue to do so until the forensic testing is complete.

The SIB are working very hard to assimilate a complete and accurate list. It may not become clear until that point if there are indeed certain personal items that are missing.

The BoI was held in camera; for the families to attend would have been unprecedented. After being told their presence might compromise witnesses' evidence the families suggested a video link between the court and another room where they could watch. That, too, was rejected. Under Colonel John Hickson's presidency the BoI sat first in Germany, where many RMP witnesses were stationed after Op TELIC, and at the Army's Courts Martial Centre at Risborough Barracks, Folkestone. The Board's members also visited Majar al-Kabir.

Every witness's questioning was intense – some were recalled to give further testimony – with members of 8 Platoon, the ARF, QRF and Ops Room staff asked, 'Did you abandon the RMP?'

And specifically to 8 Platoon: 'It was one of your last patrols; you went into that town to get some kills, didn't you?' Both accusations were vehemently denied.

Ross had initially denied that any of his men fired warning shots at the police station on 22 June, knowing his second-in-command in Alpha, Mark Weadon, had done. Brought before the BoI for a second time, the platoon commander admitted this first testimony had been misleading.

As the Board of Inquiry later reported: 'The Board felt that this failure to give a true account of the events could potentially taint the evidence of the whole of call sign Two Zero Alpha. As a result the Board recalled a number of Two Zero Alpha to ascertain whether their initial evidence was indeed correct.'

The threat of a court martial hung over Lieutenant Kennedy. For Tony Hamilton-Jewell, his dishonesty tainted every 1 PARA witness statement and he announced his intention to sue the Ministry of Defence for corporate manslaughter.

The BoI subsequently became the army's proverbial legal minefield as a restricted document conceded, 'The BoI has taken place prior to any potential disciplinary action. Concerns over possible negligence in the Operations Room [at Abu Naji on 24 June] and the concerns of witnesses potentially self incriminating themselves [Letters were sent to Lieutenant Colonel Beckett, Lieutenant Colonel Tootal, Captain Todd, Captain Bosley and Captain Palmer reminding them of their legal situation] has resulted in a number of delays as the Board awaited legal advice from Comd Legal HQ 1 (UK) Armd Div.' Lieutenant Colonel Beckett attended the BoI only to be told to return later once this legal advice was received.

Shut out of the BoI but fighting a high-profile media campaign, the families felt the government was washing its hands of the incident when, in July 2004, Geoff Hoon transferred the cases over to the Central Criminal Court of Iraq (CCCI). Although he insisted this step represented the best chance of bringing about prosecutions – Iraqi law barred any of its citizens being extradited to a foreign state for trial – he did not sound confident of trials proceeding. 'Whatever the outcome of these cases I would like to pay tribute to the efforts of the SIB senior investigating officers and their teams for their hard work.'

Reg Keys said:

> Tom was betrayed in life and now betrayed in death. I'm incensed by it. Geoff Hoon reassured me twelve months ago that they had the killers' names. They've had twelve months to arrest them. Now they have an excellent excuse to wash their hands of it. The killers will never be found.
>
> The line of investigation the Ministry of Defence took was to pursue it as a murder inquiry – we would have accepted Tom as killed in action. I expected more from the MoD than the lacklustre investigation which followed, one which was merely 'window dressing' for the army.

PAYGAN Aston was a baby when her father kissed her for the last time – it now fell to her mother to ensure she knew who Russ was.

Though the boy in the year below her at school had had a disarming grin, Anna had proclaimed him 'too obviously good-looking' and 'too cheeky'. She was right; when her friend Lorraine met him for a drink, he spent most of the evening playing pool with his mates. Anna wouldn't see him for ten years, in which time Russ became a Grenadier Guardsman and she had befriended his sister Adele. Anna was reluctant to date him, telling Adele, 'Oh no, not that cocky guy from school!' She conceded; and as the three of them sat in a pub Adele put her brother's hand on Anna's. They married in 1999 and Paygan, their only child, was born in 2002.

As the weeks and months passed after Russ's death Anna saw Paygan's likeness to her father grow. It was difficult to read Russ's next-of-kin letter:

> Hello my precious wife and daughter. I will always love you very much. Well sweetheart we are told to write these letters in case anything happens to me.
>
> So in a good old fashioned quote, 'If you receive this letter then I'm afraid I've kicked the bucket!!!' I am going to try and make the letter a bit cheeky because I know how you must be feeling. I will always be there for you and Paygan. I will always watch over you both. It has been an absolute pleasure being your husband. You make me a very happy man. I'm so glad that we have our little daughter. She is the apple of my eye. I'm so proud of you both. It's very strange writing this letter. I can only hope there's a god and I will be waiting for you when it's your time. I know sometimes I've been a bit of a grump but I really love you with all my heart and I cannot wait to see you again in heaven if there is one.
>
> I will never ever forget you Anna. You are my life and my soul mate; all you have to do is call me and my spirit will be near you. I really could not have wished for a better wife. You made me so happy Anna and we really did have some laughs together didn't we. Like the glass smashing in the Mess in Surrey. Poor old Stephen, you really did terrorise him.
>
> Tell Paygan about me when she is old enough to understand. Tell her to stay away from anyone called Dwain. Anyway, I've got to have my wings and halo fitted. I would like to have some cheery music played at my funeral and a mother of all piss ups for my mates.
>
> I love you with all my heart and soul,
> Your loving husband,
> Russ

Simon Hamilton-Jewell's next-of-kin letters revealed hidden depths of his character and his paternal nature:

> Dear Mum,
>
> If you receive this then I have been killed in the conflict. Don't be sad for me because I died doing the job that I enjoy. I have had a good life and that was thanks to my upbringing. I valued right from wrong and I believe that what I was doing was for the purpose of good and my life is a small price to pay for peace.
>
> Just because I didn't always show that I cared doesn't mean that was the case. I always cared and appreciated you and how you were always there for me. It is just that I am not always good at showing my emotions. I hope you are proud of me and realise there is nothing to regret in my passing, because my life has been good and my ambitions fulfilled. Good memories of me will ensure I am always there and if there is a God, which I do believe, then we will be reunited one day.
>
> No one really knows every part of my life; some people know some things and other people know other things. No one person knows it all and the sum of everyone's knowledge is not a true reflection of my life. I am the only person who knows the whole truth and believe me I have no complaints about my life and only a few regrets. I hope that anyone who cares about me has not been too upset by anything I have said or done.
>
> I don't really know what else to say, other than I love you and I don't want you to be too sad because I did my duty and loved life. There are a lot of people in the world who have not been blessed with the great life I've had.
>
> Love Simon,
>
> x
>
> Dear Katie,
>
> If you receive this then I'm dead, so I've just got a few things that I don't want left unsaid. I have no doubt that I am in love with you, because you're on my mind every waking moment and I know that

if the situation had arisen, I could have happily spent the rest of my life with you even though we haven't actually known each other that long.

I know I trust you and feel happy and comfortable in your company. I would have loved to have spent the summer with you, it would have been great, and I would have loved to have tried to make you happy. I think I could have. You are lovely.

So what now? I want you to grip your life, get fit, have some adventures and live life to the full; make a plan as to what you want to do then make it happen. Don't let anyone treat you like shit and ensure you don't take second best. Choose your mates well and then look after them. You can be happy if you want to be. I would ask though that just occasionally you think of me and try to have good thoughts. If I am anywhere good I will watch over you and always wish the best for you.

You are so gorgeous, if I meant anything to you, please, please, please have a good life full of fun and humour, excitement and adventure. AND ALWAYS SMILE!

I love you,

H xxx

In one of his last letters home, H-J had told Katie, 'I cannot wait to take Ollie to the park to feed the ducks!' When they heard a helicopter Ollie looked up. 'Look, Mummy, Chinook!' H-J had taught him well.

Tributes

THANK you for 21 wonderful years you gave us Si, the bravest man we ever knew. We will miss and think of you every second of the day, till we meet again, Mum, Dad and Jon xxxx

WE love you Tom – Rest in Peace. Mum, Dad and brother Richard, xxx

WE are proud to have had the privilege of being Russ's mother and father and I know his brother and sister are also proud to have had such a fine brother. We miss him more than any of us can express. Russ's death leaves an empty gap in our family and community and a great black hole in the world. Mike, Glenice and Anna Aston

A NOD, a wink or a smile; a one hundred per cent human being dedicated to life in full. He was a man keen to help anybody; a fearless man, biker, hiker and climber. But, above all, a man dedicated to the Army, his regiment, his unit and to his comrades. He was a very human person who will be dearly missed for the rest of our lives. For a soldier never afraid to do his duty – we love and miss you. God bless. Teresa and Tony Hamilton-Jewell

OUR brother Paul Graham Long, known affectionately by all his family, friends and Army colleagues as Paul, joined the Royal Military Police in

1999. He wanted only to help others less fortunate than himself. The Army was his life; he died doing what he did best, helping others. Our hearts and prayers go out to the families and friends of all the Royal Military Police killed in Iraq.

BEN was an extremely charismatic person who lightened the mood whenever he walked into a room. All he ever wanted was to become a military policeman and he worked very hard to become one. He was very career-minded, with bags of potential and had been recommended for early promotion. The red beret was all he ever wanted. It was his life, so he gave his life doing the job he loved most. He was also a loving son who will be sorely missed. John Hyde

The place seemed to be fairly quiet … the situation had stabilised, the police force [Iraqi] was starting to come together. Things looked rosy…

Major Bryn Parry-Jones (OC 156 Provost Company)

If everyone had come home from Iraq and we hadn't lost guys that day, it would have been a massive stroke of luck…It was on the cards; something was going to happen.'

An RMP

Epilogue

THE Board of Inquiry convened on 15 March 2004, publishing its findings eight months later. Its central conclusions were that the tragedy was unpredictable, and despite difficulties with communications and equipment, there was no conclusive evidence that the six fatalities could 'reasonably have been prevented'. A number of recommendations were presented.

Board of Inquiry recommendation: 'That Command Relationships are clearly articulated in Operational Orders and that the whole chain of command is clearly briefed as to whom they report to and who tasks them.'

As witnesses before the Board, military policemen claimed that during May and June 2003, the post-war phase, it was unclear to whom they were responsible: the RMP hierarchy or 1 PARA.

By the fateful day, the command and control system at Abu Naji had broken down; there was little supervision, clarity or direction over the working relationship between 156 Provo and the rest of the Battle Group. The result was C Section, as was suggested at the BoI, 'falling through the cracks'.

Board of Inquiry recommendation: 'That any Operations Room operating in this sort of environment adopts a uniform booking out system. It further recommends that the system be checked on a regular basis to ensure that all attached units are complying and that an all-informed matrix is being maintained.'

The RMPs had their own, more relaxed, set of standard operating procedures than those practised by other units. While H-J told Warrant Officer Marley of his destination on 24 June – Al Uzayr via Majar al-Kabir and Qalat Salih – the Board heard his booking-out sheet included no estimated timings of how long C Section would spend at each town.

At 1037hrs, when the Operations Room was notified of the contact involving call sign Bravo, Marley was unsure whether H-J and his men were in danger.

The Board was told by Captain John Palmer, second-in-command C Company, that, on previous occasions, he:

> had to remind his RMP Section [C Section] to book out through the Company Operations Desk. In addition only cursory information was ever passed to the Company. The pin was not always placed on the BG [Battle Group] bird table mapboard [it was placed correctly on 24 June] and RMP Section Commanders rarely went to the G2 desk [the Int Cell].
>
> The Board believes that the RMP Sections regularly failed to update the Ops Room on the progress of their visits/patrols.
>
> In practice, nobody kept track of the RMP call signs when they were on visits/patrols and the RMP call signs did not report in their progress.

The Board determined that the decision by Major Stuart Tootal and Captain Richard Todd not to 'factor' the RMP into the rescue mission was correct. 'Until WO2 Marley or the C Coy Ops Desk confirmed that the RMP were in the town, the Board believes that the Battle Group Ops Room staff could not have deployed assets to assist their extraction.'

Board of Inquiry recommendation: 'That watch keepers are trained in maintaining a Log and that it is made clear to them that Logs could potentially become an exhibit in legal proceedings.'

It is worth noting how busy the watch keepers were on the day. They were not just in the Ops Room to record events, but were actively involved in the rescue mission.

Board of Inquiry recommendation: 'That a review be conducted of RMP Officer training to ensure that their young officers are better trained to command small isolated detachments.'

This was an indictment of Lieutenant Richard Phillips, who was the senior rank among the twenty-five-man RMP 'stay-behind party'. Lt Phillips claimed it was Sgt Hamilton-Jewell who dictated C Section's tasks*.

> No, I did not send them down there [to Majar al-Kabir on 24 June]. Regarding the area to the south [of Abu Naji] my knowledge base about what was going on came directly from Sergeant Simon Hamilton-Jewell. He knew the area. I took his direction for what goes on a daily basis; it came from him.
> He would say to me how he is progressing each night. 'This is what I've done,' 'This is what I am planning for the next week,' 'This is what I am going to do tomorrow.'
> He [H-J] said his order for the day was to be down in Al Uzayr for the afternoon and he said that he would be going to this place and this place. I can't recall anyone coming back to me and voicing concerns of that nature and it would only be H-J doing that.

According to Major Bryn Parry-Jones, Lieutenant Phillips was right to afford H-J such freedom of action*:

> These [H-J and his men] were not people who have to be ordered to do things. That is the thing we pride ourselves on as military police is that our guys are thinking individuals.
> They know the broad parameters they've got to work in; they know the rules but they're bright enough to think, 'Well, I'm heading that way I might as well pop in to see whether the painting is being done.'

* Interviews with Lieutenant Phillips and Major Bryn Parry-Jones were conducted by Reg Keys. Other interviews by the author.

Obviously they wouldn't have gone in if they thought it was dangerous. The guys would not just have followed orders blindly; if they thought they were at risk they would not have done it. We're not in the First World War days now where people blow whistles and we all head over the top. They knew the personalities; they knew some of the people they were dealing with. I honestly think it just came as a complete surprise to them.

Board of Inquiry recommendation: 'That thought is given to the RMP carrying out more infantry training, specifically focusing on infantry skills.'

This suggestion followed consideration of whether C Section were adequately trained and equipped to repel the mob as the BoI report stated.

If an individual knows that he has back-up close by, he is confident in his military skills and he has sufficient ammunition to sustain a firefight until that back-up arrives, then he may well initiate that firefight. If however he has no means of knowing when his back-up will arrive, if at all, has limited ammunition and a training regime that recommends negotiation rather than conflict, then he may not.

On June 24th 2003 the six RMP had approximately 50 rounds of ammunition each and may well have felt that this was insufficient to initiate a firefight.

Major Byrn Parry-Jones was, perhaps unfairly, more critical of C Section: 'Whether you have got 50 rounds or 250 rounds, if you don't fire any rounds it doesn't matter how many rounds you've got – 50 rounds for each man is 300 rounds, that's an awful lot of rounds.'

The army's official position is that the RMPs did not fire their weapons and an examination of Si Miller's rifle supported this conclusion. The only one of C Section's A2s to be recovered, it had not been fired since it had last been cleaned. However, that the crime scene, i.e. the police station, was not secured by British forces for several days casts a shadow over the army's position that the Red Caps were merely passive in their response to the attack upon them. The evidence is inconclusive.

With no impartial observers present it is simply impossible to tell precisely what happened. Some Iraqi eye-witness accounts told of them handing over their weapons, others said the military policemen had started the gunfight before being overwhelmed.

The Iraqi interpreter's account stated that when the mob began attacking, the RMP 'moved their wagons behind the fence of the police centre to give them more protect [sic] and took their light weapons to defend themselves as well as the centre and its personnel'. Allowing for the interpreter's poor command of English, this suggests the RMP had left their rifles in the Land Rovers.

One Red Cap (interviewed by the author) explained:

> We weren't supposed to have our gats [slang for guns, from Gatling gun] with us. It wasn't like that; we were supposed to be softly, softly. They're [the Paras] the ones who should be tooled up and that, looking after us. 1 PARA's task was to look after us. It was like a big chain: we were there to look after the Iraqis, the Paras were there to look after us. We weren't supposed to be there in an aggressive stance; we were there to make a visual impact and to deter looters and such like.

Did it matter if they left their weapons in vehicles as long as infantry were in attendance? 'We didn't go on to do things on our own,' said Major Parry-Jones. 'We operate within a cordon; there was always to be a satellite patrol around them [the six].' On 24 June the satellite patrol which was in Major Parry-Jones' words 'always to be around them' did not know they were there.

Without such a cordon, H-J and his men acted valiantly – as policemen, pacifiers, but not as infanteers, who would have sought either to engage the crowd of extract from the area.

The level of skill at arms across 156 Provo was low, according to one RMP interviewed by the author:

> The only infantry training we get, officially, is in phase one training and it's called 'pairs fire and manoeuvre'. As 156 Provo you do a little bit of extra training but it's something that the unit just chucks in

because they think it will come in handy, nothing official, section attacks and that. But because we are multi-skilled, jacks of all trades, you don't get enough confidence; people don't know how to do it.

The RMP role is so difficult and the soldiering is a pretty small part of it. Most of the people in the RMP regard themselves as policemen first and soldiers second.

Lots of people said to me after the war how much respect they had for the RMP and what they had to do – they never knew before how vulnerable we were and what we did.

The Army insisted 156 Provo were adequately trained. As the Board reported:

'Pre-deployment, it was believed that the RMP were being deployed in their traditional policing role and that the extra training they conducted in infantry skills was more than adequate to cover expected eventualities. The members of C Section were generally experienced soldiers, certainly Sgt Hamilton-Jewell had infantry experience and Cpl Aston and LCpl Keys had both served in the infantry.'

Board of Inquiry recommendation: 'That a detailed communications estimate is carried out on entering theatre which is then regularly updated. Additionally, Urgent Operational Requirement (UOR) funds should be made available to purchase additional, off the shelf, communication assets as required. This is particularly relevant for operations in an urban environment.'

Given the poor radio communications across Maysan province and in built-up areas such as Majar al-Kabir, the failure of the 156 Provo hierarchy to equip its sections with satellite phones was all the more extraordinary.

As the Board noted:

The principal alternative means of providing communications within 1 PARA Battle Group was the Iridium phone. The Battle Group held 29 of these phones, a number of which had been purchased by 16 A A Bde on an Op FINGAL Urgent Operational Requirement (UOR). Phones were held centrally to enable them to be charged on the limited power points available and to ensure that they were available to patrols as required.

A phone booking-out system was used within the BG Ops Room and Comms Ops to control the issue of the phones. Phones were signed out prior to deploying on patrol and returned on completion. Less the RMP, all commanders interviewed by the Board stated that they always deployed with an Iridium phone and that phones were always available when requested.

The only means of semi-guaranteed communication from Majar al-Kabir to Abu Naji was via Iridium phone. The Board accepts that call signs 33J and 33K [the radio call signs for H-J's section] had no Iridium phone with them on June 24th 2003.

If the RMP call signs at the police station had been equipped with an Iridium phone, as per 1 PARA BG Op O, then they may have phoned the BG Ops Room when the initial contact in the town took place. This would have given them some situational awareness and it may have enabled them to make a decision to extract or to call for assistance.

There was no all-informed communications network available. The RMP should therefore have had an Iridium phone. This would have allowed the BG Ops Room to know that they were in the town and would have resulted in different actions being taken by the BG Ops Room, which may have allowed the RMP to extract. The BG Ops Room could have tasked the ARF differently and even though it would have been difficult, they could have tasked call sign Alpha or Bravo to try and reach the police station [this would have been asking too much of either call sign, considering their situation on the ground].

Call signs Alpha and Bravo were both rescued having used satellite phones to communicate with the Ops Room, while C Section were unable to talk to the Ops Room and nobody there was able to talk to them.

On Op TELIC and in the immediate post-war period, the Red Caps were too exposed and poorly led at officer level. The corps should accept some level of culpability for the tragedy.

Board of Inquiry recommendation: 'An assessment be carried out as to the suitability for the RMP to train and operate GPMG.'

The army dismissed the Board's advice claiming there was no evidence to suggest a lack of firepower had any bearing on the tragedy, and that issuing heavy weapons to RMPs would have detracted from their ability to perform their primary function as policemen. The army also declined the Board's suggestion that RMPs receive more infantry training.

These two recommendations warranted, at the very least, much further consideration – it is the author's view that in future, Red Caps should be ready, better trained and equipped to respond more aggressively than they had on 24 June.

Board of Inquiry recommendation: 'That all personnel issued with grenades must be trained in their operating procedures before issue.'

However, as the Board noted: 'The BoI has concerns over the issuing of grenades to the RMP in the first place. A number of members of 156 Pro Coy have stated that they had grenades issued to them for the war-fighting phase yet they had received no training in their use.'

Board of Inquiry recommendation: 'That the scaling of ammunition should be set at Battle Group level and that individual detachment commanders should be able to dictate ammunition holdings. The scalings then need to be confirmed across the BG.'

On 23 May the RMP handed in their own stocks of ammunition and were re-supplied with 1,050 rounds by 1 PARA – approximately fifty rounds for each military policeman on patrol.

Lieutenant Phillips claimed he questioned the de-scaling: 'We had been reduced down a month earlier [prior to 24 June]. It [the order] came from the G4 chain. There is only so far you can keep on questioning.

There were concerns – it wasn't my decision to de-scale them [C Section].'
The Board's report suggested otherwise:

> At no stage did any member of the RMP Platoon hierarchy approach
> 1 PARA and ask for the additional ammunition or for clarification as
> to what the PARA BG were carrying. If the RMP hierarchy had
> requested an increase in ammunition there is no reason to believe
> that it would not have been granted. QM [Quartermaster] 1 PARA
> BG has stated that there was plenty of ammunition available and it
> would have been issued if requested. On 28 May 03 the RMP also
> handed in Signals kit, pyrotechnic pistol (red) and smoke grenades of
> various colours. They did not ask for these to be reissued from 1
> PARA BG. Again, QM 1 PARA BG states that they had reserves
> available and they would have been issued if requested.

Major Parry-Jones supported the de-scaling:

> The Brigade was scaling down as a whole. 16 Air Assault Brigade
> had done its bit in the area; the place seemed to be fairly quiet and
> we were getting ready to hand over to a different brigade that was
> coming in. Things looked rosy when we were leaving.
>
> I had left two weeks before the guys did; they were left with 1
> PARA to provide support to the CO [Lieutenant Colonel Beckett].
> The de-scaling of ammunition is something which routinely
> happens in theatre – the Quartermasters have got to take huge
> amounts of bulk ammunition out of theatre and as the tactical
> situation changes and things get more stable we reduce the amount
> of ammunition we are carrying.
>
> The ammunition scales were reduced because the situation was
> stable enough to allow this to happen; it's the old question of how
> much is enough.
>
> Hindsight is a wonderful thing. We had not had this kind of
> attack, where we have got crowds building up and taking on the
> security forces. All you had had the entire time we had been in the
> Maysan Province and Al Amarah was the odd lone gunman having a
> pop-shot.

We were not in the business of taking on 400 people. If that was the case, if the threat state had gone up then the ammunition scales would have been re-looked at.

His men did not share his 'rosy' assessment of the security situation:

If we'd have had an open forum I would have said, 'No way am I going out there as vulnerable as we are.' It had been like that for a month and a half, working with the Iraqi militia. Fucking fifty rounds each? And they [the Iraqis], they had AKs. They weren't short of ammunition; they had a lot more than us.

My experience being on the ground with 156, it's fucking dangerous, really dangerous. You go out on your own, without any infantry, we don't even have any side arms – there weren't enough pistols to go around. How are you going to get a long [rifle] out of the window [of a Land Rover]. The stuff that we don't have is a joke.

The post-war phase was probably more dangerous than the war itself. They're [the Iraqis] uneducated, they're like badly behaved school children. Them people, it makes me angry talking about it.

The Board concluded it was impossible to state categorically that had C Section carried more ammunition the outcome of 24 June would have been different.

Board of Inquiry recommendation: 'That morphine is made available to soldiers operating in potentially hostile environments. If there is concern about misuse then it may be appropriate to centralise morphine. However, all sections deploying on the ground should have immediate access to morphine.'

The Board noted: 'The Board is concerned that morphine was not issued to members of the RMP in a potentially hostile environment, in a country where roads and driving standards were poor and RTAs could take place in isolated areas.'

THE Board deliberately downplayed the significance of the attack on 22 June to support its position that the events of 24 June 'could not have been predicted' and that the RMPs' deaths 'could not reasonably have been prevented'.

The Board claimed:

> The QRF, made up of WMIKs and a Troop of the HCR in light armoured vehicles arrived in the town [on 22 June] and as they did so the crowd was already dispersing under the guidance of Abu Hatim [Hateem].
>
> Indeed the QRF, on arriving at the police station, questioned call sign 20A as to why they had been called out, as there was no disturbance by the time they got there. In the Ops Officer's War Diary it states that baton rounds were fired at this stage. The Board has not found concrete evidence to support this.

At least two baton rounds were definitely used – one of which struck an Iraqi on the head. These would not have been fired had there been 'no disturbance'. Aggressive Iraqis swarmed around the police station as the QRF arrived. WMIKs and Scimitars were driven in a wedge formation to push the locals back and facilitate Alpha's extraction – there was also unarmed combat between Paras and Iraqis. Without question, the disturbance was continuing when the QRF arrived and for the BoI to have suggested otherwise was deeply misleading. The action at the police station a mere 48 hours before the deaths of the RMPs at the same location was far more violent and prolonged than the army is ready to admit. More caution should have been exercised by the RMP heirarchy after this incident before it was decided that C Section would stop in Majar al-Kabir en route south.

The Board's report continued:

> Call sign 20A and the QRF then returned to Abu Naji Camp and the incident was recorded in the Ops Officer's War Diary, reported up to Div and was briefed at the Ops updates that night.

The incident was however not deemed to be a significant event and whilst the stoning had been more intense than usual the BG believed that it was an issue that required a meeting with the Town Council rather than anything else.

The attack on the 22nd was significant enough to be reported to 1 (UK) Division in Basra. Both Alpha and Bravo – a doubling of manpower – were redeployed on the 24th to show a strong presence in Majar al-Kabir.

The Board merely concluded: 'The incident on June 22nd, in the absence of any intelligence to the contrary, was not an indicator that the unrest in the town was going to escalate to such a scale and the meeting on June 23rd was thought to have appeased the situation.'

Were members of C Section aware of the attack on 22 June? Major Parry-Jones stated:

> I cannot see how they could not have been aware of it, if it had happened two days earlier. Everybody knows what's going on. It's such a small place, it's a small province; there's few people on the ground so a firefight in somewhere like Al Majar, there's no way that people would not have known that.
>
> If it was considered to have been a dangerous place I would have thought that somebody would have thought, 'It's out of bounds.' I don't think anyone would have ordered them [C Section] into the town; that's my personal feeling, because that place had been on their patch all the way through and because they had got good relations with the police and because it was their pet project.

According to Lieutenant Phillips, Majar al-Kabir was dangerous but not out of bounds:

> If I was told not to go into that town then I would not have done, or I wouldn't have allowed H-J to make the decision to go in there. It was a joint decision by ourselves; we assessed the risk there and then. I did not send them out [to Majar al-Kabir]; it was Sergeant Hamilton-Jewell's decision to go down. On that morning I discussed

with H-J what he needed to do. The main thing was to be down at that southern police station [Al Uzayr] at a certain time and he said that he wanted to go down to Majar and Qalat Salih on his way down and what he was going to do at each police station and I agreed with him.

A member of 8 Platoon (1 PARA) remarked:

What the hell were they doing? They don't have an inkling about fighting and had fuck-all firepower. It was an absolutely crazy thing to do. We knew it was going to be dangerous, after what had happened two days earlier. That was a warning and it should have been heeded. It wasn't; so they died and we only just fought our way out. Even the least experienced Toms knew Majar was a mad place. They didn't shoot at us that day [the 22nd] but it was like, if we came back, they would.

OC C Company Major Chris Kemp's view of the threat state in Majar al-Kabir was more understated, as he later wrote:

At the time of the incident conditions in the town were basic. There were regular power cuts and consequently drinking water was in short supply. There was very little paid employment and the surrounding area was still very tribal and proud of its lengthy history of resistance to the Ba'athist regime.

There had always been a somewhat hostile atmosphere in the town, mainly because the high regeneration expectations of the population were not being met. Stoning of patrols by children had become commonplace and there was strong evidence to suggest that this was deliberately being instigated by anti-Coalition elements. Rumours were also rife in the town. As an example I was authoritatively told in a town meeting that the Coalition and Saddam Hussein were working together to repress the people and steal the oil. In the weeks immediately preceding the incident a number of searches for high-calibre weapons had taken place in the surrounding villages and there was intelligence to suggest that these searches were being used to fuel further anti-Coalition propaganda; in fact, there were reports that one of the leading town clerics was also preaching against these searches.

Despite this undercurrent of threat towards the British, Kemp concluded, 'There was no intelligence to indicate that anti-Coalition groupings were preparing to use physical force against us.'

THERE was little love lost between the Paras and RMP. As one Red Cap admitted:

Everyone knew something was going on and the relationship wasn't very good. I knew that things weren't all they should have been.

The Paras were trying to bubble [report] us for all sorts of things. The Paras had their whole battalion; they were getting all this down time and sunbathing and working out, all the old Para meathead stuff. I would have liked to have seen some of those plucked out of the Paras and joined to our lot for a fucking month and a half to see how they got on. The Paras? I don't think they're that fucking good. They operate well when they're surrounded by other Paras but they don't mix well.

Whilst none of the RMPs felt the Paras would have abandoned any Red Caps in Majar al-Kabir, there was a general feeling that the Paras' approach to patrolling had stirred up the locals.

As the Board reported: 'The RMP were carrying out hearts and minds operations, they were liaising with locals and they were building up a Police Force. They had the ability to increase their firepower by taking PARA escorts with them whilst on patrol. They chose not to because the more robust stance of the PARA Regt did not suit the RMP aims.'

Were the Paras itching for a contact? Some Red Caps thought so: 'The fucking Paras? They've taken bets on that [getting a contact]. They love it, I tell you.'

Whilst the Paras were aggressive, neither Lieutenant Kennedy nor Robbo would deliberately have angered the mob on 24 June.

Notwithstanding the high-profile court martial of three members of the Royal Regiment of Fusiliers for abusing locals caught stealing aid supplies and the murder charges against members of 3 PARA, the fact remains that British forces were well behaved and tolerant towards the population of Iraq. There was no systemic misbehaviour by any members of the 1 PARA Battle Group and isolated indiscretions were summarily dealt with. For example, troops from 9 Squadron Royal Engineers were made to dig trenches all day after one of their ranks threw a packet of biscuits at an Iraqi child who had been begging for food. In Baghdad, a member of 1 PARA who had deployed to guard the British Embassy was put on cleaning duties after he was caught using a sling to fire stones at Iraqis.

TOWARDS the end of the tour, the RMP were fighting among themselves:

> After we'd been in Amarah for a while, we got a fridge and it was
> located in the rear echelon room, people like the MT [motor
> transport, technicians, etc.] and the Q [Quartermaster] and that.
> We'd be out on the ground fucking grafting and you couldn't keep
> the water cool, it was like boiling; it was like drinking hot water.
> So you'd come in and everyone would like to get a bottle of cold
> water – the fridge only ran off a generator so it wasn't that cold
> anyway but it was a lot better than nothing – and all the rear
> echelon guys and that had been writing their names on the bottles
> 'So and so's bottle, don't touch' so we'd come in and we'd have no
> fucking water.
>
> Fucking hell, we're out on the ground doing all the fucking
> grafting and there's people taking the piss. And that's our own
> people, fellow RMPs. That's what it's like when you're on Ops,
> mate, fucking terrible; you learn who the real guys are and who the
> fuckers are. You get a few good lads but otherwise it's terrible.

The Red Caps were tired and overworked. Their operational burden was too great for a platoon of twenty-five – especially as the 'stay behind party' included female RMPs who could not patrol due to the abuse from Iraqi men.

The deployment of females in forward areas showed a lack of awareness of Arab and Iraqi culture. The women were eventually confined to tasks at Abu Naji, forcing the male RMPs to spend longer on the VCPs.

Warrant Officer Marley bore the brunt of much of the junior RMPs' misgivings:

> He [Marley] wasn't there for any of the war-fighting or the build-up. By the time he came out everyone was bollocked [tired]. He came out and said, 'Right, I know you're all pissed off but we're going to have a change of leadership. The OC [Parry-Jones] is leaving, the RSM is leaving; I'm going to be the new sergeant major; etc., etc.' And after he had been there a while he wanted to charge people and put it on orders that people needed to shave in the morning.
>
> But we weren't getting any time to do it. Everyone was fucked; we didn't have time to admin ourselves up. Land Rovers were being crashed out there and it was purely and simply down to fatigue. The hours we were doing were ridiculous. There were only a couple of females going out on the ground because the others either wouldn't go or couldn't go because they weren't allowed, because they were getting stoned.

As company sergeant major responsible for discipline, it is difficult to see what else Marley could have done:

> He [Marley] made himself very unpopular pretty quickly. We'd been out there, we'd done all the prep, all the build-up, all the training in Kuwait, went over the start line; he then comes out a quarter of the way through the peacekeeping phase in Amarah and he's trying to be some sort of authoritarian. If he'd been through what we had for the last four months he wouldn't have been so keen.
>
> We just couldn't physically stay awake. Anyone falling asleep on stag was getting reported, not being out on the road during the day, that kind of thing.

THE Board's remit precluded detailed examination of the ARF flight, which had come within inches of being downed. Had an RPG struck either set of rotors – or if small arms had penetrated the Chinook's engine – the helicopter would have crash-landed, in all likelihood killing its passengers and crew. Wing Commander Guy van den Berg flew the unarmoured CH-47 into the teeth of enemy resistance – opinion is divided over whether this constituted heroic or reckless flying.

The initial plan, as devised in the Ops Room, had been for the Chinook to lay up short of Majar al-Kabir to allow Sergeant Jason 'Buck' Rogers' men to advance towards Bravo's location.

The Board noted:

Somewhere in the passage of information the grid reference given to the Chinook crew did not match that recorded in the Battle Group Log. The Chinook flight followed the recognised practice of flying low and fast over built-up areas, however flying directly over the contact area was always likely to attract small arms fire. The crew attempted to avoid built-up areas and the Board believes that their flight path was logical. In hindsight it is easy to state that they should have avoided the area and landed some way off.

The Chinook flew past call sign Bravo and circled to the south of the town. On hearing call sign Bravo on the net [radio] the Chinook flew back over the town towards the call sign.

Call sign Bravo were calling the Chinook to their location and the decision to go to the call sign was made on the basis of the information available to the Chinook crew at the time. The Board believes that they made the right decision.

The Board considers that the damage sustained by the Chinook and the critical condition of the seven casualties on board provides ample evidence of the severity of the firefight in Majar al-Kabir. The Board agrees that due to the casualties it was imperative that the Chinook return to the DS [Abu Naji] as soon as possible and this was the right decision.

On the Air side, there was no top cover immediately on call to support British call signs on the ground. Once the US assets were scrambled to Majar al-Kabir, there was no forward air controller available to guide air missiles towards enemy targets.

THE Board defended Lieutenant Kennedy's failure to update the Ops Room that a vehicle patrol rather than a foot patrol was to take place following Zubaida's objections – a criticism made of him by the families of the six:

> In hindsight it would be easy to state that he should have reported the incident, however, Mission Command [the army's doctrine on leadership and principles of operation] dictates that as he was the Commander on the ground, he should make the decision based on the facts and the atmosphere pertaining at the time. This is what he did.
>
> In the light of this the Board believes that Lt Kennedy took the correct course of action. At this stage there were no signs that this incident was going to escalate to the level that it did.

As Lieutenant Kennedy later wrote:

> Having met up with the militia [in Majar al-Kabir on 24 June] my multiple [Alpha] set off on foot towards the town centre. When we were only a couple of hundred metres into the patrol the fawj commander rushed up to me in his pick-up truck and warned me that if we continued on foot we could be shot at. He did not give any specific reasons for this concern but agreed that a joint vehicle patrol would be a good idea and reduce the likelihood of a confrontation.

As events unfolded, it did not.

The report also commended Lieutenant Colonel Beckett's controversial decision to withdraw his forces:

> Once the Iraqi doctor stated that the Coalition Forces at the police

station were dead it was entirely appropriate for the doctor to recover the bodies rather than 1 PARA BG mounting a major offensive to do so. Equally the decision not to re-enter the town immediately to secure the police station for forensic evidence was correct. Any move into the town would have resulted in a major battle and, in his view, Coalition Forces casualties. He ordered Battle Group personnel to return to Abu Naji Camp.

Beckett's decision, unpopular with his men, saved lives on both sides. Losses had been particularly high on the Iraqi side – an issue which has scarcely been mentioned. Eighty to a hundred Iraqis were either killed or severely wounded. Alpha and Bravo accounted for approximately twenty to thirty locals each, with the QRF taking out at least as many. Beckett chose humanity over revenge.

Among his men, Privates Freddy Ellis, Tim May and Jason Davidson were unlucky not to be decorated for their heroism in the line of fire.

THE Ministry of Defence's decorations do not recognise the gallantry and the commitment to duty shown by C Section.

But imagine being surrounded by the gun-toting mob and hearing their baying voices reverberate around the courtyard. You sense they don't just want to kill you; no, that won't do...They intend you to suffer a humiliating death. Perhaps by this point you have seen them empty a full magazine of rounds from an AK47 into one or more of your colleagues, then batter his corpse with rifle butts.

Maybe you recognise the sound of a British helicopter above the police station and believe you might be saved.

Then you can't hear it any more...and your last hope of salvation fades.

Glossary and notes

A2 SA-80 Mark II, standard issue British assault rifle

Abu Naji The name of the 1 PARA Battle Group camp, 5 kilometres south of Amarah and 23 kilometres north of Majar al-Kabir.

16 Air Assault Brigade (16 Air Asslt Bde) Formed in September 1999 as an amalgamation of 24 Airmobile, 5 Airborne Brigade and 9 Regiment Army Air Corps, the brigade is the army's newest, largest and most potent: over 5,500 of 16 Air Asslt Bde personnel deployed on Op TELIC.

The brigade's primary war-fighting role is strike operations, usually in depth and over protracted distances. The brigade consists of four infantry battalions (1 PARA, 2 PARA, 3 PARA and a fourth battalion from outside the Parachute Regiment – 1st Battalion, the Royal Irish Regiment on Op TELIC) of which one is always at a permanent state of high readiness (2–5 days' Notice to Move); Pathfinder Platoon; 216 Signal Squadron; 3, 4 and 9 Regiments Army Air Corps (AAC); 7 PARA Royal Horse Artillery (RHA); 21 Air Defence Battery; 23 Engineer Regiment, which includes 9 Parachute Squadron (RE); the Household Cavalry Regiment (HCR), equipped with Scimitar and Spartan armoured vehicles; 13 Air Assault Support Regiment; Royal Logistics Corps (RLC); 7 Air Assault Battalion, Royal Electrical and Mechanical Engineers (REME); 16 Close Support Medical

Regiment; 156 Provost Company, Royal Military Police; and the Brigade Parachute Squadron.

On Op TELIC 16 Air Assault Brigade was commanded by Brigadier Jonathan 'Jacko' Page, a bespectacled Oxford graduate commissioned into 2 PARA in 1981. He led a platoon during the assault on Goose Green during the Falklands War. Brigadier Page has a breadth of service across airborne forces and assumed command of the brigade in December 2002. Intellectual and, to his critics, aloof, he is tipped as a future Chief of the General Staff (CGS) or even Chief of the Defence Staff (CDS) – and has made the right career moves thus far. Op TELIC was the brigade's largest and most significant operation, proving its potency as a quick reaction force.

AK47 *Avtomat Kalashnikova* automatic rifle

'Ally' Look or act in a battle-ready manner. A piece of kit can also be described as 'ally' if it is destructive and/or functions effectively.

Alpha/Two Zero Alpha The first of two multiples of soldiers from 8 Platoon, C Company, 1 PARA. On 24 June 2003 it was commanded by Lieutenant Ross Kennedy with Lance Corporal Mark Weadon as his second-in-command.

Amarah (Al Amarah) Capital city of Maysan province straddling the River Tigris and positioned 50 kilometres from the Iranian border. The city marked the northernmost tip of the 16,000-square-kilometre triangle of marshlands before their destruction by Saddam Hussein through which both the Tigris and Euphrates rivers flowed. The local economy is based mainly on farm products including rice, dates and sheep. During the 1980s the government built new docks in Amarah and the city benefits from a Japanese-built hospital. Amarah was founded in the late 1860s as a military outpost of the Ottoman Empire. From Amarah, the Ottomans tried to control warring tribes such as the Al Bou Muhammed and the Banu Lam.

AO Area of operations

ARF Airborne Reaction Force

'Bagging' Arrest

Bergen Rucksack

Bone Stupid

Bravo/Two Zero Bravo The second of two multiples consisting of soldiers from 8 Platoon, C Company, 1 PARA. On 24 June 2003 it was commanded by Sergeant Gordon Robertson with Corporal John Dolman as his second-in-command.

'Buckshee' Free or spare. A march or 'tab' may also be described as buckshee if it is less than the distance or easier to complete than claimed.

'Bug out' Leave

CAS Close Air Support

Casevac Casualty Evacuation

CBA Combat body armour, aka combat body warmers – so called because it makes the wearer hot

CDS Chief of the Defence Staff. The CDS is the officer responsible to the Secretary of State for Defence for the coordinated efforts of all three fighting services: British Army, Royal Air Force and Royal Navy. At the time of Op TELIC this was General Sir Michael Walker, formerly of the Royal Anglian Regiment.

CENTCOM United States Central Command. CENTCOM, based at MacDill Air Force Base, Tampa, Florida is the most important of the US's worldwide combat command centres, orchestrating the invasions/liberations of Afghanistan and Iraq and Gulf War I in 1991. The campaigns in Afghanistan and Iraq were led by General Tommy Franks, a three-times-wounded Vietnam veteran with over three and a half decades of military experience. General Franks told the US Senate Armed Services Committee in 2001 that CENTCOM, 'promotes regional stability, ensures uninterrupted access to resources and markets, maintains freedom of navigation, protects US citizens and property and promotes the security of regional friends and allies'.

CGC Conspicuous Gallantry Cross. Second only to the Victoria Cross in the order of medals for courage in the line of enemy fire. Instituted in October 1993, it was first awarded in 1995 to Corporal Wayne Mills of the Duke of Wellington's Regiment serving in Bosnia. After Majar al-Kabir, Sergeant Gordon Robertson became the first Parachute Regiment soldier to be decorated with a CGC.

CGS Chief of the General Staff, the officer at the top of the army's chain of operational command. On Op TELIC this was a former 1 PARA CO, General Sir Mike Jackson.

'Chins, chinstrapped, ragged' Exhausted

'Chunter' Moan

CIMIC Civil–Military Cooperation Team

CINCENT Commander-in-Chief CENTCOM, General Tommy Franks

CO Commanding officer

COIN Counter Insurgency

Coy Company. 1 PARA was organised into six companies, A, B, C, D, HQ and Support. A–C were rifle companies which each separated into three platoons, e.g. A Company consisted of 1, 2 and 3 Platoons, armed with the SA-80 A2, Minimi light machine gun, General Purpose Machine Gun (GPMG) and light mortars. Support Company (Sp Coy) provided heavier firepower: MILAN anti-tank weapon, Browning .50 cal, GPMG and 81 mm mortars. The Intelligence, Surveillance and Target Acquisition Company (D Company) provided recce and signals elements while Headquarters Company (HQ Coy) supplied adminis-tration, motor transport, vehicle maintenance and chefs. Each company was commanded by a major, known as the OC (Officer Commanding). On Op TELIC, 1 PARA's OCs included: Major Andy Harrison (A Coy), Major Tim Clegg (B Coy), Major Chris Kemp (C Coy), Major Mark Goymer (D Coy) and Major Kieron McManus (Sp Coy).

'Crash out' Leave in a hurry

'Crow' A recruit at Depot PARA, formerly at Browning Barracks, Aldershot, now Catterick. 'Crow' sticks as a generic name during recruits' first months posted to a battalion when they are otherwise known as 'Toms'.

CSM Company sergeant major

Cyalumes Luminous shafts used to signal a location

DAF 'Deliverer of Airborne Forces' or 'Heli-Bedford', the make of 4 tonne trucks used by 1 PARA on Op TELIC.

'Dicked'/ 'Spammed' Selected for an unpleasant task

DPM Disruptive Pattern Material

'Drama' Difficult or dangerous situation

DSF Director Special Forces, a brigadier responsible for liaison between UKSF and various bodies such as MI6 and the Cabinet Office.

DSO Distinguished Service Order, awarded in recognition of command of battle but not necessarily enemy fire.

Dushka Soviet-made 12.7 mm heavy machine gun

DZ Drop Zone

Ex Saif Sareea At the time the largest deployment of UK military forces since Gulf War I, this exercise demonstrated the capability to deploy an expeditionary force overseas. In September and October 2001 22,500 British personnel were involved. As the National Audit Office reported, 'The ability of men and equipment to perform in desert conditions was severely tested, which led to lessons being indentified where things worked well and where improvements can be made.' How much of this did the Ministry of Defence take on board, as operations in Iraq were beset with logistical and equipment failings? In its report on Op TELIC (*see* Op TELIC in this section) the NAO concluded, 'The Department should review its process for implementing lessons learned to ensure that, subject to issues such as affordability, technical feasibility or other priorities, lessons are implemented as quickly as possible and that war-fighting lessons do not unjustifiably slip down the list of priorities during peacetime.'

Exfil Exfiltration. Withdrawal from territory (held by the enemy).

FAC Forward Air Controller. The role of the FAC, whether on the ground or stationed in the air, is to guide munitions onto an enemy target.

'Fair one' Acceptable

Fallschirmjaeger The elite German paratroopers of World War II remain a cultural force in today's Parachute Regiment. Fallschirm-jaeger tattoos are common and their drinking songs are commonly heard in Aldershot, Colchester and Dover. The Fallschirmjaeger was a large, independent and elite force, as the Paras continue to consider themselves. The Fallschirmjaeger made the first airborne infantry assaults capturing strategic targets across western Europe. In 1941, in their greatest operation, 6,000 Fallschirmjaeger invaded and conquered Crete without support. But their losses were such that Hitler decided against any further mass airborne operations. The Fallschirmjaeger were retained as an elite infantry unit, proving themselves again at Monte Cassino in 1944, Normandy and against the newly formed British paratroopers at Arnhem.

FAWJ Abbreviated name for the militia headquarters in Majar al-Kabir.

Flap sheet Document filled out by groups of British troops before they left Abu Naji, detailing their route and listings the individuals in each group, their blood groups and nick numbers, radio details and vehicles being used.

FSB Fire Support Base

FST Field Surgical Team

'Full Screw' Corporal

FUP Forming up point

GOC General Officer in Command. The GOC 1 (UK) Division in Basra on 24 June 2003 was Major General Peter Wall.

GOSP Gas/Oil separation plant

GPMG General Purpose Machine Gun aka 'Gimpy', or 'the gun'

'Hat'/'Craphat' Para slang for non-Parachute Regiment personnel

'Head shed(s)' Those in charge, the 'bosses'

HF High frequency

HLS Helicopter landing site

HMG Her Majesty's Government

HUMINT Human intelligence, as opposed to intelligence gathered by 'artificial means', satellite or Predator drone

IC In command, e.g. 'IC Wagon'; also Intelligence Corps

2IC Second-in-command

Infanteers Infantry soldiers

Infil Infiltration (of enemy territory)

INTBRIEF Intelligence briefing

INTREP Intelligence report

IRT Immediate Response Team

1 KOSB 1st Battalion, the King's Own Scottish Borderers, the infantry battalion which replaced 1 PARA at Abu Naji

'Lance Jack' Lance corporal

LSW Light Support Weapon, aka 'Crow's Cannon' or 'L-S-Trouble U'

LZ Landing zone

Maysan Iraqi province that includes the town of Majar al-Kabir and the city of Amarah

Medevac Medical evacuation

'Mega' Used sarcastically to describe something bad.

MiD Mention in Dispatches

MILAN Anti-armour missile system carried on Support Company WMIKs. Range approximately 2 kilometres.

Minimi Gas-operated support weapon/light machine gun. Used by the SAS in Gulf War I in 1991, now issued at section level outside Special Forces.

MoD Ministry of Defence

'Monging' Idle, or doing nothing

MSG Manoeuvre Support Group, consisting of eight heavily armed WMIKs.

MSR Main Supply Route, e.g. Route 6, which passes north–south through Maysan province.

MSS Manoeuvre Support Section. Half an MSG, four WMIKs.

Multiple 8 Platoon was split in half to form two multiples, each of approximately twelve soldiers, Two Zero Alpha and Two Zero Bravo.

NATO North Atlantic Treaty Organisation

NCO Non-commissioned officer

NVG Night Vision Goggles

OC Officer commanding

ODA Operating Department Assistant

Op Operation

Op BARRAS Mission to rescue British hostages in Sierra Leone

Op GRANBY British contribution to the liberation of Kuwait in 1991, which remains the largest conventional war operation launched by the British Army since the end of World War II.

Op JASMINE Arms amnesty in Maysan province

Op KEIR 8 Mission to repatriate the RMPs killed in Majar al-Kabir

Op TELIC The name given to British military operations in Iraq. British forces accounted for a fraction under 10 per cent of the total number of Coalition Forces deployed to remove Saddam Hussein's regime – 46,000 of the 467,000 deployed. Though the National Audit Office determined Op TELIC to have been a 'significant military success' in that the key military objectives – contributing to the overthrow of the Ba'ath Party regime, overcoming organised military resistance, securing key economic and civil infrastructure, deterring wider conflict in the region and denying Saddam Hussein use of WMD – were achieved within four weeks, the post-war-fighting stage proved more demanding and complex, as the six Royal Military Policemen found to their cost. 'On a United Kingdom Government wide basis, the nature and size of the post-conflict task was extremely difficult to predict and plan for. There were gaps in both the coordination of the planning and in the capability to do more in the short and medium term than patch up the existing inadequate infrastructure.'

Logistical problems in the build-up to and during Op TELIC were widespread and widely reported. To provide just one example, medical supplies, drugs and vaccines had to be thrown away because they were temperature sensitive yet had not been transported in cooled containers.

Op VERITAS UK operations in Afghanistan 2001

ORBAT Order of Battle

OSA Official Secrets Act

The Parachute Regiment Consisting of four battalions, 1, 2 and 3 PARA are regular and full-time, while 4 PARA is part of the Territorial

Army. 1 PARA is known as 'sporty and red', 2 PARA, 'immaculate blue' and 3 PARA, 'grungy green', nicknames derived from the colours of their DZ flashes. After 1 PARA had stayed in the UK while 2 and 3 PARA recaptured the Falklands, the saying '2 PARA on phase one, 3 PARA on phase 2, 1 PARA, phased out' became popular. 2 PARA and 3 PARA are both in barracks in Colchester.

1 PARA Also known as 'weird Para' or 'strange Para' the 1st Battalion was much maligned through the 1980s, a legacy of its absence from the Falklands Islands in 1982. The battalion's reputation and future was not secure until operations in Kosovo and Sierra Leone, culminating in Op BARRAS. 1 PARA also supplied a mortar platoon to support SAS operations in Afghanistan in 2002 after Ex ROCKY LANCE in Oman. Commanded by Lieutenant Colonel T. A. Beckett QRH on Op TELIC, former COs include Lieutenant General John Reith, General Sir Mike Jackson and Brigadier Paul Gibson. In December 2004 it was announced that 1 PARA was to be removed from the infantry's ORBAT and re-tasked as a permanent support unit for the UKSF.

4 PARA The Parachute Regiment's volunteer branch compulsorily mobilised 119 soldiers for Op TELIC 1 – the battalion's biggest deployment since Suez. Some of those involved on 24 June were TA soldiers.

'5 PARA' One of the major private security companies in Iraq has been so nicknamed as so many Paras have left the regiment to join it.

Pegasus (Journal of the Parachute Regiment and Airborne Forces) Its Winter 2003 edition included a typically amusing account of the fighting in Majar al-Kabir:

> For the Company [C Company] the last few weeks had its share of surprises. 8 Pl gave a practical demonstration of 'fire and manoeuvre' in the town of Majar al-Kabir. This also included a lesson not normally covered in Brecon and Warminster – how to bump start a 4-tonner when surrounded by RPG and AK wielding

maniacs. We would like to extend our thanks to CSgt Fordell Luke and his MSG for their prompt arrival and liberal quantities of .50 and 7.62mm 4BIT.

The tragic loss of six members of 156 Provost Company RMP who were also serving in Majar al-Kabir on the same day touched all within the Battle Group. They will be sadly missed by both friends and comrades alike.

PF Pathfinders

PJHQ Permanent Joint Headquarters, Northwood, Middlesex. PJHQ was established in April 1996, combining the previously separated tri-service intelligence, planning, operational and logistics staff required to put together a British task force overseas. Lieutenant General John Reith was the Chief of Joint Operations based at PJHQ during Op TELIC. PJHQ planned and exercised operational command of all UK forces deployed on Op TELIC.

Pl Platoon. Each 1 PARA rifle company (A–C) divided into three platoons of approximately twenty-four men. Platoons are usually commanded by lieutenants, but not always. While 7 and 8 Platoons (C Company, 1 PARA) were led by Lieutenant Rick Lewin and Lieutenant Ross Kennedy, 9 Platoon was headed by Warrant Officer Tony 'Darth' Hobbins on Op TELIC.

POL Petrol, oil and lubricant. To 'pol-up' is to service a vehicle ready for its next user.

PRR Personal Role Radio

PSO Peace Support Operations

QBO Quick Battle Order

QM Quartermaster

QRF Quick Reaction Force

QRH Queen's Royal Hussars

RAMC Royal Army Medical Corps

RAP Regimental Aid Post

RE Royal Engineers

'Regted-up' Very enthused and proud member of the Parachute Regiment

REME Royal Electrical and Mechanical Engineers

RHQ Regimental Headquarters

RLC Royal Logistics Corps

RM Royal Marines

RMO Regimental Medical Officer

RMP Royal Military Police/Royal Military Policeman. The first incarnation of the RMP was the Cavalry Staff Corps, formed at the behest of Wellington in 1813, who had been alarmed by the extent of looting and drunkenness by the British Army in Portugal the previous year. The Military Mounted Police was formed in 1855 and in 1877 it became one of the British Army's permanent corps. The RMP's distinctive scarlet headdress was first worn in 1855 on the advice of the wife of the then Provost Marshal, Mrs Major C. Broakes, who recognised it was necessary for them to be distinctive from the rest of the British Army in order to fulfil their law enforcement role. The British Corps of Military Police was made a Royal Corps in 1946 by King George VI and the title Royal Military Police came into popular use. In 1992 the RMP was one of six small corps amalgamated into the newly formed Adjutant General Corps. In crude terms the RMP is split into three branches: General Police Duties (GPD), the Special Investigation Branch (SIB) and Close Protection teams (CP). After basic military training, RMP recruits receive police, driving, first aid and law instruction. On completion of training Red Caps then join a Provost company. The SIB is the RMP's equivalent of the Criminal Investigation Department (CID) of any civilian constabulary.

'Rock up' Arrive

RPG Rocket-propelled grenade

RSM Regimental sergeant major

'Rupert' Young officer

SA-80 Standard-issue British Army rifle (*see* A2).

SAS Special Air Service, of which half the manpower is provided by the Parachute Regiment

SATCOMMS Satellite communications

SBS Special Boat Service

Scimitar A three-man light armoured vehicle equipped with one 30mm cannon and a GPMG

SCIRI Supreme Council for the Islamic Revolution in Iraq

'Screw the nut!' Parachute Regiment expression used to suggest somebody should make a better job of whatever they are doing.

SFOR Stabilisation Force, referring to British forces deployed in the Balkans

SIB Special Investigation Branch, part of the RMP

Sitrep Situation Report

'Snap' More severe form of chuntering

SOP Standard Operating Procedure

Souk *(Arabic)* Market, intensely populated central area of most Iraqi towns with narrow dusty streets filled with tradesmen.

Sp Coy Support Company

Spartan A seven-man armoured reconnaissance vehicle armed with a 7.62mm cannon

Sqn Squadron

SSM Squadron sergeant major

'Stitch cadre' Unpopular training course, such as Signals

'Surrey Highlander' English, or at least English-sounding officer from a Scottish regiment, such as 1 PARA second-in-command, Major Stuart Tootal.

TA Territorial Army. Its members are known as 'Stabs': stupid TA bastards.

Tab Tactical Advance to Battle

TACSAT Tactical Satellite

TCP Traffic Control Point

TLF 'Toms Liberation Front', the potential for mutiny among a mass of disaffected Toms

'Tom' Parachute Regiment private soldier

Two Zero Alpha *See* Alpha

Two Zero Bravo *See* Bravo

UKSF United Kingdom Special Forces, the umbrella organisation that includes the Special Air Service and Special Boat Service.

VCP Vehicle Check Point

VHF Very high frequency

'Warry' *See* 'Ally'

Wilco Will comply

WMD Weapons of Mass Distruction

WMIK Weapon Mounted Installation Kit, i.e. a Land Rover armed with .50 cal Browning heavy machine gun, GPMG or MILAN weapons systems. A GPMG is mounted on the front of all WMIKs.

Yellow 2 Northern bridge in central Majar al-Kabir

Yellow 3 Southern bridge in central Majar al-Kabir

List of Characters

Abu Hateem Warlord courted by British forces, alias Karim Mahoud or 'Lord of the Marshes'. One of the most powerful figures in Maysan province, also revered for his resistance to Saddam Hussein. According to Ministry of Defence documentation seen by the author, Abu Hateem ran Amarah with the 'tacit approval of British Forces'.

Aspinall, Del, Private, ARF, wounded (Anti-Tank Platoon, Support Company).

Aston, Russ, Corporal, 156 Provost Company RMP. Aged 30, former Grenadier Guardsman from Derbyshire and a married father to Paygan.

Beckett, Tom A., Lieutenant Colonel and CO 1 PARA. Formerly of the Queen's Royal Hussars (QRH). The operational announcement confirming his appointment as CO 1 PARA was made in late 2000. He had previously been second-in-command 2 PARA. Left 1 PARA in late 2004.

Brown, Billy, Corporal, driver, Two Zero Bravo.

Chambers, Paul, Private, ARF, wounded (Anti-Tank Platoon, Support Company), aka 'Mr Jingles'.

Clegg, Bryn, Lance Corporal, ARF (Anti-Tank Platoon, Support Company).

Clement, Richard, Private, Two Zero Alpha.

Connolly, Danny, Private, Two Zero Alpha.

Cormie, Robbie, Corporal, RAF, ARF.

Coyle, Chris, Private, Two Zero Alpha.

Davidson, Jason, Private, Two Zero Alpha.

Dawes, Jesse, Private, Two Zero Alpha – not in Majar al-Kabir on 24 June.

Dolman, John Eric, MiD, Corporal, second-in-command Two Zero Bravo, aka 'The Dolmanator'.

Ellis, Freddy, Private, Two Zero Bravo.

Fasal, Firas, Doctor at the hospital in Majar al-Kabir.

Gallagher, Martin, WMIK driver, QRF.

Granger, Pat, Corporal, attached to 8 Platoon, 1 PARA on Op TELIC and the platoon's radio commander at Abu Naji on 24 June.

Griffiths, 'Grif', Private, Two Zero Alpha.

Haines, Mick, Private, Two Zero Alpha.

Hamilton-Jewell, Simon, Sergeant, 156 Provost Company RMP, aka 'Hammy' or 'H-J'. Aged 41, from Chessington, Surrey.

Harvey, 'Ginge', WMIK driver, QRF.

Healy, John, Private, wounded, QRF.

Hibbert, James, Lieutenant, 156 Provost Company RMP.

Hicks, Danny, Private, Browning gunner, QRF.

Hilditch, Dave, Sergeant, WMIK commander, QRF.

Holland, Steve, Private, Two Zero Alpha.

Hull, Gary, Private, Two Zero Bravo.

Hyde, Benjamin, Lance Corporal, 156 Provost Company RMP. Aged 23, he had wanted to be a civilian policeman. From Northallerton, North Yorkshire.

Johnson, Phil, Lance Corporal, ARF, wounded (Anti-Tank Platoon, Support Company), aka 'Tubs'.

Jones, Paul, Private, Two Zero Bravo.

Jones, Mick, Private, ARF (Anti-Tank Platoon, Support Company).

Kemp, Chris, Major, OC C Company.

Kennedy, Ross Alexander, MiD, Lieutenant, OC 8 Platoon, aka 'Ross the Boss' or 'Mr Kennedy'.

King, Mike, Private, Two Zero Alpha – not in Majar al-Kabir on 24 June.

Knighton, Lawrence, Lieutenant, second Ops Room watch keeper on 24 June.

Keys, Thomas, Lance Corporal, 156 Provost Company RMP. Aged 21, the youngest of the six-man RMP section.

Lewin, Rick, Lieutenant, OC 7 Platoon, C Company.

Lewis, Mark, Private, Two Zero Bravo.

Long, Paul, Corporal, 156 Provost Company RMP. Aged 24, a married father of one.

Luke, Fordell, Colour Sergeant, first MSG commander into Majar al-Kabir, aka 'Lukey'.

Lynch, Serge, Private, Two Zero Bravo.

Marley, Matthew, Warrant Officer, RMP representative in the Ops Room, 24 June, aka 'Bob'.

Marsh, Dan, Lance Corporal, ARF (Mortar Platoon, Support Company).

Mason, Damien, Private, ARF, wounded, aka 'Mr Pebbles'.

May, Tim, Private, DAF driver, Two Zero Alpha.

McAdam, Barry, Private, Two Zero Alpha.

McCallum, Gavin, RAF anaesthetist, ARF, wounded.

McCann, Sergeant, QRF.

McManus, Kieron, Major, OC Support Company.

McKenna, Neil, Private, Two Zero Alpha.

McMahon, Gary, Lance Corporal (Anti-Tank Platoon, Support Company).

Miller, Si, Corporal, 156 Provost Company RMP. Aged 21, from Washington, Tyne and Wear.

Morris, Emma, Lance Corporal, 156 Provost Company RMP, fiancée of Si Miller.

Murray, Private, ARF, wounded, aka 'Ruby'.

Naylor, Grant, Company Sergeant Major, C Company.

Oellerman, Steve, Corporal, Pinzgauer driver, South African, Two Zero Bravo.

Palmer, John, Captain, second-in-command C Company (on attachment from Irish Guards).

Parry-Jones, Bryn, Major, OC 156 Provost Company RMP. Promoted to lieutenant colonel after Op TELIC and posted to Whitehall as a Schools Liaison Officer. Replaced as OC by Major Meredith.

Phillips, Richard, Lieutenant, OC of the stay-behind 156 Provost Company RMP party.

Robertson, Gordon, CGC, Sergeant, commander of Two Zero Bravo, aka 'Jock Robbo'.

Rogers, Jason, Sergeant, ARF commander, aka 'Buck'.

Savage, Jon, Private, Two Zero Bravo – not in Majar al-Kabir on 24 June.

Sekwalor, Eric, first Ops Room watch keeper on 24 June, aka 'Bobsleigh Bob'.

Smith, 'Smudge', Private, Two Zero Bravo.

Thorne, Lenny, Corporal, medic on the ARF.

Thurtle, Steve, Corporal, 2IC ARF, second-in-command, wounded.

Todd, Richard, Captain, Battle Group Ops officer.

Tootal, Stuart, Major, second-in-command 1 PARA.

van den Berg, Guy, Wing Commander, 27 Squadron RAF. Chinook pilot.

Weadon, Mark, Lance Corporal, second-in-command Two Zero Alpha.

West, Andy, Captain, RAMC, 1 PARA Regimental Medical Officer.

Wilson, Gordon, Sergeant, WMIK commander, QRF.

Zubaida, Talal Abid Ahmed, militia leader in Majar al-Kabir.

Briefing on Iraq received by British troops

Introduction to Iraq:

The objective of the pocket aide memoire is to give our staff a brief insight into Iraq. It has been produced from open sources so therefore it should only be used as a guide and not as an authority.

History

Mesopotamia, modern Iraq, is often referred to as the 'cradle of civilisation'. In the ancient world it was home to many of the world's earliest cultures and empires: Sumerian, Babylonian, Assyrian etc, which all developed along the floodplains between the Tigris and the Euphrates rivers.

Ancient Mesopotamia was religiously diverse and polytheist. The first modern world religion to impact the country was Christianity. The first churches were established in the first century and by the seventh century the indigenous Assyrian Christian culture was firmly established and thriving. Today's Assyrian Christian church is the oldest ethno-religious group in the country.

In the seventh century the region was conquered for Islam by the Arab armies and the gradual conversion of most of the population began. In 1534 it became part of the Turkish Ottoman Empire. The gradual conversion of the majority Sunni Arab population to Shia Islam took many centuries. It was not until the 19th century that the majority of the population became Shia Muslims through the widespread conversion of many of the main Sunni tribes.

At the end of World War One the region passed into British hands. In 1921 Emir Faisal ibn Hussain was appointed as monarch and in 1932 modern Iraq became nominally independent. However, British influence remained strong until the overthrow of the monarchy in 1958. In 1968 Saddam Hussein's Ba'ath Socialist Party seized power in a coup. In 1980 power disputes and Iranian backing for Iraq's rebellious Kurds led Saddam Hussein to unleash the devastating Iran–Iraq war, which did not end until 1988, with little gain and the deaths of 1.5 million people. Two years later Saddam Hussein invaded Kuwait in an attempt to seize its oil fields, leading to the first Gulf War.

Throughout the 1990s Saddam Hussein's resistance to the United Nations incurred sanctions which, combined with the continuing ruthless policies of the Iraqi regime, devastated the population of Iraq resulting in the deaths of half a million Iraqi children (according to UNICEF) and a massive decline in the standard of living. Rebellion among the Kurdish population in north Iraq and Shia Muslims in the south in the years following the 1991 Gulf War meant the country had effectively reverted back to its three traditional ethno-religious zones, even before the collapse of Saddam Hussein's regime. These were a northern Kurdish autonomous region, a central region where Saddam Hussein's regime remained in strong control and a Shia south under nominal central authority.

Culture, notions of honour and shame

Honour (*sharaf* or *'ird*) and shame (*hashama*) are two of the most fundamental principles governing social organisation and interaction in Arab and Iraqi society. They are involved in almost every social contact from a casual interaction between friends on a street corner to blood feuds between families. Numerous aspects of social behaviour can be traced to a universal need to uphold the honour of the individual and his or her family, the preservation of which is considered a basic duty of all

Iraqi males. Honour is the collective property of a family and once lost is difficult to regain.

Honour determines social status, forms the basis of social etiquette, underpins relations between family lineages and tribes and can often mean the difference between life or death. The concept is at once a central element in the value system of the society, a method of regulating social relations, an organisational principle for social behaviour and means of social control. The socio-psychological need to escape or prevent negative judgement upon one's character is of paramount importance in Iraqi society and is inculcated from an early age. The imperative to avoid a loss of face (*wajh*) or be subject to shame and a consequent diminution in social status in the eyes of society to such an extent underpins social behaviour and interaction between Iraqis, at least in public.

Honour among Arabs is often described as being 'more important than facts', a phrase which implies a general tendency to deny truths which may be self-evident to Westerners, for the consequences of not doing so would be a loss of honour. Iraqis are therefore said to have 'two faces', referring to the image which is projected to the outside world and that which is experienced only by members of an individual's close family. 'Face' refers to the outward appearance of honour and Arabs describe the face as being 'blackened' when honour is undermined – conversely, the face is said to have been 'whitenened' when honour is restored. A loss of face may occur when someone refuses someone else's hospitality, ignores their authority, behaves disrespectfully towards them or in some way transgresses a behavioural code.

Shame, although a closely related concept, is of a somewhat different order to a loss of face, pertaining to situations in which honour has been more seriously compromised. In the case of a man whose wife or daughter has been guilty of an illicit sexual liaison, for example, the man – together with his immediate kin group – will be said to suffer the shame.

There are a number of different aspects of honour in Arab and Iraqi society, some of which include: virility, dignity, work, blood-purity, bravery, hospitality, authority, sexual honour and family tribe.

Guidance on interaction with Arabs

No beer, no pornography, shake hands whenever meeting an Arab and when leaving him. Sitting: never sit with the soles of your shoes or feet facing an Arab. Visiting: when offered tea or coffee, it is polite to accept, but if you accept more than 3 cups you may outstay your welcome. If tea or coffee is served in a meeting expect polite conversation – business will be conducted later. At dinner, long silences are normal. Do not belch. Arabs will want to wash their hands before dinner. Conversation: try to take the lead from what an Arab brings up in conversation and avoid asking personal questions. Never ask questions about the women of an Arab family, even if the subject is broached by them. Arabs stand very close to one another when talking – do not back away even if you find this uncomfortable.

Touching: touching, kissing and holding hands between members of the same sex is normal and demonstrates friendship – do not laugh at it. Touching or kissing members of the opposite sex in public is considered to be in extremely bad taste. Time: do not be impatient with local people – if hurried, nothing will get done. You should never be late for an appointment but do not be surprised if an Arab is. Expect and accept flexibility. Criticism: Arabs do not give or accept criticism directly. Even constructive criticism is considered an insult. An Arab's ideas should always be given consideration. If criticism is required, it should be given privately and in a tactful manner. Face-saving is very important in Arab society.

On drinking water: 'drink before you feel thirsty, up to 3 gallons a day, don't drink water that's too cold, it'll cause cramps, and sip it, don't gulp it. Add salt to your food to replace what you lose through sweat.

APPENDIX B

1 PARA Operational Deployment Personal Equipment Lists and Dress Codes

RESTRICTED

Enclosed in this letter are the kit lists and dress codes for the 1 PARA operational deployment. All members of 1 PARA Group participating in the operation are to comply with these kit list and dress codes for the duration of the deployment. Any amendments to these lists are to be cleared through the Bn Ops Officer or RSM before action taken.

WO2

Ops Warrant Officer.

NOTE: The following to be clearly marked with the individual Coy/Unit colour and Zap No. applicable.

ON THE MAN (field work)

FULL DPMS (DESERT) [Disruptive Pattern Material trousers and shirts]

BOOTS (COMBAT HIGH/DESERT)

BERET (SILVER CAP BADGE)

AK/DESERT HAT (BN TYPE TAILORED)

SMOCK PARA OR WINDPROOF (IF NOT IN BERGEN)

HELMET PARA – ELASTIC FITTED NBC (IF NOT ATTACHED TO
  WEBBING)

ID DISCS/ID CARD

MORPHINE AS ISSUED

WATCH

SILVA COMPASS

NOTEBOOK AND PENCIL

CLASP/POCKET KNIFE

SMALL TORCH

2 x FIELD DRESSINGS

PERS WPN AND ANCILS (SLING ATTACHED)

CBA [Combat Body Armour] (CARRIED AND WORN AS ORDERED)

COMD KIT (FOR COMDS)

WHISTLE

MAPS AS ISSUED

TAMS/SOP/SOC [Tactical Aide Memoire, Standard Operating Procedures,
  Secure Order Cards]

MODEL KIT [counters, string, etc. for making models of enemy positions]

BINOS

PRISMATIC COMPASS

RADIO & ANCILS

BATCO AS ISSUED

WEBBING (FOR FIGHTING THROUGH)

WEBBING/POUCHES AS PER INDIVIDUAL PREFERENCE – COMD
  POUCH

AMMO AS ISSUED

4 x MAGS (12X LSW)

SMALL WPN CLEAN KIT/OIL/FLANELETTE

MAG CHARGER

BAYONET (IF NOT ON WPN)

2 x WATER BOTTLES

PRR [Personal Role Radio] AND SPARE BATTS

1 x FIELD DRESSING

DAYSACK (FOR 24HRS SURVIVAL)

PONCHO/BUNGIES & BIVVI BAG

ETH [Entrenching Tool Hand – i.e. collapsible spade]

24 HRS RATIONS & HEXI/COOKER

CAM CREAM/INSECT REPELLENT/FOOT POWDER

SMALL PERSONAL MED KIT & SUN BLOCK

30M COMMS CORD [A system of pulls on the cord was used
    between sections in defence or ambush positions.]

MESS TIN/METAL MUG AND SPOON

1 x WATER BOTTLE

WARM LAYERS (IF REQUIRED)

1 x SPARE SOCKS

SPARE BATTS (TORCH /PRR & CWS)

CWS AS ISSUED [Combat Weapon Sight]

SMALL SHAVE KIT (FOR NBC IE RAZOR ETC)

RESPIRATOR AND NBC IPE AS ISSUED

BERGEN

SLEEPING BAG

ROLL MAT

SPARE SET DPM (DESERT) CLOTHING [You should be so lucky!]

PARA SMOCK OR WINDPROOF (IF NOT WORN)

GLOVES (OUTER & CONTACT)

SPARE WARM CLOTHING (IF REQUIRED)

SPARE SOCKS & UNDERWEAR (ENOUGH FOR DURATION
    OF OPERATION)

1 x WATER BOTTLE

SMALL WASH/SHAVE KIT

SMALL BOOT CLEANING KIT

HOUSE WIFE [Sewing kit]

LARGE DIGGING TOOL (WRAPPED IN SAND BAG)

1 x SAND BAG

EXCESS RATIONS (IF ISSUED)

SPARE BATTS

GRIP/BAG (FOR SPARES AND COMFORT)

SPARE DPM CLOTHING (1X SET COMBAT 95)

SPARE BOOTS

STABLE BELT

MAROON BN T-SHIRTS

GREEN BN SHIRT

GORTEX (OPTIONAL)

SPARE SOCKS & UNDERWEAR

BN PT KIT & RUNNING SHOES (2X BLACK RUNNING SHORTS)

SWIMMING SHORTS/TRUNKS

SPORTS CLOTHING ETC

LETTER WRITING MATERIAL/BLUEYS

READING MATERIAL

LARGE TOWEL & WASH/ SHAVE KIT/ BOOT CLEAN KIT

MARK 6 HELMET STRAPS FOR NBC

PLATOON/SECTION EQUIPMENT (FOR PACKING AT PL AND SECT LEVEL)

1 x FIRE FLY PER PL

1 x AIR MARKER PANEL PER PL

1 x MED PACK PER SECT

1 x LIGHTWEIGHT STRETCHER PER SECT

2 x RA [Right angle] TORCH & FILTERS PER SECT

2 x WIRE CUTTERS & GLOVES PER SECT

CYALUMES VARIOUS COLOURS

SPARE EXTRACTORS AND FIRING PINS FOR PERSONAL WPNS

Dress Codes

Working Dress No. 1

Full desert DPMs (sleeves up and down as per first and last light)

Beret (Silver cap badge) or desert hat

Stable belt

Boots (Combat High/Desert)

Working Dress No. 2

Green BN T-shirt

DPM (desert) trs

Stable belt

Boots (Combat High/Desert)

PT Dress

Maroon BN T-shirt or vest

Black shorts

Socks

Running shoes

Field Dress

As per working dress No. 1 (Less stable belt)

Webbing

Daysack

Bergen

Above to be packed as per deployment kit lists – any additional equipment as per BN CSS orders depending on type of operation/mission.

Rest period (within tented camp areas) dress

As per working dress above or:

Tracksuit or sports kit, etc.

NOTE: All above (where applicable) will have BDE and BN badges correctly tailored as per direction from BDE and BN HQs.

Secretary of State for Defence Geoff Hoon's written statement as placed in *Hansard* on 2 July

On 24 June last week, I informed the House that six Royal Military Police soldiers had been killed, and eight other United Kingdom service personnel had been wounded in incidents in Iraq earlier that day.

Since then, we have been working hard to establish what took place. It may be some time before we have a full picture; indeed, we may never know with absolute certainty precisely what happened. However, we will do all we can to establish the facts, and to hold to account those responsible. Accordingly, we have launched an investigation, and the Special Investigation Branch have appointed a senior investigating officer. We are also looking at the wider, operational aspects of what took place, to determine whether there are any lessons we need to learn. It may be some time before this work is complete, and we do not therefore intend to respond to every piece of media speculation or conjecture in the interim.

It would, however, be right for me to set out our current understanding of events leading up to, and on the day of the incidents themselves. In doing so I should point out that our understanding may change as new information comes to light.

The RMP were engaged in assisting with the regeneration of the local Iraqi police service, by ensuring that they had proper training, equipment and infrastructure to operate as professionally as possible. This task included routine visits to police stations in the area. The police station in Al Majar Al Kabir is one of a number that the RMP planned to visit last Tuesday.

Al Majar Al Kabir is a town of approximately 60,000 people, situated to the south of Al Amarah, in Maysan province. The town has always been fiercely independent and was free of Saddam's regime by the time Coalition Forces reached it. The main focus of military operations in the area in recent weeks had been the implementation of a weapons amnesty, and thereafter, the recovery of illegal weapons.

These weapons searches were unpopular with the local population, although none had been conducted in the town itself. Local religious leaders had called for further searches to be resisted, and on 22 June, a 1 PARA patrol in the town were faced with a hostile crowd of some 500 people. The soldiers fired baton rounds in order to enable them to be able to withdraw from the town. At a meeting the next day, officers from 1 PARA agreed with the town council that weapons searches would be suspended, and that the council would themselves take responsibility for recovering 'heavy' weapons.

With this agreement in place, the following day the RMP section 'booked out' at around 0910, planning to visit three towns in the area – Al Majar Al Kabir being the first. Routine force protection measures in place required that they should all be armed, should have their body armour and helmets with them, should have working communications, and that there should be at least two vehicles – in fact they had three.

We judge that they would have reached the town at around 0940–0955, shortly before a 1 PARA patrol also entered the town.

We cannot yet be certain, but it may be that the attack on the PARA patrol took place before the attack on the RMP. The attack on 1 PARA commenced at around 1030, when the patrol was stoned by a large crowd. At some point a crowd also appears to have massed outside the police station. While attempting to move their vehicles inside the police compound, the RMP came under fire, and it seems at least one of them was killed at that point. The crowd evidently then stormed the police station. British forces were informed a short while later by local Iraqis that all six of the RMP personnel had been killed.

We understand that attempts were made to contact the RMP section as events unfolded. This is one of the details we will be trying to establish as part of the investigation.

In the follow up to these incidents, Iraqi leaders in the province are continuing to work closely with us. We will not lose sight of our overall aim to support a better Iraq, and an Iraq that is for the Iraqi people. British forces in Iraq continue to do an excellent job in taking this important work forward.

As they do so, our thoughts remain with those that have lost their lives, and their loved ones who mourn them.

Chronology

All timings are estimations based on anecdotal evidence – there is insufficient evidence to provide an accurate breakdown of events at the police station.

24 June 2003

0630–0700hrs Support Company drive through Majar al-Kabir. The town is 'eerily quiet'.

0800hrs Update of Battle Group issues and planning the day ahead held at the BG bird table. It was intended to provide an 'all-informed update on patrol activity and current intelligence'.

0840hrs 8 Platoon call signs Alpha and Bravo book out of the Operations Room.

0850hrs Sergeant Hamilton-Jewell approaches the 156 Provost Company desk to book out and provide details of C Section's intended movements. He states his time of departure from Abu Naji as 0910hrs, to return at 1700hrs.

0900hrs Alpha and Bravo leave Abu Naji for Majar al-Kabir. Also the time of the CO's daily briefing.

0910hrs C Section leave Abu Naji for Al Uzayr via Majar al-Kabir and Qalat Salih.

0930hrs Alpha and Bravo arrive at militia headquarters (FAWJ building) in Majar al-Kabir.

0940hrs C Section arrive at the police station in Majar al-Kabir

0940hrs–0950hrs Alpha begin foot patrol through the town with the militia in tow. Lead members of the patrol cross the northern bridge and turn right at the crossroads.

1005hrs Foot patrol is called off after Lieutenant Kennedy is warned of 'bad men' in Majar al-Kabir by Zubaida. Lieutenant Kennedy radios Sergeant Robertson, the Bravo commander, instructing him to patrol the town in vehicles.

1010hrs Call sign Bravo depart militia headquarters driving two Pinzgauers.

1020hrs Bravo enter the souk and the stoning begins. The attack is prolonged and intensifies before Bravo fire baton rounds and warning shots.

1025hrs Bravo engaged by small arms fire. There is a firefight before the call sign extracts north. Alpha recognise the sound of British rifles. Lieutenant Kennedy and Lance Corporal Weadon order the call sign to remount the DAF. The sound of shooting also interrupts C Section's meeting at the police station. Sergeant Hamilton-Jewell orders the three RMP Land Rovers to be driven inside the compound. Bravo drive north past the crossroads as a mob give chase, armed with RPGs and AK47s.

1035hrs Alpha arrive at the crossroads, approximately 100 metres from the police station, and are engaged. The call sign debus and adopt all-round defence.

1037hrs Bravo establish a position on the eastern riverbank and receive fire from the east, west and south. Sergeant Robertson gives the Ops Room a contact report and requests a QRF and ammunition re-supply. Sergeant Rogers (QRF commander) called to Ops Room; Captain Todd and Major Tootal are alerted.

1040hrs The DAF has to be bump-started under fire at the crossroads. The vehicle is then engaged from an alleyway. Threats are neutralised. Bravo remain under sustained fire on the riverbank. Lieutenant Knighton briefs Captain Todd. Warrant Officer Marley suggests C Section might be in Majar al-Kabir.

1045hrs Plans for the rescue mission firm up. There will be an Airborne Reaction Force and a Quick Reaction Force (to infiltrate by land). WO2 Marley tries unsuccessfully to radio C Section.

1050hrs Lieutenant Kennedy is requested to re-insert into Majar al-Kabir to assist Bravo's extraction. Captain Todd briefs Sergeant Rogers, the duty Chinook pilot and the commander of Gaz 1.

1055hrs Major Tootal instructs Major Kemp (OC C Company) to drive to Majar al-Kabir and establish an Incident Command Post (ICP) on the town's northern perimeter.

1100hrs Wing Commander Guy van den Berg arrives from Basra by Chinook. The female flight lieutenant requests use of his helicopter. He declines and says he will fly the mission. Gaz 1 leaves Abu Naji. Sergeant Rogers' men cross-deck between Chinooks and the medics arrive at the HLS. Alpha are engaged with RPGs as they re-insert into Majar al-Kabir.

1105hrs Van den Berg's Chinook leaves Abu Naji. Colour Sergeant Luke's Manoeuvre Support Group (MSG) see it fly above them as they take on additional ammunition supplies. 1 (UK) Division are notified of the alarming situation in Majar al-Kabir.

1110hrs Colour Sergeant Luke's MSG depart Abu Naji. Gaz 1 hovers above Majar al-Kabir.

1115hrs approx Having lost both Pinzgauers, Bravo seek refuge in a house. They are surrounded and repel waves of enemy attacks for over half an hour. The Chinook makes its second pass over Majar al-Kabir and prepares to land. It is engaged by small arms fire and RPGs.

1120hrs The Chinook comes under heavy fire, causing the ARF mission to be aborted.

1138hrs The ICP has been established as the MSG sweep past the HCR and into enemy fire in the town. Alpha remain engaged in heavy fighting with Iraqis streaming towards them from the sugar factory.

1145hrs Bravo break the enemy cordon around its position, running to an irrigation ditch and another building. Sergeant Robertson instructs Private Ellis to run across open ground to the QRF positions.

1200hrs Dr Fasal arrives at the Incident Command Post (ICP) in an Iraqi ambulance and reports four Coalition Forces hostages at the police station. Major Kemp requests the doctor return to the police station and facilitate their release.

1230hrs Dr Fasal returns to the ICP to report there are now three dead Coalition Forces at the police station. He offers to collect the bodies; Major Kemp agrees. Ops Room hear report of three dead. WO2 Marley requests a TACSAT message be sent to Al Uzayr for Sergeant

Hamilton-Jewell to radio in on his arrival. Gaz 1 is replaced over Majar al-Kabir by Gaz 2.

1250hrs Bravo join Alpha in the vicinity of the ICP. Dr Fasal brings the bodies of Sergeant Hamilton-Jewell, Corporal Long and Corporal Aston to the same location.

1308hrs Dr Fasal recovers Corporal Miller, Lance Corporal Hyde and Lance Corporal Keys. The six bodies are transferred to a British military ambulance. Lieutenant Colonel Beckett is briefed on the tragedy by Major Kemp.

1340hrs With all Coalition Forces accounted for, Lieutenant Colonel Beckett orders all personnel to withdraw.

Bibliography

Military publications and documentation

Operation Telic – Infantry Urban Close Combat by Major C. P. Kemp (Restricted)

Pegasus, Journal of the Parachute Regiment and Airborne Forces: Yearbooks 2000, 2003 and seasonal editions Winter 2000, Summer 2001, Autumn 2002, Summer 2003, Winter 2003, Summer 2004

RAF News, 11 July 2003

Royal Military Police Journal August 2003 and December 2003

Special Investigation Branch (SIB), 'Witness Brief, Photographic Supplement', 2003

Special Investigation Branch (SIB), 'Brief to the immediate families of the six RMP NCOs killed at Al Majar al-Kabir, Iraq', January 2004

Aide Memoire, J2, HQ MND (SE).

Citation, Conspicuous Gallantry Cross, Sergeant G. Robertson CGC

'Findings, Recommendations and Options, Board of Inquiry into the circumstances leading up to the deaths of Sgt S. Hamilton-Jewell, Cpl R. Aston, Cpl P. Long, Cpl S. Miller, LCpl B. Hyde and LCpl T. Keys'

Non-military publications

Dabrowska, Karen, *Iraq, The Bradt Travel Guide*, 2002

Patai, Raphael, *The Arab Mind*, Hatherleigh Press, 2002

Stallworthy, Jon, *The Oxford Book of War Poetry*, Oxford University Press, 1988

The Daily Telegraph: War on Saddam, Robinson, 2003

Thesiger, Wilfred, *The Marsh Arabs*, Penguin, 1967

National Audit Office, *Report on Operation TELIC, United Kingdom Military Operations in Iraq*, 2003

National Audit Office, *Report on Exercise Saif Sareea II*, 2002